Official
Microsoft®
Internet
Explorer 4
Book

Microsoft Press

Official Microsoft Internet Explorer 4 Book

Published by Microsoft Press
A Division of Microsoft Corporation
One Microsoft Way
Redmond, Washington 98052-6399

Library of Congress Cataloging-in-Publication Data pending.

Printed and bound in the United States of America.

1 2 3 4 5 6 7 8 9 MLML 2 1 0 9 8 7

Distributed to the book trade in Canada by Macmillan of Canada, a division of Canada Publishing Corporation.

A CIP catalogue record for this book is available from the British Library.

Microsoft Press books are available through booksellers and distributors worldwide. For further information about international editions, contact your local Microsoft Corporation office. Or contact Microsoft Press International directly at fax (425) 936-7329. Visit our Website at mspress.microsoft.com.

Acquisitions Editor: David Clark
Project Editor: Barbara Moreland
Technical Editor: Dail Magee, Jr.

for Suzanne, always

Acknowledgments

Writing a book like this one isn't a lonely, solitary task done by an isolated writer typing away in an attic. I get lots of help, and I get to meet and work with some great people. (Lucky for me, because I'm such an extrovert, I couldn't survive if the attic myth were true.) I'd like to give special thanks to David Clark, acquisitions editor, for his confidence and support at every stage; to Barbara Moreland, project editor, for great editing, good cheer, and those very precious moments when we took time to indulge ourselves in pure, unabashed love of the English language; to Dail Magee, technical editor, for a fantastic job of helping me deal with a rapidly evolving product; and last but not least, to the Internet Explorer 4 team for creating the best browser package available. I'd also like to thank the other members of the Microsoft Press team, especially Abby Hall and Teri Kieffer. Thanks to my family, too, for their support and encouragement—and yes, you can have your very own copy of Internet Explorer. Now let me have my computer back!

Table of Contents

Browse

PART II

Communicate

PART III

Publish

Introduction

What happens when the world's leading software publisher focuses its considerable expertise on figuring out how to improve Internet software, and then puts its best people to work on creating the ultimate package for Internet users? Internet Explorer. In review after review, the experts agree: This is the best software you can use to access the Internet. If you've never used the Internet before, you'll find that Internet Explorer 4 is genuinely easy to learn and to use. And if you've used some other browser or a previous version of Internet Explorer, you'll be amazed at the innovations in this new version. Internet Explorer 4 will redefine the standard for Internet software.

The *Official Microsoft Internet Explorer 4 Book* shows you how to use Internet Explorer 4 like a pro and how to make full use of the Internet. By reading this one book, you'll gain so much Internet expertise that friends and colleagues will think you've been using the Internet for years. You'll learn to pinpoint information on the World Wide Web by taking advantage of Internet Explorer 4's new Search explorer. You'll master electronic mail, including advanced security features such as digital signatures and encryption. You'll even be able to create and publish your own home page, without knowing any HTML (the language that specifies the appearance of pages on the Web). In other words, with this book you can unlock all the tools of Internet Explorer 4—and with them, all the treasures of the Internet.

With Internet Explorer 4, the Internet becomes more useful and fun than ever because you can bring it home, right to your desktop. You can turn your personal computer into an extension of the Internet, as if there were no distinction between your computer and the external Net. You have the option to use one set of navigation skills and make everything available, whether it's a file on your desktop or a page on a Web site halfway around the world. You no longer have to change gears conceptually when you go from your computer to the Internet, or from the Internet back to your computer.

The *Official Microsoft Internet Explorer 4 Book* is your key to harvesting the Internet's riches and to transforming your desktop so that it's seamlessly integrated with the World Wide Web. If you're a total beginner, you'll find that this book's concise, plain-English explanations will get you up to speed quickly and painlessly. If you're an Internet veteran, this book will enable you to master all of the convenient new features of Internet Explorer 4 and to increase immeasurably your enjoyment of the Internet.

Introducing the Internet

If you've never used the Internet before, you're probably wondering what all the fuss is about. This section offers a brief, jargon-free explanation of the Internet and insight into why it's becoming so increasingly indispensable. Skip to the next section if you're already familiar with the Internet.

What Is the Internet?

When telephones were new there were only a few telephone exchanges, all based in towns and cities. Each used its own proprietary signaling system. If you had a phone provided by Company A, you couldn't place a call to somebody who was using one from Company B. Naturally, phone usage didn't grow very fast. Then somebody had the excellent idea to get all phone companies to agree to use just one technical standard. With standards, a user of Company A's phone could call one of Company B's subscribers—or any other telephone user. The rest is history; international telephone standards led to explosive growth in telephone usage. Today nearly one billion telephones are in use worldwide, and the amazing thing is that you can dial almost any of them directly.

The Internet offers the same kind of compatibility for computer networks. Before the Internet, there were many different types of computer networks, and a computer on Network A couldn't exchange data with a computer on Network B. The Internet is a set of standards that enable differing computers and computer networks to work with one another. In the same way that telephone standards led to the emergence of a worldwide telephone system, Internet standards are creating a worldwide computer network. It's not as big as the telephone system—not yet, anyway—but it's still pretty big. According to recent estimates, the Internet currently has about 75 million users in 132 countries worldwide.

Most people connect to the Internet at work via a local area network or by using a modem and telephone line to dial an Internet service provider (ISP). Others connect by means of an online service, such as America Online or The Microsoft Network. Once you're connected to the Internet, something wonderful happens: You can make contact with any of hundreds of thousands of computers that are set up to provide information via the Internet.

Why Use the Internet?

Many people use the Internet for communication. By far the most popular application for the Internet is electronic mail, which is faster and less expensive than the postal service (derisively called "snail mail" by Internet users). You can also use the Internet like a telephone. Microsoft NetMeeting enables you to place free long-distance "telephone calls" to other Internet users, provided each of you has equipped your system with a sound card and a microphone. But the Internet also enables you to access data stored on other computers—and that's where the World Wide Web comes in.

The Internet is fast becoming a worldwide public information system, and the Web is this system's delivery service. When you use the Web, you're requesting a copy of information that's stored on one of an estimated 250,000 Web servers—computers that are set up to fulfill requests for Web information. These servers collectively house an estimated 55 to 75 million resources, including pictures, sounds, videos, and Web pages. Although there's a lot of nonsense on the Web—anyone can publish anything—there's also useful information on practically any subject you can imagine.

To understand what you can do with the Internet, it's best to think in terms of differing Web services. As you read this list, note that Internet Explorer 4 includes everything you need to make use of all of these services, and each will be explained fully in this book.

World Wide Web. To use the Web, you need a program called a browser; the browser displays Web pages. On most pages, you see underlined and colored text (called hyperlinks) that you can click to go to a different page. What's amazing about the Web is that the new page you see might be stored on the same computer as the original page, or it might be coming from halfway around the world. The Web transforms the Internet into a global information system of astonishing richness and vitality. Internet Explorer 4 is the best browser you can use to access those treasures.

🌐 **FTP.** Short for File Transfer Protocol, FTP enables Internet users to receive (download) as well as send (upload) computer files, including graphics, audio, video, and software. The FTP standard ensures that the files are transferred without error. Using FTP, you can access and download an estimated 250,000 free or shareware programs from the Internet. With Internet Explorer, you don't need a separate FTP program to download files; Internet Explorer can access FTP data directly and automatically.

🌐 **Electronic mail.** Generally known as e-mail, electronic mail is fast becoming indispensable for personal and professional communication. With e-mail, you can type and send a message to somebody, and it's received almost immediately. You can also attach documents, images, voice recordings, and videos to your message. New security standards enable you to send confidential messages, which can be read only by the intended recipient. The handwriting is on the wall for the postal service: Last year in the U.S., the number of messages exchanged by e-mail exceeded the number sent by first-class mail. Internet Explorer 4 lets you communicate using a really great e-mail program called Outlook Express.

🌐 **Usenet.** Something like a letters-to-the-editor column on a global scale, Usenet enables an Internet user to send a message to many people. But there's not just one newspaper. Usenet includes more than 25,000 topically named discussion groups, called newsgroups, which contain messages from people all over the world. You'll also see replies to these messages, and your Usenet software—called a *newsreader*—groups these messages so you can see the flow of debate on a topic. Although there's a great deal of nonsense on Usenet, you'll also find thousands of serious newsgroups devoted to practical and technical subjects. Every day, Usenet generates enough new text to fill an entire set of encyclopedias! You can use Outlook Express to read Usenet and to post your own messages.

🌐 **Internet Relay Chat (IRC).** Can you socialize on the Internet? You bet. IRC enables you to join real-time chat groups with other Internet users. This interchange is strictly text-based; you type a message, and everyone in the chat group sees it. You get replies, and soon you're in the middle of a conversation. If you'd like to talk privately to somebody, you can "whisper" so that just that one person hears, or the two of you can go to a private room.

Using Microsoft Chat, a free add-on program available from Microsoft, you can join the party.

- **Internet telephony/videoconferencing.** You can use the Internet like a telephone—and what's more, it's free, even for long distance. (You place your "call" to somebody's computer, though, so this option is limited to exchanges between people who both have Internet connections and suitably equipped computers.) Advances in compression technology enable you to send and receive video, too. Those "picture telephones" you see in science fiction movies are close to becoming a reality! Microsoft Net-Meeting, part of the Internet Explorer 4 suite of software, is the most advanced program available for Internet telephony and videoconferencing.

- **Web publishing.** One of the best things about the Internet is that you can create your own Web pages. Millions of people have created home pages, and so can you. In the past, you had to learn Hypertext Markup Language (HTML) to do this. But no more. Now publishing a professional-looking Web page is as easy as using basic word processing and creating simple tables. Thanks to Microsoft FrontPage Express, you can become a published Web author without writing a single line of code.

Introducing Internet Explorer 4

Internet Explorer 4 is a suite of programs that work together harmoniously to enable you to take full advantage of everything that's available on the Internet.

- **Internet Explorer.** The best browser currently available, this component enables you to browse the World Wide Web, sub-scribe to channels, and download software to your computer. The program's Search, Favorites, History, and Channels explorers make it much easier to find cool Web pages, to keep tabs on your favorite sites, to go back to previously visited sites, and to have fascinating content come directly to your desktop. Once you install Internet Explorer, you have the option of installing the Web Integrated Desktop, which allows you to browse your desktop the same way you browse the Web.

- **Outlook Express.** Combining e-mail with Usenet newsgroups, Outlook Express provides a complete Internet messaging system. All your messages, whether they're from e-mail or Usenet, are grouped in a single message panel and organized neatly into folders. A real plus is that this program uses the standard Windows Address Book, which is available to other Windows applications. Among this component's very cool features are the ability to check multiple mail and Usenet accounts, to send and receive secure (encrypted) e-mail, and to send and receive messages with rich (HTML) formatting. Glowing reviews call this the best e-mail program you can get at any price.

- **Microsoft Chat.** This easy-to-use program enables you to join real-time discussions on Internet Relay Chat (IRC). If you want, you can even view the conversation as an ongoing comic strip! Microsoft Chat is the easiest way to try out IRC and see what it's all about.

- **Microsoft NetMeeting.** By far the leading program in the Internet telephony/videoconferencing area, NetMeeting enables you to place and receive long-distance audio and video calls via the Internet. In addition, you can create collaborative discussions (involving two or more people) in which every user has access to a shared whiteboard space, a text chat window, and shared Windows applications.

- **Microsoft FrontPage Express.** An easy-to-use version of Microsoft FrontPage, a leading Web authoring program, this component enables you to create great-looking Web pages without knowing any HTML. You can use the FrontPage Express tools to create your own home page and to send richly formatted e-mail messages.

Using This Book

The *Official Microsoft Internet Explorer 4 Book* has three parts.

Part I: Browse. Internet Explorer—the browser component of the Internet Explorer suite—is the focus of Part I. You'll learn how to extract the maximum from the Web, including how to find great content, how to save your favorite sites so you can get back to them later, how to subscribe to live content so that it appears on your desktop, and much more. You'll also learn how to bring your Internet skills back home, as you browse your own computer's contents using the Web Integrated Desktop.

Part II: Communicate. Messaging is the theme of Part II. You'll fully explore Outlook Express, and as you do, you'll become an expert in electronic mail and Usenet. You'll also learn how to use Microsoft Chat so that you can join real-time discussions on Internet Relay Chat and how to use Microsoft NetMeeting for Internet telephony and videoconferencing.

Part III: Publish. The topic of Part III is creating your own Web content. You'll learn how to use FrontPage Express to make jazzy-looking Web pages, complete with graphics, sounds, and video. You'll also learn how to publish your pages on the Internet and how to create customized folders for the Web Integrated Desktop.

You don't need to read the parts in order. For example, if you'd like to get started with e-mail right now, flip to Chapter 11. Also, you don't need to read all the chapters; read just the ones that interest you. For example, Chapter 12 discusses great features in Outlook Express for adding digital signatures to your e-mail and encrypting your messages so that only the intended recipient can read them. If you're not interested in sending or receiving confidential e-mail, you can skip this chapter.

Connecting to the Internet

If you don't already have an Internet connection, you need to get one before you can use Internet Explorer 4. This section explains your options and shows you how to get hooked up in short order.

What You Need

To connect to the Internet and use the version of Internet Explorer discussed in this book, you'll need the following:

- **Microsoft Windows 95, Microsoft Windows 98, or Microsoft Windows NT.** Versions of Internet Explorer 4 are currently planned for Microsoft Windows for Workgroups, Microsoft Windows 3.1, and the Apple Macintosh operating system. Although these versions closely resemble the product that's discussed in this book, the focus here is placed on the Windows 95/98/NT version.

- **High-speed modem.** If you plan to connect to the Internet by means of a telephone line, you need to equip your computer with a high-speed modem. A modem is a device that modifies outgoing and incoming computer signals so that they can travel over the telephone system. Your modem should be capable of sending and receiving data at a speed of at least 28,800 bits per second (28.8 Kbps).

- **Separate phone line for the Internet.** Unless you plan to log on sporadically, consider getting a separate phone line that's set aside for Internet use. Otherwise, people will get busy signals when they try to call you.

To get the most out of the Internet, investigate these options:

- **An ISDN connection.** Short for Integrated Services Digital Network, ISDN is a digital telephone service. To find out how to get this, call your local phone company. To hook your computer up to your ISDN line, you'll need an ISDN adapter instead of a modem. You'll get a connection with speeds of up to 128 Kbps. The downside is that the ISDN connection and needed equipment cost much more than an ordinary phone connection and a modem.

- **Sound card and stereo speakers.** The Web is loaded with audio. To hear it, you need to equip your system to play back recorded sounds.

- **Microphone that plugs into your sound card.** If you would like to place and receive free long-distance phone calls via the Internet, buy a microphone that's designed to work with your sound card. With most sound cards, you can use any microphone with a small, portable-stereo–sized plug.

- **Microsoft IntelliMouse.** Internet Explorer version 4 is optimized specifically to take full advantage of this advanced mouse, which includes a roller between the mouse buttons. For example, you can scroll up or down in a Web page by moving the roller. This option is convenient and reduces the amount of mouse and keyboard fussing that you'll otherwise have to do.

- **A 17-inch or larger monitor.** Although you can browse the Web quite happily with a smaller monitor, it's great to have a bigger one. You can enlarge the page so that the author's overall design comes into view.

Connection Options

To connect to the Internet, do one of the following:

If you use a computer at work, find out whether you can connect to the Internet using your office computer. Talk to your system administrator. Bear in mind, though, that you should use this connection only for work-related browsing. Ask your system administrator for guidelines on acceptable use. (It's probably OK to do Internet research related to your job, but it's probably not OK to browse www.playboy.com!) For personal use of the Internet, get a dial-up connection for your home computer.

Check the Yellow Pages to find local Internet service providers (ISP). Look under Computers–Networks or Computers–Online Services. ISPs are just about everywhere these days. If you find a local ISP, give them a call and ask what they charge. You should be able to get an unlimited connection, plus an e-mail account, for about $20 to $25 per month.

Consider a national service provider, such as Mindspring or Earthlink. These ISPs have local dial-in numbers (called points of presence, abbreviated POP) in thousands of localities. As with local ISPs, you should be able to get an unlimited connection to the Internet and an e-mail address for about $20 to $25 per month.

Check out the online services. America Online, The Microsoft Network, and other online services provide Internet access. You also get to take advantage of the premium services that these companies offer. In general, though, this option is more expensive than using an ISP.

The easiest way to get connected to the Internet is to pop this book's CD into your computer's CD-ROM drive. After the software starts, you can search for national ISPs that have points of presence in your dialing area. When you find one, you can sign up using your credit card information. You'll be on the Internet within a half hour.

From Here

Let's get started.

- Are you new to Internet Explorer? Flip to the next chapter for a beginner's level introduction to Web browsing.

- Are you new to the World Wide Web? Find out what all the fuss is about by reading Chapter 2.

- Having trouble finding anything useful on the Web? Check out Chapter 3, which shows you how to take full advantage of the new Search explorer in Internet Explorer 4.

- Would you like to subscribe to content so that it appears on your computer's desktop? Flip to Chapter 4.

PART

Browse

1 Get Ready

Before you drive an unfamiliar car, you need to figure out some basic but very important things, such as how to adjust the stereo so you can tell which Beatle is singing—John, Paul or George. The same principle applies to Microsoft Internet Explorer. This chapter introduces the basics of using Internet Explorer, including understanding what's on the screen and getting a grip on the fundamentals of navigation. Take a quick look, adjust the program to your liking, and then get ready for some serious surfing (in Chapter 2).

NOTE Have you installed Internet Explorer? If not, do so now. Instructions are on the CD-ROM included in this book.

Connecting to the Internet

To start Internet Explorer for the first time, double-click The Internet, an icon you'll find on your desktop. You'll see the Sign-In dialog box, shown in Figure 1-1. Carefully type your user name and password, just as your Internet service provider (ISP) gave them to you—including capitalization. When you're sure you've typed your user name and password correctly, click Connect, or just press Enter.

Figure 1-1

To connect to the Internet, type the user name and password that your Internet service provider gave you.

If you want to avoid typing your password every time you connect to the Internet, you can choose the Save Password option in the Sign-In dialog box (or just press Alt + S). But think twice before you do this. Although your password will remain invisible, this option would enable anybody to sit down at your computer and get connected to the Internet. If you have curious kids at home, and you haven't enabled site rating protection (see Chapter 7), you might want to type the password manually. It's a pain, I know, but at least you'll be sure that your kids aren't visiting the Oral Excitement page.

Assuming all goes well with your connection, you'll see the Internet Explorer start page (Figure 1-2). This page will look different by the time you access it. In fact, it changes every day. That's part of the fun. You'll explore this page in detail later.

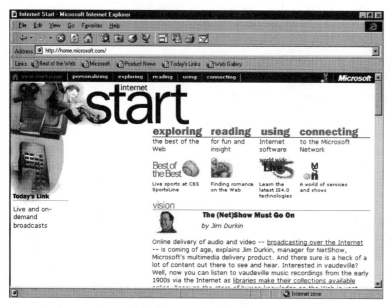

Figure 1-2

You see the start page when you launch the program. You also see it when you click the Home button or choose Home Page from the Go menu.

HELP

The connection didn't work!

This problem isn't unusual, especially if you're connecting for the first time.

Is your modem turned on? If you have an external modem, be sure you've turned on the power.

Is the phone line plugged into the modem, and is it plugged into the right connector? Some modems have different connectors for "line" and "phone."

Are you getting a dial tone? If not, there's something wrong with the way the phone line is hooked up.

Did your ISP reject the logon attempt? You might have typed your user name or password incorrectly. Try again.

Still doesn't work? Call your Internet service provider and ask for help. They'll walk you through a status check of all your Internet settings to make sure everything's correct.

1

Understanding What's on the Screen

Take a seat and get oriented. Look at Internet Explorer's screen. Figure 1-2 shows what you'll see with all of the toolbars brought into view. Let's examine the screen from top to bottom.

- **Title bar.** Positioned at the top of the window, the title bar shows the name of the Web document you're currently accessing. You also see the standard Windows buttons for minimizing, restoring, and maximizing the window, as well as a close button, which enables you to quit the program. (I'm assuming you know how to perform the basic window calisthenics with the version of Windows that you're using.)

- **Menu bar.** On the menu bar, you'll find the names of Internet Explorer's menus. If you select one of the menu names, a menu drops down, giving you additional options. The menus contain all of Internet Explorer's commands. However, the most frequently used commands appear on the toolbars. You probably won't use the menus much, and only for commands that aren't on the toolbars. This book will discuss these as they come up.

- **Program icon.** The Microsoft Internet Explorer insignia (the big *e*) becomes animated while Internet Explorer is retrieving a document for you. (Retrieving a document is sometimes called *downloading*.) The animation ceases when the whole document has been downloaded.

- **Standard buttons.** This toolbar contains the most frequently chosen commands. You'll use these funny little icons a lot.

- **Address bar.** The address bar shows the current Web address of the page you're viewing. You'll learn more about Web addresses later in this chapter.

- **Links bar.** The links toolbar contains links that you can click to go to a specific Web page quickly. You'll find five predefined links, but you can customize this bar with your own favorite links. You'll learn how to do this Chapter 2.

- **Explorer bar.** The Explorer bar—more like a window panel, actually—appears only if you click one of the Explorer bar buttons on the standard toolbar. The Explorer bar can show favorite sites, search tools, recently visited sites, or sites you can subscribe to. There's a little close button on the Explorer bar's title bar that enables you to close this panel if it gets in the way.

- **Workspace.** In the workspace, you see the Web document you're currently accessing. If the document is bigger than the window size, you'll see active scroll bars, which you can use to bring additional portions of the document into view.

- **Status bar.** In the status bar, Internet Explorer talks back. You'll learn more about Internet Explorer's messages as they come up.

Understanding the Standard Toolbar

Look closer now at the standard toolbar, which you'll use often. The toolbar, shown below, provides quick access to many of Internet Explorer's most frequently accessed commands—especially Web navigation commands. Here's a quick overview of the tools and a brief description of what they do.

Name	Action
Back	Goes back one document in the list of documents you have retrieved in this session and displays the document in the workspace. (This tool is unavailable if you've just started Internet Explorer and haven't accessed anything but the start page.)
Forward	Goes forward one document in the list of documents you have retrieved in this session and displays the document in the workspace. (This tool is unavailable if you haven't clicked the Back button.)
Stop	Stops downloading the current document. This tool is handy if the document you're downloading seems to take forever or doesn't look very interesting.
Refresh	Downloads a new, fresh copy of the current document from the Internet. This tool is useful if you've clicked the Stop tool and then decide you'd still like to see the whole document.

(continued)

1

Name	Action *continued*
Home	Re-displays the default start page, the one you see when you start Internet Explorer. You can change this page, as explained in Chapter 5.
Search	Displays the Search Explorer bar on the left side of the window. This Explorer bar enables you to search the Web for information. You'll learn how to use this window (and perform searches) in Chapter 3.
Favorites	Displays the Favorites Explorer bar on the left of the window. This Explorer bar enables you to access your favorite sites quickly. You'll learn how to save favorite sites in Chapter 2 and how to organize them in Chapter 5.
History	Displays the History Explorer bar on the left side of the window. This Explorer bar enables you to see all the sites you've recently visited. You'll learn how to use this cool, new feature later in this chapter.
Channels	Displays the Channels Explorer bar on the left side of the window. This Explorer bar enables you to subscribe to Webcasting sites. You'll learn how to use this *extremely* cool feature in Chapter 4.
Full Screen	Zooms the window to the full size of the screen and hides all toolbars except the standard toolbar. Learn all about this new feature later in this chapter.
Mail	Opens Outlook Express for sending and receiving e-mail. Other options enable you to send a link or a page to someone, or to start reading newsgroups. You learn about e-mail and newsgroups in Part II.

Adjusting the Toolbars

Each of Internet Explorer's toolbars can be adjusted to suit your fancy. To bring hidden toolbars into view, choose Toolbar from the View menu, and then select the toolbar you want to display. After the toolbar appears, you can adjust it by moving the *drag handle,* the vertical line on the toolbar's left edge. Try moving the drag handle left and right, and also up and down. As you can see, you can stack the toolbars any way you like. You can also combine toolbars.

While you're learning Internet Explorer, it's best to display all three toolbars in full width. Later, you can hide the ones you don't want to use. (To hide a toolbar, choose Toolbars from the View menu and then select the toolbar's name.)

NOTE

What's the ideal toolbar setup? I like to see all three of them in full width, with the standard toolbar on the top, the address bar in the middle, and the links bar at the bottom. I like the standard toolbar on the top because it's near the menus, and I like to have all the commands grouped together. I like to have the links bar on the bottom because it can be customized. In Chapter 5, you'll learn how to add your own links to the link bar—links you'll use every day. They're easy to reach when they're on the bottom.

Grasping a Few Basic Terms

You'll hear people talking about "Web servers," "Web sites," "Web pages," and "home pages." Let's clarify these basic terms.

- 🌐 **Web server.** A program that listens for requests from browsers for a particular Web page (or the computer that's running the program). The server dishes out the page and then listens for more requests. If the server can't find the page, it sends an error message that says "not found" or something similarly vague and unhelpful.

- 🌐 **Web site.** A collection of Web pages. A Web site has a unique Internet address that unambiguously identifies its location. Most Web sites contain dozens, hundreds, or even thousands of Web pages.

- 🌐 **Web page.** A Web page is a single Web document. In actual length, some are shorter than a page, while some are longer— lots longer. Most Web pages average about two screenfuls of text and graphics.

- 🌐 **Home page.** People use this phrase in different ways. It basically means "home base." In Internet Explorer, you click Home (on the toolbar) to go to the MSN Internet Start page. This phrase also refers to the welcome page of a Web site that includes many linked pages, so you might see a Home icon on somebody's pages. If you click this icon, you see the welcome page, not the MSN Internet Start page. When people say, "I can't wait to put

1

my home page on the Web," what they're talking about is a personal page, which is likely to contain their resume, picture, favorite hobbies and pets, and a few favorite links.

HELP

Is it a *site* or a *page*?

As you'll quickly discover, people use the terms *site* and *page* more or less synonymously. Somebody who says, "Hey, check out this awesome site," is usually referring to a specific Web page or document, not an entire collection of documents. This isn't done just by *newbies,* people new to the Internet, but by seasoned vets, too. I suspect it's because *site* sounds more high tech than *page* or *document.* Still, you'll have a better grasp of the Web if you keep the distinction in mind.

Taking Internet Explorer for a Spin

Try a bit of Web navigation. In this mini-lesson, you'll learn about the all-important Back and Forward buttons, which are about as crucial as the gear-shift lever in your car. It makes good sense to understand these features thoroughly.

Try the following tutorial:

1. On the start page, you'll see some text. (It changes every day, but there's always something.) In the text, some words are underlined and displayed in a different color. Move the pointer to the underlined text. When you have positioned the pointer over the underlined text, note that the pointer changes shape. It becomes a hand. This tells you that you have positioned the pointer over a *hyperlink.* A hyperlink enables you to select another Web document to display. Don't click yet.

2. Move the pointer over some of the graphics. As you can see, many of them are hyperlinks, too. Don't click yet.

3. Where will you wind up when you click a hyperlink? When the pointer changes to a hand shape, the status bar shows the link's destination. Look at the status bar as you're moving the pointer over links.

4. OK, now click a link. Internet Explorer displays the new page, and some other things happen, too. On the status bar, the ever-

talkative Internet Explorer tells you what it's doing: opening the page. If the page has lots of graphics or other resources and is taking a while to download, the program tells you how many items remain to be downloaded. When the page is finished, you see "Done."

5. On the page you just accessed, click another link. You'll see another new page. Fine! Now, how do you get back?

Going Back

To get back to the start page, use any of the following techniques:

🌐 Click the Back button like crazy until you see the start page. (You can also press Alt + Left Arrow.) This technique works to get you back to where you started, but it's really slow if you've visited a lot of pages.

or

🌐 Click the little down arrow next to the Back button. You'll see a little drop-down menu listing the pages you've displayed in this session (Figure 1-3). Choose Internet Start to go back to the start page.

or

🌐 Click the Home button (or choose Home Page from the Go menu).

You'll see the start page again.

Figure 1-3
To go back to a recently visited page quickly, click the down arrow next to the Back button and choose a page from the drop-down menu.

Going Forward

One thing about Web browsers that's really confusing for new users is the Forward button (same as selecting Go and Forward or using the Alt + Right arrow keyboard command). In the previous section, you clicked a number of hyperlinks and then went back. If you did this, try clicking the Forward button. As you can see, this re-displays the sites you just went back from.

1

A little confusing? It is, at first. It's sort of like trying to ride a bicycle for the first time. After a little practice though, the movements come naturally. Again, here's what the Back and Forward buttons do:

 Back. Click Back to see the document from which you just jumped via a hyperlink. If you keep clicking Back, you keep going back in the series of jumps you made in this session. When the Back button dims and becomes unavailable, you're looking at the first document you saw in this session. To go back to a particular site, it's easiest to display the Back button's drop-down menu, which enables you to choose the page you want to go back to.

Forward. Click Forward to re-display documents you've gone back from. If you haven't clicked Back, Forward is dimmed.

TIP
The Forward button has a drop-down menu just like the Back button does. You can click this button to display a list of the sites you can go forward to. This option is a real time-saver when you need to jump forward several pages.

Did you notice that, when you click Back, pages re-display much more quickly than they did when you first accessed them? That's because Internet Explorer stores recently accessed Web documents in a *cache* (pronounced "cash"), which is a special folder on your hard disk. It's called Temporary Internet Documents, and it's located in the Windows folder. When you return to a recently accessed document, Internet Explorer retrieves the document from the cache rather than downloading it from the Internet, which would take more time.

Refreshing a Page

When you go back to previously viewed pages, Internet Explorer retrieves the page from the cache, as you've just learned. But what if the page has changed? If you'd like to make sure you're viewing the most recent version of a page, click the Refresh button. Doing so forces Internet Explorer to retrieve a new copy of the page from the network.

Returning to Previously Visited Pages

Internet Explorer gives you additional ways to go back to previously visited Web pages. Try these out to see whether you like using them.

You can return to previously visited sites by going to the menu bar and selecting File. On the File menu, you'll see the last several documents you accessed (Figure 1-4). You can return to any one of these documents by choosing it from the menu.

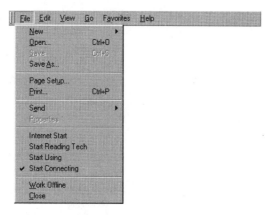

Figure 1-4

The File menu enables you to choose from recently accessed pages.

Here's another way to see a list of previously visited sites. Click the down arrow on the right of the Address bar. You'll see a list of sites in the order you've visited them. This method isn't as convenient or as complete as using the History Explorer bar, though.

Using the History Explorer Bar

Do you feel lost? That's the downside of the Web. Thanks to the innovative History Explorer bar in Microsoft Internet Explorer 4, you'll find out where you are quickly enough—and you'll find your way back to sites you've previously visited with ease.

To view the History Explorer bar, just click the History button on the standard toolbar or go to the View menu and choose Explorer Bar. Select

1

History from the submenu. The screen splits, and you see the History Explorer bar in the left pane (Figure 1-5). This is a really neat feature—so neat, in fact, that it's reason enough to prefer Internet Explorer over any other browser. Listed under Today are all the sites you've visited in the current day's searching; if you click on one of them, Internet Explorer expands the hidden list of pages at the site—pages you viewed in previous surfing sessions. You can also view items from previous weeks' history.

To return to a page listed in the History Explorer bar, just click it.

NOTE

By default, Internet Explorer stores history items for the previous 20 days. You can increase or decrease the retention period, if you wish. To do so, choose Options from the View menu and click the General tab. In the History area, type the number of days you want the program to retain history list items, or you can use the spin controls. If somebody else is using your computer and you'd prefer to cover your tracks, you can clear the history list by clicking the Clear History button. Click OK to exit.

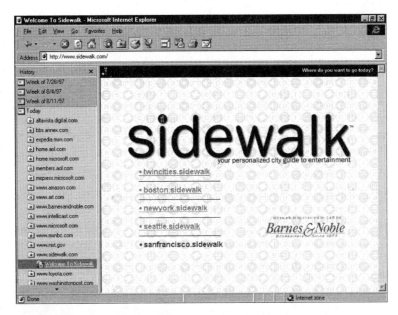

Figure 1-5

The History Explorer bar makes it a snap to return to previously visited sites.

Browsing Offline

If you'd like to visit History pages while you're offline, do the following:

1. Go to the File menu and choose Work Offline.

2. In the History Explorer bar, click the site you want to visit.

How does this work? When you choose Work Offline, Internet Explorer doesn't go to the network to see whether the page has changed. Instead, it loads the copy of the page that was made on your hard disk when you first downloaded the page. Once you choose Work Offline, this option remains in effect until you again choose Work Offline from the File menu to remove the check mark next to this option. Be sure to do this when you next log on to the Internet.

Going to a Web Page
by Typing Its Address

Once word gets around that you're using the Internet, somebody will rattle off a Web address and say, "You've *got* to see this!" Don't try to find the page by surfing. That would be like trying to find somebody in New York City by knocking on doors and asking around. You need to go to the page by typing its address.

Using the Address Bar

The best way to find a site you want is to use the Address bar. (If you don't see the Address bar, go to the View menu and select Toolbars. Then click on Address Bar. If you can't see the address box, locate the toolbar's drag handle—it's a vertical line at the left edge of the bar—and drag until the box comes into view.) Click in the address box to select the current Web address. Then type the address (note that you don't have to type the *http://* part). For example, to access http://www.amazon.com, you just type www.amazon.com. If you don't have a cool site to go to, try this one; it's the Web address for one of the Internet's most successful and interesting online businesses (Figure 1-6 on page 19).

1

You can often find a company's home page just by typing *www* followed by a period, the company's name, another period, and *com*. Try some of these: www.pepsi.com, www.toyota.com, and www.washingtonpost.com.

Web addresses are also known as URLs, short for Uniform Resource Locator (URL). Some people pronounce this "Earl," while others spell it out ("you-are-ell").

What's in a URL?

URLs have three parts: the protocol, the domain name, and the resource location and name. In *http://www.microsoft.com/ie/default.asp*, for example, the *http://* part is the protocol, *www.microsoft.com* is the domain, and */ie/default.asp* is the resource location and name.

The first part of the URL indicates the *protocol* that's supposed to be used to access the data. A protocol is a communications standard that specifies how computers can exchange data over the network. Microsoft Internet Explorer is a Web browser, and it can work with the basic Web protocol, HTTP (the Hypertext Transfer Protocol). But it can work with other protocols, too, such as FTP (the File Transfer Protocol), which enables you to copy files to your computer. Chapter 11 discusses FTP.

The second part of the URL gives the *domain name* of the computer that's running the server. A domain name is a user-friendly version of a numerical Internet address (which looks something like 228.137.190.15). An Internet service called the Domain Name Service (DNS) translates between these user-friendly alphabetical names (such as www.microsoft.com) and their numerical equivalents.

The third part of the URL gives the exact storage *location and name* of the specific resource you're after. This might include a directory path similar to the ones you use on your computer. Sometimes the third part of the URL is omitted. If so, you will go to the server's main welcome page. For example, if you type only *http://www.microsoft.com*, you will see Microsoft's home page.

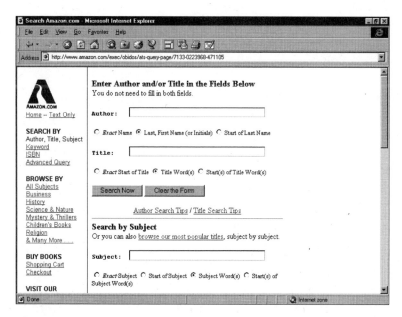

Figure 1-6

You can get to Amazon.com—or any other Web site—by typing its address in the Address bar.

Typing Web Addresses Correctly

Suppose you type the address and press OK, but nothing happens. The animation just runs and runs, and still nothing happens. Finally you see an alert box informing you that Internet Explorer couldn't open the site or the document. Chances are you didn't type the address correctly.

To avoid errors when you type Web addresses, note the following guidelines:

- 🌐 URLs are case-sensitive, so be sure to copy the capitalization pattern exactly.

- 🌐 Don't place any spaces within the address.

- 🌐 Check to make sure you've put periods and slash marks (/) in the correct places.

- 🌐 Most Web documents are named with an *extension* (the part of the filename that comes after the period). Most of the time this is *.html,* but sometimes it's *.htm,* or *.asp.* Make sure you type the extension correctly.

1

If you're trying to visit somebody's home page, the URL might contain a tilde (~), which is often used to indicate the name of somebody's home directory on a Unix computer. It isn't a typo. Be sure to include the tilde.

 If you grew up with DOS, you poor thing, remember that these slash marks are forward slashes (/), not backward slashes (\).

 Check your typing. You have probably made some tiny, human, forgivable typing mistake that's hardly noticeable—except to computers.

 Maybe you didn't make a mistake. Sometimes Web pages disappear, leaving a *stale link* behind. (A stale link is a hyperlink that takes you to a "page not found" message.)

TIP

By means of the History list, introduced earlier in this chapter, Internet Explorer remembers the Web pages you've visited. The next time you type a previously visited address, the program will try to complete what you're typing. Called AutoComplete, this is a really cool feature—try it. Click Home to get back to the start page, and then type the address of the page you were just looking at. As you can see, the program tries to guess where you're going. If it guesses right, just press Enter.

Stopping an Unwanted Download

Suppose you click the wrong hyperlink—and off Internet Explorer goes, obediently downloading some huge page with tons of graphics. It's taking forever, and you don't even want to see it. What to do? Simple: Click Stop (or press Esc). This button stops the download, enabling you to click Back so that you can try again.

Using Internal Navigation Aids

You've learned how to use the Back and Forward buttons. As you know, these buttons enable you to re-display pages you've previously viewed. Sometimes, though, they don't provide the best way to get around a site with multiple pages. If the site is well designed, you can use *internal navigation aids*. These are links, usually given in a list, that work like a table of contents. They show you the structure of the site and enable you to move around within it.

Web authors provide internal navigation aids in different ways. One of the best is shown in Figure 1-7: a row of navigation buttons running down the side of the page (or across the top or bottom). The best sites use this design consistently. No matter which page you're viewing, you still see the same list of links. This aid really helps to prevent disorientation.

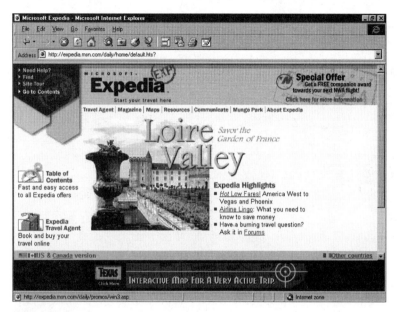

Figure 1-7

Look for internal navigation aids, such as the buttons on the left side of this page. They enable you to move around the site easily.

Navigating Framed Documents

Framed documents (Figure 1-8 on the following page) have two or more independent panels. Depending on how the page's author set them up, you might be able to scroll the frame and adjust its border; this can be prevented, though, if the author prefers. You know you can scroll a frame if you see a scroll bar. To find out whether you can adjust a border, move the pointer to it and see whether it changes to an arrow shape.

The page shown in Figure 1-8 uses one of the frames—the one on the right—to display internal navigation aids. These aids stay put, even if you scroll the other panel. That's a very good reason right there to like frames. You click one of the links in the navigation aid list, and you see a new page in the adjacent panel.

1

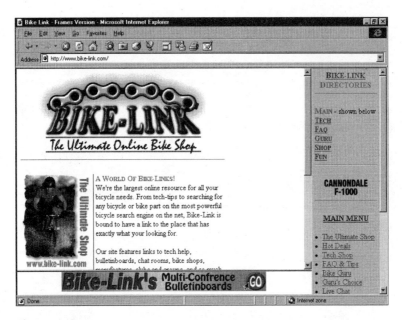

Figure 1-8

Frames can be used to provide internal navigation aids.

Some people don't like frames, though. They find them confusing to use. For example, when you click the Back button, you see the previous panel. But you don't actually leave the page until you've gone back to the first panel you saw and then clicked Back once more. It isn't so confusing once you understand what's happening.

🌐 Many sites let you choose between a framed and a non-framed version. If you just don't like fussing with frames, choose the non-framed version.

🌐 Some frames are scrollable, and others aren't. You can tell the difference by looking to see whether there's a scroll bar.

🌐 Sometimes Web authors enable you to adjust the frame borders. You can tell whether a border is adjustable by moving the mouse pointer to the border. If the pointer changes shape to arrows, you can adjust the border.

🌐 Only one frame is active (selected) at a time. When you click Back or Forward, your action affects only that frame, not any others.

🌐 If you've viewed many pages within the frame site and want to go back to the previous site you viewed, it's faster to choose the previous site from the history list than to click Back. You might have to click Back many times to exit the framed site.

🌐 If you're at the beginning of the framed site (the welcome page), clicking Back takes you out of that site to the previously viewed site.

🌐 Sometimes panels don't have borders. (Authors can hide the borders if they want to.) But you can tell that the page uses frames if scroll bars appear that don't run the length or width of the window.

Using the Pop-Up Menus

Microsoft Internet Explorer makes good use of the right mouse button. Try right-clicking various things within the program's window—a graphic, the page background, a link. As you'll see, a pop-up menu appears with options that are relevant to what you're pointing at (Figure 1-9). For example, when you point at a text link, you can choose from the following options: Open, Open In New Window, Save Target As (save the document referenced in the link), Print Target (print the document referenced in the link), Copy Shortcut (for pasting elsewhere), Add To Favorites, and Properties (information about the page).

Figure 1-9
Don't forget that the right mouse button displays a pop-up menu such as this one, from which you can choose commonly used commands.

Using the Full Screen View

When you click the Maximize button on the Internet Explorer title, Windows zooms the window to full size. But there's another way to get the big picture—the Full Screen view. Like Maximize, the Full Screen view zooms the screen to full size, but it also hides all the toolbars except the standard toolbar.

To see the Full Screen view, just click the Full Screen button on the standard toolbar. To return to the normal view, click the Full Screen button again.

TIP The Full Screen view is the ideal environment for using the Explorer bars (Search, Favorites, History, and Channels). There's plenty of room to see the Web page you're viewing. Plus, the Explorer bars behave dynamically in the Full Screen view. They appear when you move the pointer toward the left side of the screen and disappear when you move the pointer away.

Navigating with the Keyboard

If you would prefer to use the keyboard instead of your mouse, you can use keyboard shortcuts (also called *hotkeys*). Here's a list of hotkeys you can use for navigation:

To do this:	Press this:
Go back (same as clicking Back button)	Alt + Left arrow or Backspace
Go forward (same as clicking Forward button)	Alt + Right arrow
Move to next hyperlink	Tab
Move to previous hyperlink	Shift + Tab
Jump to the page referenced in currently selected hyperlink	Enter
Scroll down	Down arrow
Scroll down in larger increment	Page Down
Scroll to end of document	End
Scroll up	Up arrow
Scroll up in larger increments	Page Up
Scroll to beginning of document	Home
Refresh the current page	F5
Stop downloading	Esc

PART

Getting Help

Microsoft Internet Explorer comes with a standard Windows help utility, similar to the ones you've probably seen in other Windows applications. To get help, go to the Help menu and choose Contents And Index. You'll see the Help window shown in Figure 1-10. To explore the contents, just click one of the plus signs to expand the list of topics; click the minus sign to collapse a topic list. To see a page concerning a topic, just click it.

You can also search for information. To do so, click Index. In the text box, start typing a word or phrase. The Help window tries to match what you're typing. If there's a Help page relevant to the word or phrase you typed, you'll see it in the panel. Just click Display to see the page.

The Help window's toolbar enables you to hide the topic list (click Show to bring it back), go back to a previously displayed page, or print the current help page. If you're done with Help, just click the close button.

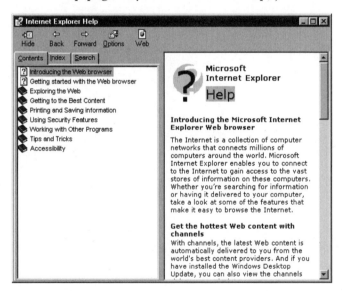

Figure 1-10
The Help window provides information about Microsoft Internet Explorer, including how-to instructions and some neat tips and tricks.

From Here

- Get some practice by doing some serious surfing. Chapter 2 gives you a taste of what's out there.

- Learn how to find information on the Web and turn the Internet into a really useful tool. Chapter 3 shows you how.

2 Dig the Web

Some people have the impression that the Web is just a waste of time and that there isn't much quality content out there. But people who say this probably haven't seen the best of what the Web has to offer. It's a really good idea to start your surfing by visiting the best and most useful sites on the Web. Once you've seen the best of the Web, you won't waste your time on inferior Web pages, and you'll be on your way to transforming the Web (and Microsoft Internet Explorer) into a tool of genuine value to you, personally and professionally.

As you explore the Web, you'll find some sites that you will want to visit time and again. Internet Explorer makes it easy to do this, as this chapter explains. You can save your favorite sites to the Links bar, to the Favorites menu, and to the Windows desktop. You can even create keyboard shortcuts to your favorite sites. This chapter explains how to customize Internet Explorer so that your favorite sites are a click or two away.

HELP **I've been up all night surfing—quick, I need an excuse!**

Here are a few excuses I've tried. For some reason, they didn't work very well, but maybe you'll have better luck.

> "I just lost track of time. I couldn't believe it when I saw the sun come up."
>
> "The information superhighway will change society. I must be prepared."
>
> "I realize that finding every Star Trek site on the Web could be seen as a waste of time, but I'm learning highly marketable computer skills."
>
> "A new form of consciousness is emerging, and I want to be part of it."
>
> "It beats watching old movies, doesn't it?"

Judging a Site's Quality

You'll have your own ideas about site quality after browsing for a while, but really great sites have several or all of these characteristics:

- 🌐 **Rich content.** You want more than just a bunch of splashy graphics (which take forever to download) and a few words here and there. A great site offers entertaining and useful information. It takes a lot of work to make a great site—which is why they're so rare.

- 🌐 **World-class design.** We're not talking about just good looks. A well-designed site is easy to navigate; just by looking at the page for a few seconds, you should be able to tell what's there and what you can do.

- 🌐 **Interactivity.** A great site invites exploration and gives you ways to get involved. At www.amazon.com, introduced in Chapter 1, you can add your own book reviews.

- 🌐 **Frequently updated, timely information.** The site's content changes frequently, and it's worth visiting again and again.

- 🌐 **Free, useful goodies.** A really good site offers images and software to download, on-screen calculators, checklists, rich and searchable archives, and more.

Looking at Microsoft's Top Sites

Some of the best sites on the Web are brought to you by the same company that makes your favorite browser. Take a look at Slate, Expedia, MSNBC, Microsoft Investor, and Cinemania.

Slate

Can a high-quality magazine survive on the Web? Nobody's paying for the subscription; it's going to take advertising dollars if a Web magazine hopes to survive. Most of all, though, it's going to take quality writing. That's the approach taken by *Slate* (www.slate.com), a reader's site. The table of contents page (Figure 2-1) enables you to access the articles easily. Try exploring this site, and you'll understand what the phrase *quality Web site* is all about. It's all here: great content, loads of interactivity (you can respond with letters to the editor), easy navigation, frequent updates (well, it *is* a magazine), and tons of nifty freebies (a searchable archive of past *Slate* articles).

Figure 2-1

Slate shows you what quality Web site *means.*

2

MSNBC

And now for the news. MSNBC, a joint venture between Microsoft and NBC, brings you the latest news (www.msnbc.com). To navigate the site, you can use the internal navigation aids at the top of the screen (Figure 2-2), which enable you to select news categories (such as commerce, sports, or weather). Scroll down to see more headlines.

Figure 2-2
Get the news from MSNBC.

Expedia

There's a travel agency on the Web? Yes, and it's free. At Microsoft Expedia (expedia.msn.com), you can learn about travel destinations, view maps, get travel tips, and even make air, hotel, and car reservations. As you can see from Figure 2-3, which shows one of Expedia's feature stories, this site is beautifully done. A totally cool feature enables you to search for the lowest current airfares for a trip you're planning to make. This feature lets you see the same data that travel agents see and lets you select the flight.

Microsoft Investor

If you're looking for help managing and tracking your investments, Microsoft Investor (investor.msn.com) is loaded with useful tools and information, including a portfolio tracker. You type in the ticker symbols of your stocks or mutual funds, and Microsoft Investor shows your portfolio's current value. There's more, too. You can search for information about companies, research new investment opportunities, view current market results, see an online stock ticker, and even buy and sell stocks online. You'll also find feature articles that show you how to explore the world of investments (Figure 2-4).

PART

Figure 2-3

If you're thinking about a vacation, make Expedia your very first stop.

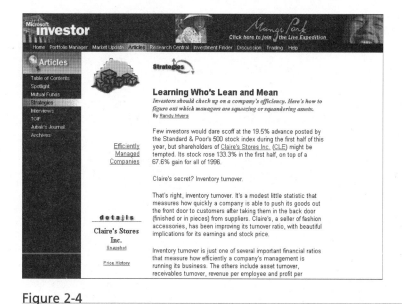

Figure 2-4

Microsoft Investor provides in-depth investment analysis, research resources, market reports, and even a portfolio tracker.

2

Cinemania

Love movies? You'll love Cinemania (cinemania.msn.com). You'll find feature articles and an enormous database of film reviews. You can even see a list of the movies playing in your area, including show times (Figure 2-5). For some films, you can view a preview right on your computer screen. (See Chapter 9 for more information about viewing movies on-screen.) Among the many features is a list of current video releases, including reviews that point you to the three- and four-star releases—and warn you about the duds.

Figure 2-5
Cinemania is required reading for movie fans.

Exploring the Best of the Web

Want to see the best of what's out there? You'll find several pages on the Web that list picks for the best pages on the Web. They vary, based on the interests and expertise of the people who put them together. Hyperlinks take you directly to pages that look interesting.

Best of the Web

Get started by surfing the following "Best of the Web" pages.

🌐 **Microsoft's Best of the Web.** This one's easy to get to. Just click Best of the Web on the Links toolbar, or choose Best Of The Web from the Go menu. Figure 2-6 shows what it looks like today (it changes often).

Figure 2-6

Microsoft's Best of the Web is easy to use and loaded with fantastic places to surf.

🌐 **WebCrawler Guide** (webcrawler.com/select). This guide lists the best sites on the Internet, as selected by WebCrawler Select's critical reviewers. Categories include arts and entertainment, business, computers, daily news, government and politics, education, health and medicine, humanities, the Internet, life and culture, personal finance, recreation and hobbies, science and technology, sports, and travel.

🌐 **WWWomen** (www.wwwomen.com/feature/bestwww.shtml). This page contains a great list of women's sites, encompassing sports, labor issues, health, networking, family issues, and more.

Top 100 Sites

The following sites offer differing views on which are the top 100 sites on the Web.

🌐 **MacUser 101 Must-See Sites** (www.zdnet.com/macuser/mu_0396/ feature/feature1.html). Although this list includes some sites specific to Macs, it's really of general interest to any Web user. The touch here is decidedly artistic and zany ("The Foolproof Guide to Making Any Woman Your Platonic Friend"), but there's some solidly useful stuff, too, including a great page of reference links ("When You've Misplaced Your Library Card").

2

- **PC Magazine's Top 100 Sites** (www.pcmag.com/special/web100/_open.htm). This site offers great links to computer companies and computer resources on the Web, particularly Windows-based systems and Windows-compatible computers. You'll also find useful sections on entertainment, news, and reference.

- **The Web 100** (www.web100.com). User ratings determine the rankings on this list, so here's a great way to find out which pages Web users prefer. You can view them by rank, in groups of 10 at a time, or by topic (including arts and entertainment, business and commerce, education and reference, government and politics, health and medicine, news and information, sports and leisure, and science and technology). In the top 10 this week are: SeniorCom, Healthfinder, CDnow, and—English teachers are going to love this—The Complete Works of William Shakespeare.

What's Cool

Apart from the gold and the dreck, there's the cool. And what does *cool* mean? As my Generation X friends say, "If you have to ask, you're never gonna know," but there is a Web-specific definition. A cool Web site captures the spirit of the Web as a new, multimedia communication medium.

Admittedly, *cool* is hard to define. At the Cool Site of the Day (cool.infi.net), you'll find a FAQ (short for "Frequently Asked Questions") that employs scientific research in an effort to pin down just what makes certain Web sites cool. According to the FAQ, a site's coolness can be attributed to a trace element called *coolium*. However, most of the sites that wind up on "what's cool" lists tend to have discovered one or more of the following secrets to success:

- **Awareness of the Internet's potential as a new medium.** One of the most popular sites on the Web, frequently named in What's Cool lists, is *Word,* an exclusively online magazine (www.word.com). A literary magazine stressing Generation X sensibilities, *Word* combines text with graphics, animations, and photographs in a full expression of the Web's multimedia possibilities (Figure 2-7).

Figure 2-7

Word *fully explores the Web's multimedia possibilities.*

IntelliMouse: A Better Way to Surf

While you're browsing through all these interesting sites, your mouse—
and your elbow—are going to get a workout. But there's a better way.
Microsoft Internet Explorer is optimized to make full use of Microsoft's
IntelliMouse, an innovative mouse that includes a scrolling wheel
button between the two mouse buttons. When you've installed
IntelliMouse, you can:

scroll through a Web page by rotating the wheel button forward or
back—no more fussing with scroll bars,

continuously scroll the page by holding down the wheel button
while moving the mouse, or

jump to a link by pointing to it and *datazooming* forward. (To
datazoom, hold down the Shift key while you rotate the wheel.)

2

- **Savvy music stuff.** I wonder how many otherwise obscure bands have become major sellers because of the Internet? Word about music that's unusual, interesting, or hip gets around quickly on "the Net." Don't miss the Ultimate Band List (<u>ubl.com</u>), which tracks pages—both amateur pages and those sponsored by record companies—about bands of all kinds, ranging from the best-known acts to obscure but up-and-coming local ensembles.

- **Techno-zaniness.** At last count, there were more than 500 devices connected to the Web, including a talking machine (what you type is spoken out loud), a lava lamp, a CD player, hot tubs, and hundreds of live cameras. For a list, go to Yahoo! (<u>www.yahoo.com</u>) and search for the phrase "Interesting Devices."

- **Secret knowledge revealed.** As you'll see in the Hidden Mickeys of Disney site, Disney Imagineers embed Mickey Mouse shapes here and there throughout the Disney theme parks as a joke; find the scoop on how to locate them at **www.oitc.com/Disney/**.

- **Hip graphics.** Some of the world's best graphic designers are working on the Web; it's an exciting new medium for them. There's currently a preference for 1950s nostalgia graphics. For an example, see the home page of the Internet Underground Music Archive (Figure 2-8) accessible from **www.iuma.com**.

Figure 2-8

Internet Underground Music Archive (IUMA)

You'll find several sites that offer lists of what's cool.

🌐 **Yahoo!'s Picks of the Week** (www.yahoo.com/picks/). The ya-hoos at Yahoo! put together a weekly list of sites that are timely, informative, or just plain wigged out.

🌐 **Cool Site of the Year** (cool.infi.net/csoty/index.html). From the folks who bring you the Cool Site of the Day, here's the Cool Site of the Year, along with some runners-up.

🌐 **Netscape Communication's What's Cool** (home.netscape.com/home/whats-cool.html). This page should be titled "What's Cool in Corporate America," but it's well worth a visit.

What's Hot

What's hot isn't exactly the opposite of what's cool: hot sites are the most popular, and some of them are cool, too. You can find out what's hot by checking out the following sites:

🌐 **100 Hot Games** (www.100hot.com/games/). This page lists the hottest sites for games of all kinds (including computer games, video games, chess, cards, role-playing, and more), based on Web traffic statistics.

🌐 **100 Hot Web Sites** (www.100hot.com). This list is compiled objectively using Web traffic statistics. The list doesn't include college sites or home pages. Categories include models and celebrities, the best of the WWW, games, show business, online services, sports, live audio, places, travel, technology, chat lines, kids, business, jobs, service providers, and shopping.

🌐 **The WebCrawler 100** (www.webcrawler.com/WebCrawler/Fun/WC100.html). WebCrawler, one of the Web's popular search services, ranks sites by the number of servers that link to those sites.

What's New

Hundreds, sometimes thousands, of new Web sites appear daily. There's no way to keep up with all of them, but the following Web services keep track of some of the most interesting and useful new sites:

🌐 **Netscape Guide's What's New** (guide.netscape.com/guide/whats_new.html). This list of interesting new sites in Netscape Communications's Guide (Figure 2-9) is well worth exploring, even if you're not using Netscape Navigator.

2

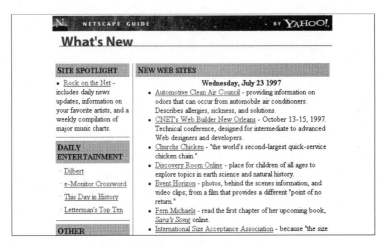

Figure 2-9

Netscape Guide's What's New lists today's new Web sites.

🌐 **New and Noteworthy (point.lycos.com/columns/new/).** Point Communication picks the most interesting new sites reviewed this week.

🌐 **Today's Links** gives Microsoft's pick of the day. (Click Today's Links on the Links bar to see what's up.)

🌐 **WebCrawler Guide to New Sites (webcrawler.com/select/nunu.new.html).** New sites that have been critically reviewed by the WebCrawler Select staff are listed here.

🌐 **What's New On Yahoo (www.yahoo.com/new).** Hundreds of new sites go online daily, and they'll appear in Yahoo, the Web's best subject tree. (There'll be more about Yahoo in Chapter 3.)

Daily Inspiration

Here are some great Web sites that change every day, bringing you new information that will make you learn and laugh:

🌐 **Cool Jargon of the Day (www.bitech.com/jargon/cool).** Those ever-enterprising technobabblers are sure to come up with ever-more-confusing terms.

🌐 **Cool Site of the Day (cool.infi.net).** Every day there's a new, cool site. Check it out!

🌐 **David Letterman's Top Ten List (www.cbs.com/lateshow/).** Did you miss the *Late Show?* Check out this site for Letterman's latest Top Ten List.

PART

🌐 **Those Were the Days** (www.440.com/twtd/today.html). You think today's news is bad?

🌐 **Urgent News of the Day** (www.yahoo.com/headlines/current/news/). Skip the newspaper, skip Dan Rather—it's all here.

Making the Web Useful

Cool, intriguing, entertaining, zany, wild, fun—these are the adjectives that you'll use to describe the sites you've visited so far. But what about *useful?* Is the information *practical?*

You bet. Here's a sample of what Internet Explorer and the Web can help you do:

🌐 **Get help with your kids' homework.** Looking for teaching resources, or for some help with homework? The Education Index (www.educationindex.com) lists hundreds of excellent education sites. It's organized both by subject and age level (lifestage).

🌐 **Look for college scholarships.** Search for colleges and scholarships—and you can even apply online, thanks to CollegeNet (www.collegenet.com).

Yahoo! Internet Life's 25 Most Incredibly Useful Sites

Don't miss this useful page: www3.zdnet.com/yil/content/depts/useful/25mostuse.html. It lists Yahoo! Internet Life's all-time favorite Incredibly Useful Sites. Here's a sample of what you'll find: how to

> avoid speed traps
> avoid tax audits
> estimate college costs
> find the closest ATM
> fix your own cable TV
> hear your newspaper
> track your packages
> unclog your drain.

There's a new Incredibly Useful Site every day, so check back often.

2

- **Find out how much your used car is worth.** You'll find this information, plus the dealer invoice cost of the new car you're considering, at Edmund's online site (<u>www.edmunds.com</u>). Don't miss the tips on negotiating with dealers; you could save thousands of dollars.

- **Learn more about diseases and their diagnosis.** The entire Merck Manual—yes, the full text of this physician's reference—is available online (<u>www.merck.com</u>). It's searchable. You type in a word and see a list of articles concerning this word.

Staying Informed

How much are you spending on magazine and newspaper subscriptions? You could possibly pay for your Internet access (and then some) by getting the news and magazine articles you want from the Web. The following *free* sites contain the *full text* of the most recent edition of newspapers and magazines. What's more, they offer search and navigation tools that enable you to find what you're looking for. At *TV Guide*'s Web site, for instance, you can set up a personal profile that enables you to list only those shows that conform to your interests, for up to a week in advance.

Atlantic Monthly <u>www.theatlantic.com/issues/current/contents.htm</u>

Christian Science Monitor <u>www.csmonitor.com</u>

Los Angeles Times <u>www.latimes.com</u>

Money accessible from <u>www.pathfinder.com</u>

New York Times <u>www.nytimes.com</u>

Time accessible from <u>www.pathfinder.com</u>

TV Guide <u>www.tvguide.com</u>

US News and World Report <u>www.usnews.com</u>

USA Today <u>www.usatoday.com</u>

Washington Post <u>www.washingtonpost.com</u>

Creating Shortcuts to Favorite Pages

By now, you have surely found some Web pages that you will want to visit again and again. Rather than navigating to these pages manually, take advantage of several Internet Explorer features that give you much quicker access to your favorite pages. Within Internet Explorer, you can add favorite pages to the Links toolbar and to the Favorites menu. You can also create shortcuts to your favorite pages and place them on the desktop. You can even create keyboard shortcuts that take you instantly to your favorite sites, without any fussing with the mouse! The following sections explain how to customize Internet Explorer so that your favorite sites are easily accessed.

Adding Favorite Pages to the Links Toolbar

The Links toolbar, introduced in Chapter 1, provides a really handy way to get to your favorite sites quickly. The buttons are easy to access. Microsoft Internet Explorer comes configured with five buttons, but you can delete them without a guilty conscience. They're duplicated (for the most part) by commands on the Go menu, or they're easily accessed from Microsoft's home page.

To delete existing buttons on the Links bar, follow these steps:

1. Point to the button, and click the right mouse button.

2. Choose Delete. You'll see a dialog box asking you to confirm.

3. Click Yes to confirm the deletion.

To add a page to the Links bar, follow these steps:

1. Display the page you want to add.

2. In the Address bar, click on the icon that's just to the left of the URL, and drag this to the Links bar. You can also drag a link from a Web page to the Links bar.

3. When you have positioned the pointer where you want the button to appear, release the mouse button.

TIP

Because the Links bar provides the quickest and easiest access to your favorite sites, use it for pages you really want to access every day. Be sure you leave room for your favorite search engine and subject directory, which you'll learn about in the next chapter.

Saving Favorite Sites

The Links bar has room for only a few of your favorite sites, but you can also save favorite sites to the Favorites menu. As you'll learn in Chapter 5, you can organize this menu with folders and subfolders. This enables you to save dozens or even hundreds of your favorite sites. Creating a well-organized Favorites menu transforms Internet Explorer into a tool of profound personal usefulness. That's no overstatement. Start the day with

2

fast-breaking news in your professional field, check your mutual funds, search for facts to back up the points you want to make in that meeting. You'll be amazed at the difference that this accessible information can make in your life.

Chapter 5 shows you how to organize favorites. For now, learn how to save them. They'll go to the top level of the Favorite's menu. Later, you'll learn how to create folders and store your favorites in them.

To create a favorite, follow these steps:

1. Display the document.

2. Choose the Favorites menu, and then select the Add To Favorites command. You'll see the Add To Favorites dialog box (Figure 2-10). Internet Explorer proposes the page's title in the Name area.

3. If you'd like to be notified when the content changes, click either of the Yes options. (You'll learn more about subscriptions in Chapter 4.)

4. Click the OK button to save the favorite. Internet Explorer creates a shortcut in the Favorites folder, using the document's title as the name. Internet Explorer also adds the document's name to the Favorites menu. To return to this page in the future, just choose its name from the Favorites menu.

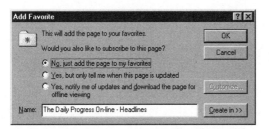

Figure 2-10

You can save any Web address as a favorite.

My favorites menu is getting too long!

Been adding lots of favorites, huh? Time to organize your favorites list. You can create categories of favorites, such as "Fun Stuff," "Research-Related Stuff," "Art Sites," or whatever you like, and create submenus that pop up when you click one of these. For the lowdown, see Chapter 5.

Adding a Shortcut to the Desktop

There's another way to save your favorite sites: create shortcuts on your desktop. After you create the shortcut, you can get back to the site very easily by dragging the shortcut into Internet Explorer's window. (In order to do this, though, you need to work with a nonmaximized Internet Explorer window so that you can see the shortcuts on the desktop.)

To create a shortcut to a particularly useful Web page, follow these steps:

1. Choose the File command; select Send and Shortcut To Desktop. If you prefer, click the right mouse button in the workspace and choose the Create Shortcut command. You'll see a dialog box informing you that a shortcut to the current site will be created on your desktop.

2. Click the OK button.

Creating Keyboard Shortcuts to Your Favorite Sites

For anyone who suffers from mouse elbow (the 90s version of tennis elbow), we have some very, very good news: Windows 95 enables you to create keyboard shortcuts to your favorite Web pages. These include pages that you've saved on the Links bar or the Favorites menu, as well as desktop shortcuts.

These keyboard shortcuts use various combinations of the Ctrl, Alt, and Shift keys. For example, you can save *USA Today* to the Ctrl + Alt + U shortcut. When you press these keys, you see *USA Today*.

To create a keyboard shortcut to one of your favorite sites, follow these steps:

1. Display the shortcut to your favorite site by one of the following methods:

    If you're creating a keyboard shortcut to a button on the Links bar, drag the toolbar to bring the favorite site's button into view, if necessary.

    or

    If you're creating a keyboard shortcut to a favorite on your Favorites menu, choose Organize Favorites from that menu. You'll see a dialog box listing your favorite sites. Scroll, if necessary, to bring the favorite site's icon into view.

    or

    If you're creating a keyboard shortcut to a desktop shortcut, bring it into view by minimizing windows, if necessary.

2

2. Move the mouse pointer to the favorite, and click the right mouse button. You'll see a pop-up menu.

3. Choose Properties. You'll see the Properties dialog box for this shortcut, as shown in Figure 2-11.

4. Click inside the Shortcut key box.

5. Type the letter that you want to use with Ctrl + Alt. To assign the page to Ctrl + Alt + B, for example, type B. (It doesn't matter whether you type an uppercase or lowercase letter.) You can create other combinations by holding down any two (or all three) of the "shift" keys (Shift, Ctrl, and Alt) while you type the letter.

6. Click OK.

NOTE

If you are running another Windows application that uses the same keyboard shortcuts, the shortcut might not work. Also, note that you can't use any of the following keys: Esc, Enter, Tab, Spacebar, Print Screen, or Backspace.

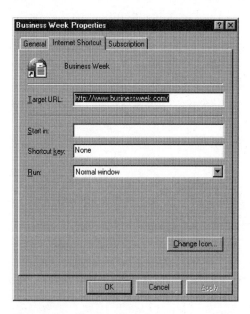

Figure 2-11

You can assign any shortcut to a shortcut key.

To help you remember your shortcut keys, try using letters that remind you of the favorite site's title:

AltaVista	Ctrl + Alt + A
Business Week Online	Ctrl + Alt + B
Charlottesville Daily Progress	Ctrl + Alt + C
Deltaville, Virginia, weather	Ctrl + Alt + D

From Here

- 🌐 Learn how to search the Web in Chapter 3. It's one of the most important Internet skills you can learn.

- 🌐 Organize Internet Explorer so that your favorite Web pages are accessible at the click of a mouse button. You'll find out how in Chapter 5.

- 🌐 Bring excellent content to your desktop, as explained in Chapter 4.

2

3   Find
It Fast

With more than 55 million Web documents in existence and thousands more being added each day, the Web is becoming one of the richest treasure troves of information in the world—but it can be difficult to find the information you're looking for. Many Web users find this situation frustrating, and more than a few give up on the Internet after trying a few searches and coming up empty-handed. But that's too bad. In many cases, the desired information really is out there, and in huge quantities. It's just that the search tools are inconvenient to use, and it takes a little knowledge to search effectively.

Thanks to Microsoft Internet Explorer 4 and the Search Explorer bar, the mechanics of searching have just gotten much easier. The Search Explorer bar enables you to search for Web sites much more conveniently than competing browsers—another one of those things about Internet Explorer that you're really going to like!

Having great tools helps, but it's also important to develop a good search strategy. In this chapter you'll learn how to use Internet Explorer's search tools, and what's more, you'll learn a series of tricks that will help you search more effectively. After reading this chapter, you'll be able to locate the information you want in ways that go far beyond the skills of the average Web user.

Understanding the Web's Search Services

Among the Web's most popular sites are two kinds of search services: subject directories and search engines. It's not surprising that they're so popular. These are the tools people *must* use to find what they're looking for. In this section, you'll learn the difference between the two, so you'll know which one is best to use for a particular search.

Subject Directories

A subject directory is like the subject catalog in a library: it groups Web sites by topic (such as art, entertainment, or chemistry). Unlike a library's subject catalog, though, subject directories contain only a small fraction of the total number of documents on the Web. All the indexing has to be done by a human being, and furiously working Yahoo! staffers are able to index only about 2000 sites per day. Yahoo!, one of the most popular subject directories, indexes less than 1 percent of the 55 million documents now on the Web. But this isn't necessarily a bad thing. For the most part, the pages indexed in Yahoo! are valuable pages. Yahoo! indexes only those pages that meet its criteria for high-quality content.

The welcome page for Yahoo! shows the top-level subjects (Figure 3-1). After you click a subject category, you see progressively more detailed subjects and lists of Web pages (Figure 3-2).

You can also search Yahoo!. Bear in mind, though, that this is not the same thing as searching the whole Web. You're just searching within Yahoo!, which contains far fewer documents than the whole Web does.

TIP Use a subject directory for an initial search. Subject directories generally list only those pages of good to excellent quality that contain meaningful information on a given subject.

Figure 3-1

Subject categories in Yahoo! are like a library's subject card catalog.

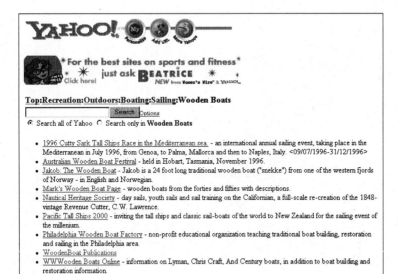

Figure 3-2

You can browse Yahoo! to find more detailed subjects and lists of Web pages.

3

Search Engines

Because subject directories index only a small fraction of the total number of available Web documents, you might not find what you're looking for in a subject directory. You might need to use a *search engine* such as AltaVista (Figure 3-3) or InfoSeek to find what you're looking for. Search engines provide "industrial-strength" database search software that is capable of searching enormous databases containing all the words used in millions of Web documents.

Figure 3-3

AltaVista is one of the powerful search engines available to you on the Web.

Unlike subject directories, which are created by people, search services rely on automated programs to detect and index Web sites. These programs, called *robots* or *spiders,* roam the Web hunting for new documents. When one of these programs finds a new document, it reports the document's address, retrieves all or part of the document's text, and adds the words to a huge database. For example, suppose you publish a page containing the word *Cleveland.* Sooner or later, a spider will detect your page and tuck it into the database so that your URL is listed (along with many thousands of others) as a Web document that mentions *Cleveland.* If users search for *Cleveland,* they'll get a list of Web documents that includes your personal Web site.

PART

This example helps to explain both what's good about search services and what's bad about them. The good thing is that a competent searcher, armed with some of the tricks you'll learn later in this chapter, can zero in on pertinent Web pages with an amazing degree of precision. For example, you can combine search words to focus your search. But even competent searchers retrieve many pages that aren't relevant to their subject. For example, suppose your page is autobiographical, and you said something like, "I was born in Cleveland, but I really don't know anything about it because we moved away when I was six months old." For somebody searching for information about Cleveland, this fact isn't going to be particularly informative. Still, these services are invaluable, if you're willing to put up with their basic inaccuracy.

TIP Use a search engine if you didn't find what you want in a subject directory. You'll need to learn some search techniques to avoid retrieving too many irrelevant documents.

Using the Search Explorer Bar

New to Internet Explorer 4 is a very convenient feature called the Search Explorer bar. When you click the Search button on the Standard toolbar, or go to the View menu and select Explorer Bar and Search, you see the Search Explorer bar, a panel on the left of the window (Figure 3-4). Here are listed the Web's best search services. (See the sidebar on page 53 for a quick introduction to these services.)

Why the Search Explorer Bar Is So Terrific

What's so cool about the Search Explorer bar? Searching by going to a search service directly is inconvenient. You type in one or more search terms and get a retrieval list. Something looks interesting, so you click it, but it turns out to be a dud. You have to click Back to return to the retrieval list. The whole procedure is time-consuming and tedious. With the Search Explorer bar, you see the results of the search in the Explorer bar itself; you can just click away at the retrieved sites until you find the one you're looking for (Figure 3-5). This is another one of those features that make Internet Explorer 4 far and away the best browser available.

3

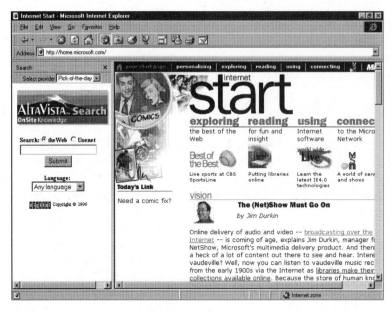

Figure 3-4

The Search Explorer bar (the panel on the left) gives you a convenient way to search.

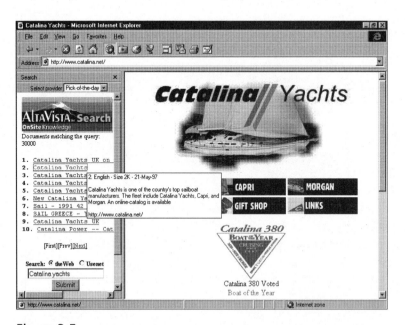

Figure 3-5

Point to a link in the Search bar to see more information.

A Quick Guide to the Web's Search Services

InfoSeek. Although this search service has a small database, you'll find that InfoSeek searches generally produce a more useful retrieval list than most other search services. However, the small database means that there are surely more documents of interest out there. My test search for "Catalina Yachts" returned 218 hits.

Lycos. This service offers a big database of Web documents; my test search returned 10,022 hits. However, Lycos doesn't index the full text of Web documents. Instead, it concentrates on important words in the first 20 lines or so of text and gives preference to titles. As a result, you may miss documents in which your subject is mentioned only peripherally. That's fine usually, but you should use AltaVista if you really want to track down every document that mentions your search terms.

Excite. This service offers a really big database (my search returned 24,133 hits), and it's easy to use. The retrieval list includes a percentage figure that indicates a guesstimate concerning the document's relevance to your interests.

Yahoo!. This is the only subject directory in the Search Explorer bar, and it's a great place to start. Because Yahoo! indexes so few sites, you don't get many hits—my test search netted only 12—but they're usually good ones.

AltaVista. This search service indexes the full text of every document that its spider detects. What this means is that many of the pages you retrieve mention your search words in a peripheral way. You get a huge list of retrieved documents (nearly 50,000 for my test search), but almost all of them are irrelevant to the research focus. Use this service when you want to make sure that you're not missing something that's out there. It's best for pinpointed searches using special syntax that works only if you search from AltaVista's home page (altavista.digital.com). With the Explorer bar, you can search Usenet newsgroups as well as the Web, and you can select a language, too.

HotBot. Combining a big database with a sophisticated search method that seems to produce lots of relevant documents, HotBot is my first choice for a quick and easy search. My test search netted 652 hits, and the first 20 or 30 seemed much more relevant to my subject than the retrieval lists of other search engines. Hotbot enables you to search Usenet newsgroups as well as the Web, and you can even do a combined search.

3

Try searching these services in the following order. Begin with Yahoo! to see if you can hit a "bingo" page—one that's exactly what you need. If Yahoo! doesn't net you anything, try InfoSeek, which won't overwhelm you with too many documents. Still can't find anything? Try HotBot, Excite, and AltaVista.

Troubleshooting Your Search

If your search didn't work out well, consider the following possibilities:

- 🌐 **Did you spell the search terms correctly?** A typo or misspelling can ruin your search.

- 🌐 **Try a synonym.** If you're searching for a wine called Shiraz, you should also search for Syrah, a different name for the same wine.

- 🌐 **Did you use the wrong capitalization pattern?** Use capital letters only when they're appropriate. Don't type your search terms in all capital letters.

Closing the Search Explorer Bar

When you're finished searching, you can close the Search Explorer bar in any of the following ways:

Click the Search button again.

or

Right-click the Search bar's title bar, and click Close.

or

Go to the View menu; select Explorer Bar and None.

This security alert says that other people can read the text that I'm sending!

It's true, they can. This Security Alert appears when you type something in a text box and press Enter (or click a Submit or Search button). I wouldn't worry about it, though. The point of this alert is really to educate you about Internet security; everything you upload is in *cleartext* (nonencrypted, readable text). That's worrisome if you upload your Social Security Number or credit card number, but not so worrisome for search terms. It's not too likely that anyone would really be interested in what you're searching for, so just click the option that hides this warning in the future.

Looking for the Needle in the Haystack

Still haven't found what you're looking for? It's time for AltaVista. This search service is the least convenient to use for quick, easy searches because it retrieves too many documents. If you're willing to learn a bit more about AltaVista's advanced search syntax, though, you can use this service with an incredible degree of precision.

🌐 **Phrase searching.** If you're looking for a phrase, surround the phrase in quotation marks. For example, search for *"Outer Banks"* rather than *Outer Banks,* so you won't get the page describing the new banking ventures in Outer Mongolia.

🌐 **Wild cards.** Use a wild card to make sure you're getting all the documents relevant to your interests. Most Web search services don't enable you to do this, but AltaVista lets you type an asterisk to match one or more characters at the end of a word. For example, you can type *kayak** to match *kayak, kayaks,* and *kayaking.*

🌐 **Requiring a certain word.** Put a plus sign right in front of your most important word. If you see lots of stuff on the Outer Banks but nothing on kayaks, for example, type *"Outer Banks" +kayak*.* The plus sign brings documents containing this word to the top of the list.

🌐 **Rejecting a certain word.** If the retrieval list is stuffed with documents pertaining to something you don't want, type a term describing these documents and place a minus sign in front of it. For example, the Outer Banks kayak search nets many documents, for some reason, that mention Asheville, N.C. To demote these documents to the bottom of the list, type *-Asheville.*

These nifty tricks enable you to perform a pinpointed search, one that works much better than just typing the terms without any special symbols. Suppose you're looking for Web pages concerning kayaking on North Carolina's Outer Banks. If you type in *outer banks kayaking,* you get over 80,000 documents—a few too many to go through! If you search for *+ "Outer Banks" +kayak,* you only get 125—and they're mostly very good. See what I mean?

3

I tried these tricks with another search service, but they didn't work!

That's right. Unfortunately, each of the Web's search services uses its own search *syntax,* the rules for typing search terms and search commands properly. But there's some overlap. For example, you can use the plus and minus signs in Lycos and InfoSeek, and you can perform a phrase search in InfoSeek by surrounding the search term in quotation marks.

Using Specialized Search Services

The Web's search engines and directories are great tools, but they don't contain all the information that's out there. Often, using a specialized directory or search engine is much better than trying to search the whole Web. In this section, you'll find some great tips concerning searching for information on specific subjects. This section isn't meant to be comprehensive but only to give you an idea of the incredible richness that's out there and why it makes sense sometimes to focus on specialized search services rather than using Web search engines.

TIP

There are two wonderful collections of Web search services that I strongly recommend you visit: Internet Sleuth (**www.isleuth.com**), which offers keyword search access to more than 2000 Web-accessible databases in every conceivable field; and the University of California, Berkeley's Index to the Internet (**sunsite.berkeley.edu/InternetIndex/**).

Government

Like to know what your elected representatives are up to? Vote Smart (**www.vote-smart.org**) tracks the voting records of more than 13,000 political leaders. You can use this service to find out the names and addresses of all the representatives in your zip code. THOMAS (**thomas.loc.gov**) provides a searchable database of current bills as well as the *Congressional Record.*

Arts

To find out what's happening in the arts, you can check out CultureFinder: The Online Address for the Performing Arts (www.culturefinder.com). CultureFinder (Figure 3-6) includes a searchable calendar for more than 900 arts organizations in the U.S. and Canada. Like to explore the arts online? World Art Treasures (sgwww.epfl.ch/BERGER/) offers a collection of 100,000 slides compiled by art historian Jacques-Edouard Berger.

Figure 3-6
CultureFinder enables Web users to search for information concerning more than 900 arts organizations in the U.S. and Canada.

Health

Healthfinder (www.healthfinder.gov) is an excellent place to start searching for medical information on the Web. If you'd like to search the scientific literature, HealthGate Medline Search (www.healthgate.com) offers free Web access to the largest database of medical research reports, Medline.

3

Business

If you're trying to track down basic information about businesses, check out Hoover's Online (www.hoovers.com), which offers a free database of more than 10,000 of the largest public and private U.S. companies. Looking for Securities and Exchange Commission (SEC) data on stocks that are publicly traded? Look no further than the EDGAR Database (www.sec.gov/edgarhp.htm). This is a fully searchable index to post-1994 SEC filings, including quarterly and annual financial reports. For a Web version of the Yellow Pages, try BigBook (www.bigbook.com), which is searchable and offers local listings for your area (Figure 3-7).

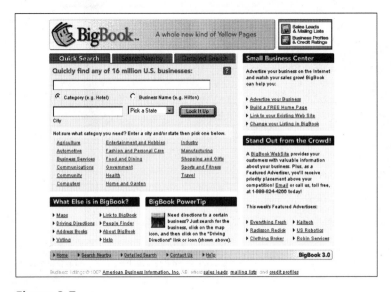

Figure 3-7

BigBook is the Web's answer to the Yellow Pages.

People

InfoSpace (www.infospace.com) provides access to 112 million U.S. and Canadian telephone listings, including businesses as well as individuals. AT&T's Toll-Free Internet Directory (www.tollfree.att.net) enables you to search for toll-free (800 and 888) numbers, but you should also try Internet 800 Search (inter800.com), which includes non-AT&T toll-free numbers as well. Other convenient people-finding services include WhoWhere (www.whowhere.com) and Bigfoot (www.bigfoot.com), which enable you to search for e-mail addresses.

PART

Jobs

Increasing numbers of people are finding jobs on the Internet. To find out why, check out America's Job Bank (www.ajb.dni.us), with a searchable database of more than 250,000 job openings (Figure 3-8). CareerMosaic (www.careermosaic.com) enables you to search for openings at specific companies.

Figure 3-8
America's Job Bank enables you to search a database of more than 250,000 current job openings.

Schools

The American School Directory (www.asd.com) is a searchable database of 106,000 schools at the K-12 level in the U.S. There's a ton of information here about public and private schools. If you're a teacher, you'll love the Eisenhower National Clearinghouse (carson.enc.org), with a searchable database of more than 7000 K-12 curriculum resources.

Weather

The Weather Channel has a great Web site (www.weather.com) that lets you see local forecasts. The U.S. National Weather Service (www.nws.noaa.gov) has a good site, too, with current weather and storm warnings.

3

Maps

MapQuest (www.mapquest.com) is a free interactive atlas of the U.S. that enables you to plan driving itineraries, with outcomes that are sometimes slightly quirky. For a map locating any street address in the U.S., see Yahoo! Maps (maps.yahoo.com/yahoo), which enables you to search by address or zip code; the result is a detailed local map (Figure 3-9). For general geographic and demographic information on the U.S., see U.S. Gazetteer (www.census.gov/cgi-bin/gazetteer). You type in a zip code and out come maps and the latest census data.

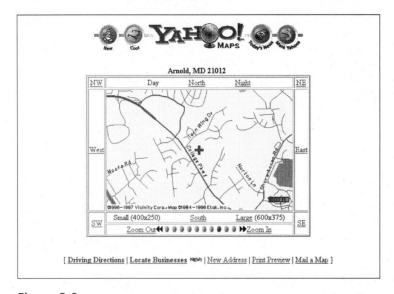

Figure 3-9

Yahoo! Maps provides detailed local maps.

Recipes

Epicurious (www.epicurious.com) is a beautiful site (Figure 3-10) that includes, among many other things, an incredible database of more than 6000 recipes. If that's not enough, try Internet Chef On-Line Magazine, with a searchable archive of almost 30,000 recipes (www.ichef.com). Wine Spectator Online (www.winespectator.com) offers an amazing database of approximately 15,000 wines containing ratings and tasting notes. If you're confused about some of the terminology you encounter in these recipes or wine-tasting notes, don't miss Epicurious's dictionary of more than 4200

PART

food, wine, and culinary terms (**www.epicurious.com/db/dictionary/terms/ indexes/dictionary.html**). If you're concerned about the nutritional value of the food you eat, check out the USDA Nutrient database (**www.nal.usda.gov/ fnic/foodcomp/Data/SR11/**).

Figure 3-10
Epicurious offers a database of more than 6000 recipes.

From Here

🌐 By the time you get to Chapter 5, you'll have a lot of favorites saved, and you'll need to get them organized. This chapter will show you how, and it includes lots of other customizing tips as well.

🌐 Get out your wallet—your Microsoft Wallet, that is—and get ready to do some shopping. It's easy and safe. Find out how in Chapter 8.

🌐 Static Web pages can be informative, but they're boring. In Chapter 9, you'll learn how to take full advantage of the Web's active content, including Java, JavaScript, ActiveX controls, sounds, and movies.

3

4 Subscribe to Cool Content

Now that you know how to search for great content, there's another way to use the Web: make the content come to you. It's possible to do that with two excellent new features of Microsoft Internet Explorer 4—subscriptions and channels. Imagine receiving HTML documents in your e-mail that show you the latest new content at your favorite sites. (HTML is short for Hypertext Markup Language.) And imagine, too, minimizing your windows and finding actively updated content on your desktop, including sports scores, a stock market ticker, and news headlines, all updated automatically throughout the day. There's no hassle involved here. You don't have to go out and find something—it comes to you! But don't worry about having stuff pushed at you that you don't want. The choice is all yours, and you can cancel your subscriptions and channels at any time.

Subscriptions work with your favorite sites and don't cost anything. When you subscribe to a favorite site, Microsoft Internet Explorer regularly checks these sites to find out whether new content is available. If so, you can choose to be notified or to have the new content automatically downloaded to your hard disk. (You can schedule this to happen at night, when the Internet isn't so busy and when your computer isn't in use.) Later, you can view the new content offline, if you wish.

Also free, channels provide another way to get great content downloaded to your computer. A *channel* is a Web site that's automatically updated according to a schedule set by the channel's owner. You can display the channel in Internet Explorer (like a Web page) or place it on your Windows desktop. The decision is up to you.

If all this sounds slightly confusing, take heart. It's really pretty simple, and you'll be amazed at how much it adds to your enjoyment of the Web. After subscribing to your favorite Web sites and especially to channels, your computer comes alive with rich, new information that's tailored to your interests. As you'll see, you use the same basic procedures to subscribe to Web pages and channels. Let's get started by subscribing to your favorite Web pages.

Subscribing to a Favorite Web Page

When you subscribe to a favorite Web page, Microsoft Internet Explorer checks the page to find out whether any new content has appeared since you last accessed that page. If so, the program will notify you by placing a *gleam* (a red star on the upper left corner of the icon) next to the page's name in the Favorites list. Another option is to have the page mailed to your e-mail account, and with Microsoft Outlook Express, you'll see the page exactly the way it looks on the Web.

Before you subscribe to a favorite Web page, take a moment to understand your subscription options. Then try setting up a partial, a full, or a custom subscription. It's so easy with Internet Explorer!

Understanding Subscription Options

When subscribing to a Web site, you have several options. You can choose how you want to be notified and whether you want the page downloaded. You can also set the schedule for updating or choose manual updating.

You can select from the following options for subscribed pages:

- 🌐 **Notify.** In the Favorites list, you'll see a change in the page's icon. This change lets you know that there's new content at that page. If you wish, you can also be notified by e-mail.

- 🌐 **Download the page.** The page is downloaded. This is the best option if you plan to visit the page while you're online.

- 🌐 **Download the page and the pages linked to it.** If the page has many links, this option might download quite a bit of material, so use it sparingly. Still, it's the best choice if you're planning to do much offline browsing.

You can also choose from the following update options:

- 🌐 **Daily updating.** This option updates your pages automatically according to a daily schedule.

- 🌐 **Custom schedule.** You choose times for updating.

- 🌐 **Manual updating.** To update your subscriptions, go to the Favorites menu and select Update All Subscriptions.

Creating a Partial Subscription

In a partial, no-frills subscription, you get notification via an icon change in the Favorites list but no downloading. To subscribe to a Web page with a partial subscription, follow these steps:

1. Display the Web page to which you want to subscribe.

2. From the Favorites menu, choose Add To Favorites. You'll see the Add Favorite dialog box (Figure 4-1).

3. Choose the first Yes option and click OK.

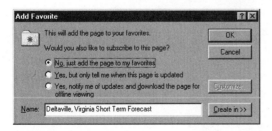

Figure 4-1

This dialog box enables you to add a favorite and create a subscription at the same time.

4

Creating a Full Subscription

In a full subscription, you get notification via an icon change in the Favorites list and downloading of the new content. To subscribe to a Web page with a full subscription, follow these steps:

1. Display the Web page to which you want to subscribe.

2. From the Favorites menu, choose Add To Favorites. You'll see the Add Favorite dialog box (Figure 4-1).

3. Choose the second Yes option and click OK.

Creating a Custom Subscription

If you would like to download not only the page you select but all the pages linked to it, receive e-mail notification when the page changes, choose an updating time, or specify a required password, you need a custom subscription. Follow this procedure:

1. Display the Web page to which you want to subscribe.

2. From the Favorites menu, choose Add To Favorites. You'll see the Add Favorite dialog box (Figure 4-1).

3. Choose the second Yes option, and then click Customize. You'll see the first page of the Subscription Wizard (Figure 4-2).

4. Choose one of the downloading options. You can download only this page or this page and all the pages linked to it.

    If you choose to download linked pages, click Next. The Subscription Wizard will ask you to specify how many levels you

Figure 4-2

The Subscription Wizard enables you to create a custom subscription with down-loading, e-mail notification, and scheduled updates.

want to download. If you choose one level deep, Internet Explorer downloads the pages that are linked on the subscribed page, but it doesn't download any more pages. If you choose two levels, the program downloads the pages that are linked on the subscribed page, and it also downloads the pages that are linked on all the pages linked to the subscribed page. And if you choose three levels—suffice it to say that you're going to be downloading a lot of Web pages! You can choose up to three levels, but this option isn't recommended unless you've got unlimited Web access and loads of disk space.

5. Click Next to continue. You'll see the next page of the Subscription Wizard (Figure 4-3).

6. If you would like e-mail notification, click Yes. If the address is not correct, click Change Address, type the correct address, and click OK.

7. Click Next. You'll see the schedule page of the wizard (Figure 4-4). You can choose from three default schedules: Daily (update every day at midnight), Weekly (update every Monday at midnight), and Monthly (update on the first day of every month at midnight). If you have enabled Dial-Up Networking for your computer, you can also check an option that allows unattended dial-up at the indicated times. If you don't want automatic updates, choose Manually.

Figure 4-3

In this page of the Subscription Wizard, you choose whether you want to be notified via e-mail.

4

If you would like to change the default schedules, choose a schedule option and click Edit. (Another alternative is to click New to create and name a new schedule option.) You'll see a dialog box that enables you to choose from a variety of scheduling options (Figure 4-5). For example, for daily schedules, you can update every second or third day, every weekday, or every day. For weekly schedules, you can choose to update every week or every other week; you can also choose the day of the week on which you want the update to occur. For monthly schedules, you can choose the day on which updating occurs. You can also choose to update every month, every other month, every third month, and so on. (Note that the weekly and monthly options aren't visible in Figure 4-5, in which the Daily options are selected.)

For all three of the options (Daily, Weekly, and Monthly), you can choose the time of the update. You can also choose to repeat the update throughout specified hours of the day.

8. When you've finished choosing schedule options, click OK. You'll see the wizard again.

9. Click Next. You'll see the password page (Figure 4-6).

10. If this Web page requires you to supply a user name (login name) and password, click Yes and type the user name and password.

11. Click Finish. You see the Add Favorite dialog box again.

12. Click OK. Your custom subscription is finished.

Figure 4-4

This page of the Web Site Subscription Wizard enables you to choose an update schedule.

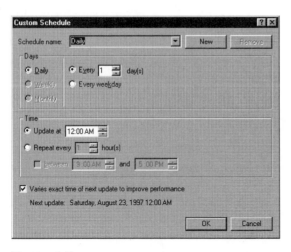

Figure 4-5

If you're creating a custom schedule, you can choose from a variety of scheduling options.

Figure 4-6

If the Web site requires a user name and password, supply these here.

Updating Subscriptions

If you chose manual updating, you must update pages manually. To do so, go to the Favorites menu and select Update All Subscriptions. You'll see a dialog box that shows the progress of the downloads. If you'd like to see more of what's going on, click the Details button.

4

You can tell right away whether Internet Explorer has detected any new content by looking at the Favorites list. You'll see a bright red gleam on the icon next to the name of each page that's changed. If you selected e-mail notification, you'll get an e-mail message informing you that there's new content at the indicated page.

Browsing Offline

If you decided to download pages so that you can browse offline, you can take a look at the new content without being connected to the Internet. Choose Work Offline from the File menu, and then open your favorite. If you downloaded linked pages, you can view all the pages that are linked within the favorite page. If you try to click a link that requires you to go online, you'll see a dialog box asking whether you would like to do this.

When you're finished browsing offline, be sure to choose Work Offline from the File menu again so that you clear the check mark from this option. You can then go online again.

Managing Subscriptions

Would you like to see a list of all your subscriptions? Go to the Favorites menu and choose Manage Subscriptions. You'll see a different Subscriptions dialog box, like the one shown in Figure 4-7. In this dialog box, you can view and edit your subscriptions.

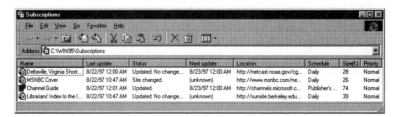

Figure 4-7

In this dialog box, you can view and edit your subscriptions.

TIP

Check out the Status column to find out whether any problems were encountered in the last update. If everything went right, you'll see "Updated" or "Site changed." If an error occurred, this column indicates what might have gone wrong, enabling you to fix it. If you don't see the Status column, choose Details from the View menu.

PART

Editing Subscriptions

The Subscriptions dialog box enables you to update, delete, and rename your subscriptions, as well as change notification, scheduling, and downloading options. Here's a quick rundown of the possibilities:

🌐 To update a subscription, select the subscription (press Ctrl + A to select all subscriptions), and choose Update Now from the File menu.

🌐 To delete a subscription, right-click the subscription and click Delete.

🌐 To rename a subscription, select the subscription, go to the File menu, and choose Rename.

🌐 To change the notification settings, right-click the subscription and click Properties. You'll see a Properties dialog box for this subscription. Click the Receiving tab, and select (or clear) e-mail notification. Click Change Address if you need to change the e-mail address.

🌐 To change the schedule settings, right-click the subscription and click Properties. In the Properties dialog box, click the Schedule tab, and choose a schedule option. You can edit the existing schedule (click Edit) or create a new one (click New), using the dialog box shown in Figure 4-5 on page 69.

🌐 You can also change downloading options.

Choosing Custom Downloading Options

If you choose the downloading option (a full subscription), you might want to customize the downloading settings. You can choose from many options, including specifying what type of content you want to download.

To choose custom downloading options, right-click the subscription (in the Subscriptions dialog box), click Properties, click the Receiving tab, and select Notify Me When Updates Occur (if necessary). Then click Advanced. You see the Advanced Download Options (Figure 4-8).

In the Content For Offline Use area, you can change the number of levels you want downloaded. You can also choose whether the program downloads linked pages if they're located outside the site.

In the Items To Download area, you choose which types of content to download. By default, Internet Explorer downloads images, ActiveX controls, and Java applets, but not sound or video. You can select Sound And Audio if you'd like this content along with the page, or you can minimize your download time by choosing not to download images or controls.

You can also choose a maximum amount to download per update. This can be especially useful when you're downloading linked pages.

4

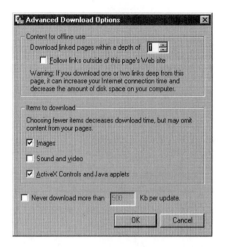

Figure 4-8

From this dialog box, you can choose advanced download options for offline viewing.

Viewing and Subscribing to Channels

Channels are much like subscribed Web pages, but there are two big differences. With subscriptions, you decide how often to update the page; with channels, the content provider makes this decision. With subscriptions, you decide how much to download; with channels, the content provider ensures that you receive everything you need to enjoy the channel.

You can enjoy channels in several ways. The first is to view a channel within the browser, just as you would view standard Web pages. Or you can subscribe to a channel, as described in this section. If a channel offers you the option, you can place the channel on the Active Desktop.

Viewing Channels in the Browser

You can view channel content without subscribing to it.

1. Click the Channels button to display the Channels Explorer bar (Figure 4-9).

2. Choose a channel by clicking a channel subject category and then clicking one of the channels within that category. You'll see the channel's Web page within the browser window.

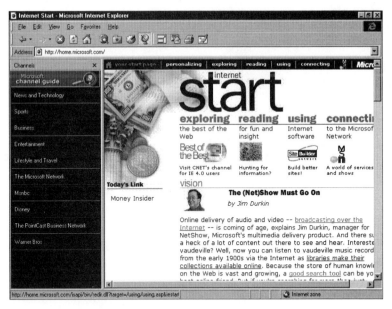

Figure 4-9.

The Channels Explorer bar shows the channels that are currently available.

Subscribing to a Channel

You can subscribe to channels the same way that you subscribe to favorite Web pages: partial, full, or customized subscription options. You'll have many of the same choices you have for subscribing to ordinary Web pages.

1. Click the Channels button to display the Channels Explorer bar.

2. Click a channel subject category to display a list of the channels in that category.

3. Right-click on the name of the channel to which you want to subscribe. On the pop-up menu, choose Subscribe. You'll see the Subscribe Channel dialog box (Figure 4-10), which is similar to the one you see when you subscribe to a Web page.

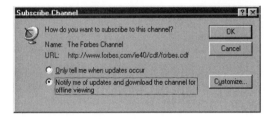

Figure 4-10

You can decide exactly how you want to subscribe to a channel.

4

4. Choose the notify-and-download option (unless you want to be notified only when an update occurs).

5. Click Customize to select custom channel options. You'll see the first page of the Subscription Wizard (Figure 4-11). This is similar to the first page of the wizard you see when you subscribe to a Web page, but in this case you choose between downloading only the home page of the channel or all the content supplied by the channel.

6. Choose one of the downloading options, and click Next. You'll see the next page of the Subscription Wizard, which is the same as the one on the Web page subscription wizard (see Figure 4-3 on page 67).

7. If you would like e-mail notification, click Yes. If the address is not correct, click Change Address, type the correct address, and click OK.

8. Click Next. You'll see the schedule options, which are the same as the ones you use to schedule Web page subscriptions (see Figure 4-4 on page 68). Set the schedule to match your preferences, or select manual updating.

9. Click Finish. You'll see the Subscribe Channel dialog box again.

10. Click OK.

Figure 4-11

The Subscription Wizard enables you to choose options for channel subscriptions.

Displaying a Channel on the Desktop

Some channels are specifically designed to be viewed on your desktop. These are called Active Desktop items. It's really neat to see the actively updated content (Figure 4-12). If something looks interesting, just click it. For example, the Microsoft Investor ticker provides stock quotes and news headlines. To get details on a stock or one of the news stories, just click it. You'll automatically see the full story in an Internet Explorer window.

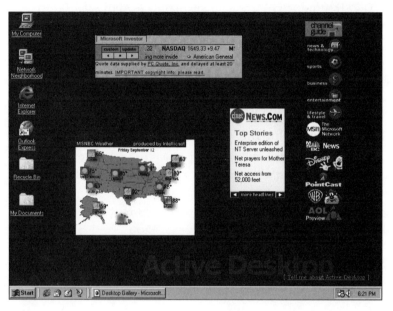

Figure 4-12

Active Desktop items appear on your desktop, with content actively updated according to the content provider's schedule.

There's already a channel on your desktop—the Internet Explorer Channel Bar, which lists the same channels you see in the Channel Explorer bar. Among the channels is the Channel Guide, which enables you to look for new channels. Try clicking it.

Placing an Active Desktop Item on the Desktop

The following instructions tell you how to access Microsoft's Active Desktop Gallery, which lists providers who are making Active Desktop items available. In the future, as more content providers broadcast content from their sites, you'll be able to find many additional goodies for your desktop.

4

1. If you have Internet Explorer open, minimize it so that you can see your desktop.

2. Right-click the desktop and choose Properties. (You can also choose Settings from the Start menu, select Control Panel, and open Display.) Click the Web tab (Figure 4-13).

3. Click New. You'll see a dialog box that asks you whether you want to go to Microsoft's Active Desktop Gallery.

4. Click Yes. Internet Explorer will display the Active Desktop Gallery page (Figure 4-14).

5. Browse through the Active Desktop items offered. When you find one that you like, look for a button named Add To My Desktop or Add To Active Desktop and click it.

6. If a Security Alert dialog box asks whether you want to add an item to your desktop, click OK. You'll see the Create New Active Desktop Item dialog box (Figure 4-15).

7. You can click Customize Subscription to change the update schedule and supply a site password, just as you did for Web page subscriptions.

8. Click OK. Internet Explorer downloads the current information for the new item and places it on your desktop.

Figure 4-13

Use the Web tab of the Display Properties dialog box to add Active Desktop items.

Figure 4-14

The Active Desktop Gallery offers a growing number of items to add to your desktop.

Figure 4-15

From this dialog box, you can customize your Active Desktop item subscription.

HELP

I don't see any channels on my desktop!

Chances are the Active Desktop is disabled. Point to the desktop, and click the right mouse button. From the pop-up menu, choose Active Desktop and then select View As Web Page.

4

Viewing Active Desktop Content

Active Desktop items are chock-full of clickable content. Try clicking something, such as a news headline, a link, or a graphic. Microsoft Internet Explorer springs into action and takes you directly to the content that's relevant to what you've clicked. No searching, no browsing—go right to the information you're after.

Managing Your Active Desktop

Once you've added Active Desktop items to your desktop, you can manage them in many ways. You can refresh and update them, move them around on the desktop so that they're positioned conveniently, change subscription options, and delete them. You can even temporarily hide or close them. The following sections explain how to manage Active Desktop items efficiently.

Refreshing the Active Desktop

If an Active Desktop item stops working, it's probably because of a network connection problem. You'll see a gray, lifeless box. To bring the item back to life, right-click the desktop (not the item itself) and choose Refresh from the pop-up menu.

Updating the Active Desktop

Default Active Desktop settings enable the Active Desktop content providers to determine update intervals. If you've been offline for a while, though, you might have missed an update. To make sure you're looking at the most recent versions of your Active Desktop items, right-click the desktop; from the pop-up menu, select Active Desktop and then Update Now.

Positioning Active Desktop Items

If you'd like to reposition an Active Desktop item, move the pointer carefully to the top of the item until you see its title bar. (Be careful not to click yet, or you'll open an Internet Explorer window; if this happens, close the window and try again.) Once the title bar appears, click within the title bar and drag to position the item on your desktop.

Changing Subscription Options

You can change your subscription options for any Active Desktop item.

1. Carefully move the pointer to the top of the item's window until the window's title bar appears.
2. Click the down arrow on the left end of the title bar, and choose Properties from the drop-down menu.

3. On the Subscription tab, you can click Unsubscribe to permanently delete your subscription. On the Receiving tab, you can change the type of subscription, whether you want to receive e-mail notification, and your login name and password. On the Schedule tab, you can modify the update schedule in the same fashion as other subscriptions.

4. When you've made the changes you want, click OK.

Hiding Active Desktop Items

Have you added too many Active Desktop items? It's easy to do because they're fun and informative. Perhaps you'd like to hide one or two of them, though, so you can concentrate on getting some work done. Without deleting the item, you can remove it from the desktop temporarily. If you wish, you can bring it back later, without having to reinstall it.

To hide an Active Desktop item, follow this procedure:

1. Carefully move the pointer to the top of the item's window until its title bar appears.

2. Click the close box on the right end of the title bar.

To bring the item back, take these steps:

1. Right-click the desktop. You'll see a pop-up menu.

2. Click Properties. You'll see the Display Properties control panel.

3. Click Web. You'll see the Web properties.

4. In the list of items on the Active Desktop, find the item you want to restore and click in the check box next to the item's name.

5. Click OK to confirm your choice. You'll see the item on the desktop again.

Deleting Active Desktop Items

If you don't like an Active Desktop item and want to remove it from your system, go to the Web page of the Display Properties dialog box. Select the item you want to remove and click Delete. If you want to remove all Active Desktop items and start over again, click Reset All. Click OK to confirm the deletion.

Temporarily Closing All the Active Desktop Items

Like to hide all the Active Desktop items temporarily? Right-click the desktop, choose Active Desktop, and then select View As Web Page to clear the check mark from this option. To bring all the content back, just repeat this procedure.

4

From Here

You've mastered the world of Web content by now. You've learned how to find the good stuff that's out there, and you've even learned how to make it come to you. Now it's time to get organized and explore some additional features of the Web.

- In the next chapter, you'll learn how to customize Internet Explorer, and in particular, how to organize your Favorites menu.

- Chapter 10 shows you how to capture all this cool stuff you're seeing by copying, saving, and printing. You'll also learn how to download shareware from the Web.

- In Chapter 9, you'll learn how to get into the exciting world of Web commerce. As you'll see, it's much more secure than ordering via telephone, despite what you may have heard to the contrary.

5   Customize It

You've conquered the Web. You've learned how to find outstanding content and how to search for specific information. You've even learned how to make content come to you. What now? It's time to customize Internet Explorer so that the program aligns with your preferences. In this chapter, you'll learn about individualizing Internet Explorer and about appearance and accessibility options that you can use to meet your personal needs.

If this sounds like drudgery, don't panic. Sure, there's some tedium involved—"organizing your favorites" and "customizing your start page" sounds like that four-letter word, *work*. But the payoff is worth it. With only a few minutes of effort, you can create a customized start page that displays news, sports, and weather, as well as other content that changes every time you start the program. Even if you decide to skip the custom start page, don't put off creating custom folders for your Favorites menu. Those folders are the key to transforming Microsoft Internet Explorer into an efficient tool for collecting your favorite Web pages.

81

Changing the Start Page

When you start Internet Explorer, it automatically displays the default start page: <u>home.microsoft.com</u>. However, you can use any existing Web page as your start page. For example, suppose you start almost every Web session with a search. Why not make your favorite search engine your start page? If you don't like the change, you can easily restore the default start page.

To change the default start page, follow these steps:

1. Display the Web page that you want to use as your new start page.

2. Choose Internet Options from the View menu, and click the General tab. You'll see the General options.

3. In the Home Page area, click Use Current. Or you can click Use Blank, if you'd rather display a blank page when you start.

4. Click OK to confirm your choice.

If you get tired of your new page, you can restore the default start page by clicking Use Default.

Personalizing the Start Page

If you'd prefer to stick with the default start page, here's another option: personalize the default start page so that it shows content that's of interest to you. Is this a big job? No. Personalizing your start page only takes a few minutes. As you'll surely agree, it's time well spent.

To get started, click Home to display the default start page and find the custom start page link on Internet Explorer's default start page (click the Home button to display this page, or choose Home Page from the Go menu). Look for "Personalizing your start page." There's currently a whole section devoted to this important subject, as well as a Personalizing button at the top of the screen. However, by the time you read this, Microsoft's ever-diligent Webmasters will have come up with an even more impressive page design. But the Personalizing links will be there, somewhere on the default start page.

Here's how the start page personalization works right now (as with all things on the Web, this is subject to change). You see a page that asks you to select a topic, select content providers, and click Next. Continue this process until you've selected content providers for all the topics listed on the page (Figure 5-1). When you're done, click Finish.

What's the result? A start page that's loaded with the content you've selected (Figure 5-2). You'll see new content from the same providers automatically the next time you log on.

Figure 5-1

You begin customizing your start page by choosing content providers for all the listed topics.

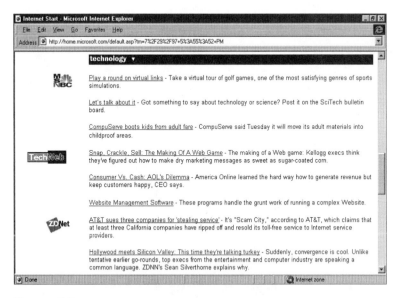

Figure 5-2

Your customized start page contains news stories and content from the providers you've selected.

83

5

It's also easy to make changes or additions to your custom home page. You do so by clicking an Update Choice link, which enables you to run through the content selection options again.

Personalizing MSNBC

The joint news venture between Microsoft and NBC, MSNBC, enables you to create a customized news page. To access the customization form, open the MSNBC home page (www.msnbc.com/) and follow the links to the Personal Front Page. Choose the information you'd like to appear on your Personal Front Page (Figure 5-3), and click the option that displays your page. The next time you access MSNBC, you'll see a Personal Front Page with the choices you've selected.

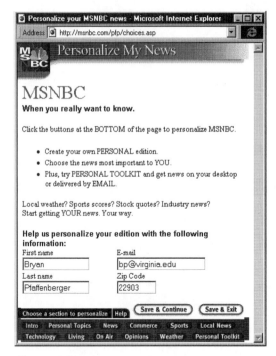

Figure 5-3

You can create your own personal MSNBC page.

Organizing Your Favorites Folder

By now, you've surely saved many sites to the Favorites folder; as a result, your Favorites menu has too many sites. The more sites you add, the longer the list grows, and the less useful it becomes. It's time to organize your Favorites list into folders. As you'll see, the folders you create appear as commands on the Favorites menu—commands that, when you click them, display submenus listing Web sites according to whatever categories you've created.

It's a little bit of work to get your Favorites list organized, but after you do, you'll be glad you did. With a well-organized Favorites list, you can add hundreds of sites without overburdening the Favorites menu. In time, your copy of Internet Explorer will become a treasure trove of the Web sites you've found most useful.

Planning Your Folders

To get the most out of Internet Explorer's Favorites, you should organize it so that few or no Web documents appear in the menu's top level. As you'll see in the section titled "Creating a Folder," this is easy to do. Every folder you create within the Favorites window automatically establishes a new top-level menu option on the Favorites menu. When you click one of these options, you see a submenu containing all the Web sites you placed within that folder (Figure 5-4). You can even create submenus within submenus (Figure 5-5). In this way, you can store dozens or even hundreds of favorite sites.

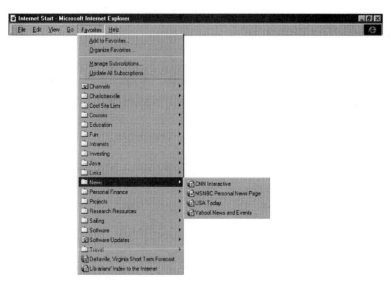

Figure 5-4

Organize your Favorites menu so that there's nothing but folders on the top level; submenus list your favorite sites.

5

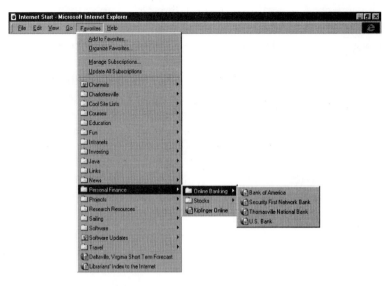

Figure 5-5

You can create submenus within submenus to store even more favorites.

Take a moment to plan the categories by which you want to organize your favorite sites. What types of Web documents are you most likely to save? Jot them down on a list, and don't forget that you can also create folders within folders. The following is a sample of folder organization.

Investing
    Bonds
        Mutual funds
        Balanced funds
        Bond funds
        Growth funds
        Income funds
        Small-cap funds
    Quick quotes
    Stocks
Sailing
    Boatyards
    Chesapeake Bay
    Marinas
    Rappahannock weather

Creating a Folder

After you decide how to organize your Favorites list, create some folders by following these instructions:

1. Go to the Favorites menu and choose Organize Favorites. You'll see the Organize Favorites window shown in Figure 5-6.

2. Click the New Folder button on the toolbar. You'll see a new folder in the window.

3. Type a name for your new folder.

Figure 5-6
Organize your favorites by creating folders and subfolders in this window.

Adding Favorites to a Folder

Now that you've created a new folder, you can move existing favorites into it. To add a newly discovered favorite site to one of the folders within the Favorites window, use these steps:

1. In the Organize Favorites window, select the favorite that you want to move.

2. Click Move. You'll see a Browse For Folder dialog box.

3. Click the folder to which you'd like to add the favorite, and click OK. Internet Explorer moves the favorite into the folder.

5

Renaming a Favorite

To rename a favorite or folder in the Organize Favorites window, select the favorite and click Rename. Windows will highlight the current name. Just start typing to replace this name with the new one.

Deleting Favorites from a Folder

Sometimes favorite sites fall out of favor. You don't visit them anymore, or you can't remember why you thought they were so hot in the first place. Others disappear or move to new locations so that the connection on your Favorites list no longer works. To keep your Favorites list well organized, you should periodically delete unwanted sites.

To remove unwanted sites from the Favorites list, follow these steps:

1. Display the Organize Favorites dialog box, if necessary, by choosing Favorites and Organize Favorites.

2. If necessary, open the folder that contains the site you want to delete.

3. Select the site you want to delete. To delete more than one, hold down the Ctrl key and click on each site you want to delete.

4. Click Delete.

5. You'll see an alert box asking whether you're sure you want to move the deleted item to the recycle bin. If you're sure you're deleting the correct site, click the Yes button. (If you're not sure, click the No button and check what you've selected.)

HELP

I deleted the wrong site!

Never fear. On the desktop, double-click the Recycle Bin. Select the site that you deleted accidentally. Choose the Restore command from the File menu. Windows will return the deleted item to the place from which you deleted it.

Additional Personalizing Options

This chapter has already covered the most important options for customizing Internet Explorer. In this section, you'll learn about some additional ways to make the program fit your specific needs. This section is strictly fine-tuning, though, so you can skip it if you like.

Choosing Toolbar and Status Bar Options

Are you strapped for screen space? Here are some tricks you can use to reduce the amount of space the toolbar and status bar take up.

🌐 To hide the text labels (thus reducing the size of the buttons), right-click the toolbar background and clear the check mark from Text Labels.

🌐 To selectively hide one or two of the toolbar panels, go to the View menu and choose Toolbars. Clear the checkmark next to the toolbars you don't want to see. (I don't recommend this, though, unless you're using a really tiny monitor.)

🌐 To hide the status bar, clear the check mark from the Status Bar option in the View menu. If you're really strapped for screen room, this is a better choice than deleting the toolbar—and what's more, you won't have to read those annoying scrolling messages that some Web authors place on the status bar using a Java trick.

Choosing Font Options

A few Web sites specify font and font sizes for their documents, but it's a chancy business because the fonts don't show up unless they're installed on a given user's system. You can assign Zapf Chancery or Garamond all you want, but not that many users have these fonts, so browsers revert to the default fonts. But you can change Internet Explorer's default font settings for your system in two ways: You can increase or decrease the standard font size, and you can reassign the default fonts to something that's more aesthetically pleasing or more readable.

To change the relative size of fonts displayed in a Web page, go to the View menu and select Fonts; then choose a font size from the submenu. You can choose a font size from Smallest to Largest (the default is Medium). Figure 5-7 shows the smallest font size, while Figure 5-8 shows the largest.

5

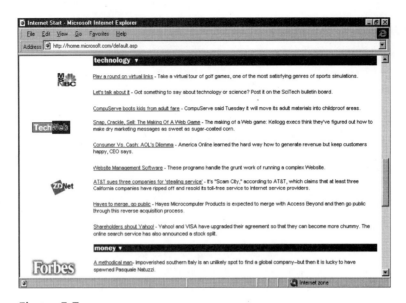

Figure 5-7

Here's how a document looks with Internet Explorer's smallest font size.

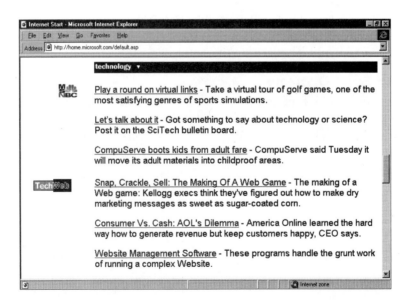

Figure 5-8

And here's how the same document looks with the largest font size.

You can also change the default font (typeface). By default, Internet Explorer displays proportionally spaced type in Times New Roman, and monospace (typewriter) type in Courier New. If you'd like to change these settings, choose Internet Options from the View menu. On the General tab, click the Fonts button. You'll see the Fonts dialog box shown in Figure 5-9.

Figure 5-9

You can change Internet Explorer's default fonts from this dialog box.

In the Character Sets list, you'll see the default character sets; these are currently Western (Latin-1) and Universal Alphabet (otherwise known as Unicode). Now most of the documents on the Web use Latin-1, which packs a potent Western European bias; the up-and-coming standard is Unicode. For now, though, select the Western character set. In the Proportional Font box, choose the font you want for the proportionally spaced typefaces you see on Web pages. In the Fixed-Width Font box, choose a font for the typewriter-like text that you sometimes see on Web pages. (For this font, you'll be wise to leave the default setting, Courier New.) You can choose a default font size, too. When you're finished choosing font options, click OK.

My font choice doesn't work!

That's probably because you're viewing a page that contains its own font choices. When a Web author chooses fonts, the author's choice overrides your own, which is justifiable since the font choice is probably part of the author's overall design.

5

Choosing Language Options

If you read languages other than English, you might want to add language support. To do so, go to the View menu and select Internet Options. On the General tab, click the Languages button. You'll see the Language Preference dialog box (Figure 5-10).

Figure 5-10

Choose languages from the Language Preference dialog box.

To add a language to the Language list, click Add, select a language, and click OK. Repeat this step until you've added all the languages you can read, and then adjust their order. Languages will be treated in order of their priority in the list. To change the order, select a language and click Move Up or Move Down. You can also remove a language by selecting it and clicking Remove. When you're done setting your language preferences, click OK.

Choosing Accessibility Options

Users with special needs will appreciate the Accessibility options. You can display these by choosing Internet Options from the View menu and then clicking the Accessibility button. You'll see the Accessibility dialog box (Figure 5-11). The options in this dialog box enable you to override Web authors' color, font, and font size settings. Comparatively few Web authors consider such things as color blindness and impaired vision when they compose Web pages, so these options are a nice touch indeed. The style sheet option enables a knowledgeable Internet Explorer to compose a *cascading style sheet* (a text file containing a list of HTML tags and the formats to associate with each) and to impose its formats on every document that Internet Explorer displays.

PART

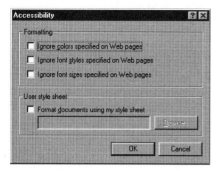

Figure 5-11

Accessibility options enable users to override Web authors' color and font choices.

Choosing Colors

If Web authors do not choose colors for text, links, and backgrounds, Internet Explorer uses its default colors: black text, gray background, reddish-purple visited links, and blue unvisited links. You can change these colors, if you wish. To do so, go to the View menu and choose Internet Options. On the General tab, click the Colors button. You'll see the Colors dialog box shown in Figure 5-12. To change the Text and Background colors, clear the Use Windows Colors check box and click the boxes to choose a color. To change the Links colors, click each box and choose a color. When you're done, click OK.

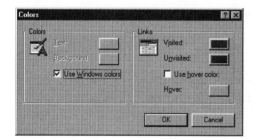

Figure 5-12

You can change the default text, background, and link colors, if you wish.

Increasing the History List's Time Depth

The history list keeps track of all the sites you've visited within a specified period of time—by default, the past 20 days. The history list comes in handy when you're trying to get back to a page you previously visited, as discussed in Chapter 1. By increasing the time depth of the history list,

5

you increase the chance that you'll be able to find your way back to a previously visited page. In addition, Internet Explorer uses the History list for AutoComplete, the function that enables it to try to guess which URL you're typing in the Address box. The more URLs you store, the better AutoComplete works.

To change the depth of the history list:

1. Go to the View menu and select Internet Options; click the General tab, if necessary.

2. In the History area, enter the maximum number of days you want to keep the links you've visited. Try increasing the number of days to 60.

3. Click the OK button.

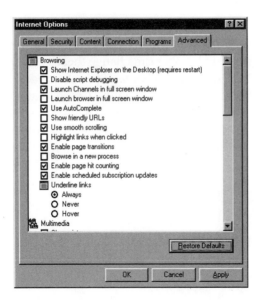

Figure 5-13

The Advanced tab on the Options dialog box offers more ways to customize Internet Explorer.

Sundry Additional Tweaks

You'll find lots more options for customizing in the Advanced page of the Options menu (Figure 5-13). To view this page, choose Internet Options from the View menu and click Advanced. Here's a quick rundown of the Browsing options (subsequent chapters examine the Multimedia, Security, and other options):

- **Show Internet Explorer on the Desktop.** This option, on by default, places an Internet Explorer icon on your desktop.

- **Disable script debugging.** If a VBScript or JavaScript in a Web page encounters an error, you'll see a dialog box that asks whether you want to continue running scripts on that page. If these messages get tiring, you can turn off this option. (You might want to notify the page's author that you're receiving errors.)

- **Launch Channels in full screen window.** When you open a channel from the Channel bar on the desktop, Internet Explorer automatically changes to full-screen mode. If you'd rather see the standard browser window, turn off this option.

- **Launch browser in full screen window.** Likewise, by default Internet Explorer opens in a window when you're viewing a standard Web page. Turn on this option to always start in full-screen mode.

- **Use AutoComplete.** This feature is on by default, but some people don't like to have it get in their way while they're typing URLs. If you feel that way, turn AutoComplete off.

- **Show friendly URLs.** This option, off by default, displays "friendly" or abbreviated versions of Web addresses (URLs) on the status bar. Experienced Web users feel that these so-called friendly URLs are actually confusing because they prevent you from seeing which URL you're accessing. Leave this one switched off.

- **Use smooth scrolling.** What's not to like about this? Sounds good, right? It does use more memory than less-than-smooth scrolling. This option is on by default, but if memory is tight on your system, you might consider switching it off.

- **Highlight links when clicked.** This option, off by default, highlights a link when you click it. The highlight makes it easier to tell that you've successfully clicked the link, but the animated program icon gives you the same information.

- **Enable page transitions.** This option, on by default, permits Internet Explorer to use cool new transitions between Web pages if the pages' author has included them.

- **Browse in a new process.** This option, off by default, enables Internet Explorer to take full advantage of Windows' sophisticated multithreading capabilities. That way, if the browser encounters

5

a Java applet or ActiveX control that crashes, no other programs are affected (including Windows). However, this option takes a lot of memory, and it rules out use of some Web Integrated Desktop features.

- **Enable page hit counting.** On by default, this privacy-related option enables channel content providers to track what you're looking at when you access their channel. If you're not comfortable with this, clear this option.

- **Enable scheduled subscription updates.** If you want to schedule your own subscription updates, leave this option on.

- **Underline links.** By default, Internet Explorer always underlines text links. You can change this option so that text links are never underlined or are underlined only as the mouse pointer passes over them.

HELP

I caught my coworker looking at my history list!

That wasn't very nice, but let's face it—people do snoop. Maybe they're looking for something that could embarrass you, or maybe they're just curious. Either way, you should be aware that even a relatively unsophisticated intruder can tell where you've been browsing by looking at your history list, just by clicking the History button on the toolbar or by opening the History folder in the Windows directory. If you'd like to cover your tracks, click the Clear History button, located on the General tab of the Internet Options dialog box.

From Here

- You've personalized Internet Explorer so that the program works the way you want. Now rev it up! The next chapter shows you a whole series of tricks that make the program seem to run a lot faster.

- Safeguard your security and privacy while you're browsing. Be sure you fully understand the security and privacy options discussed in Chapter 7.

- Have a go at multimedia, Java applets, ActiveX controls, and more, as explained in Chapter 9.

PART

6 Soup It Up

Some skeptics say, "It isn't the World Wide Web, it's the World Wide Wait." Microsoft Internet Explorer is an expertly crafted program that runs like the wind compared to its competition, but neither Microsoft, nor all the King's men, seems to be able to do anything about Internet congestion. Like it or not, the Web often slows to a crawl.

In this chapter you'll learn the soup-it-up tricks that experienced surfers use—tricks that can dramatically speed up the program's apparent speed, even in the face of sluggish Internet traffic. These tricks include using clever time-saving Internet Explorer features such as AutoScan and AutoSearch, opening multiple windows for browsing, saving passwords, switching off multimedia, and increasing the size of the program's disk cache (where temporary Internet files are stored). You'll also learn how to recover quickly if you run into one of those all-too-common (and incomprehensible) error messages, such as "404 Not Found," and how to fully exploit menu shortcuts and those nifty pop-up menus. What's covered here is strictly fine-tuning, but there are some tricks that you won't want to miss!

Using AutoScan

It's common to make mistakes when you're typing URLs—and these mistakes result in a lot of wasted time. For example, if you're trying to access www.microsoft.com and make an error (such as typing the wrong top-level or root domain, as in www.microsoft.gov or www.microsoft.edu), you get an error message after the access times out, which might take a couple of minutes. Then you might spend even more time attempting to locate the correct URL.

Microsoft Internet Explorer comes with a cool new feature called AutoScan that jumps into action when you type a URL that doesn't work. It does two things. First it tries to see whether you typed the root domain incorrectly by trying others. If that fails, it searches the default search service in an attempt to locate the correct URL.

To use AutoScan, you must turn on the two Searching options in the Options dialog box. To turn these on, choose Internet Options from the View menu and click the Advanced tab. Under Searching, make sure there's a check mark next to Autoscan Common Root Domains, and click Always Search under the next option (Search When URL Fails). Click OK to confirm your choice and return to Internet Explorer.

Using AutoSearch

Thanks to the Search Explorer bar, it's easier than ever to search the Web with Internet Explorer. But here's an even faster way to do a quick, easy search. In the Address bar, type *go* followed by a space and one or more search words. Then press Enter. Internet Explorer sends the search words to the current search provider—at this time it's Yahoo—and you quickly see a list of matching sites. Figure 6-1 shows the results of typing *go anne arundel county maryland*.

Find It Fast (on the Page)

You've searched for and finally found a document that mentions *antidisestablishmentarianism*. Fine, but it's a 50-page document. Don't drive yourself nuts searching for the word manually; use the Find command instead. To search the currently displayed Web document, choose Find from

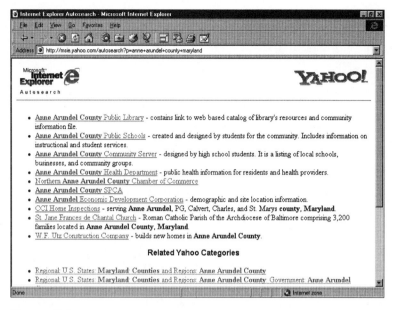

Figure 6-1

An AutoSearch can be run by typing search words directly into the Address box. Here you see the results of one such search.

the Edit menu or use the Ctrl + F shortcut. You'll see the Find dialog box. In the Find What box, type the word you're looking for and click Find Next. If Internet Explorer locates a match, the program highlights the word in the background (but leaves the Find dialog box on screen, which enables you to search again, if you wish). To search for another instance of the word, click Find Next. When there are no more matches to be found, you see a message that the whole document has been searched. To close the dialog box, click either Cancel or the close button.

You can customize your search by using some of the options in the Find dialog box:

🌐 To match what you typed as whole words (rather than as parts of words), click Match Whole Word Only.

🌐 To match the capitalization pattern you typed, click Match Case.

🌐 To control the direction of the search, click Up or Down. (It's Down, by default.)

6

Using More Than One Window

You can open two, three, or more Internet Explorer windows, displaying different Web pages in each. Here are some good reasons to open more than one window:

🌐 **Keep working while downloading a lengthy document.** Suppose you're waiting for a lengthy document to download. To keep working with Internet Explorer, you can open another Web document in a new window. The lengthy document will continue downloading in the original window.

🌐 **Keep reference information available while you're reading another document.** For example, you could display a glossary of terms in one window while reading text in another.

🌐 **Keep a page full of links in one window while you browse the links in another.** To do this, point to one of the links in the page that lists links you want to explore and click the right mouse button. From the pop-up menu, choose Open In New Window. You can easily go back to the original page by clicking within its window.

How to Open a New Window

You can open a new Internet Explorer window by right-clicking or by using the menu.

If you see a hyperlink that you'd like to display in a new window, you can do so by first right-clicking the hyperlink. From the pop-up menu, choose Open In New Window. Internet Explorer opens the document in a new window.

To open a new Internet Explorer window using a menu, go to File, select New, and then click Window. You can also use the Ctrl + N shortcut.

Stopping an Unwanted Download

After you click a hyperlink, Internet Explorer starts downloading a new document. If you decide you're not interested in seeing the document, you can stop the download before it's complete. To stop downloading a document, click Stop or choose the View menu and select Stop. Or you can simply press Esc.

TIP If you're trying to access a site and there's no response after about 20 or 30 seconds, click Stop or press Esc. Chances are you're not going to get through; perhaps the Internet is congested, or the site's down temporarily. Try again later.

Switching Off
Graphics, Sound, and Video

Sure, multimedia's great. But multimedia files are often huge, and they take time to download. Are you more interested in the text than the pictures and design glitz? If so, consider turning off the automatic downloading of multimedia files. The Web won't look as pretty, but you won't believe how much faster you can browse. You can still view individual pictures, if you wish.

Turning Off Multimedia

Here's what to do. Choose Internet Options from the View menu, and click the Advanced tab. In the Multimedia area of the options list (Figure 6-2), remove the check beside Show Pictures, Play Animations, Play Videos, Play Sounds, and Smart Image Dithering by clicking each one. Click OK.

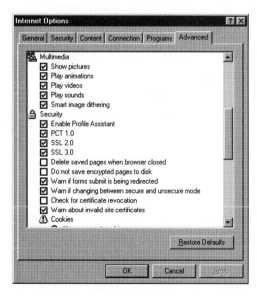

Figure 6-2
You can turn off multimedia effects from the Internet Options dialog box.

6

NOTE

> If the page you were viewing contains pictures, you'll still see them after turning off multimedia, but don't worry, Internet Explorer is still working just fine. Your choices in the Internet Options dialog box affect only the new pages you download after turning multimedia off. To hide the pictures in the current page, click Refresh; this forces Internet Explorer to download a new copy of the page from the network.

After you turn off graphics, sounds, and video, the Web won't look or sound as nice, but it will download so much faster. In place of graphics, you'll see *placeholders* (Figure 6-3). In well-designed sites, you'll see text that describes what the pictures show.

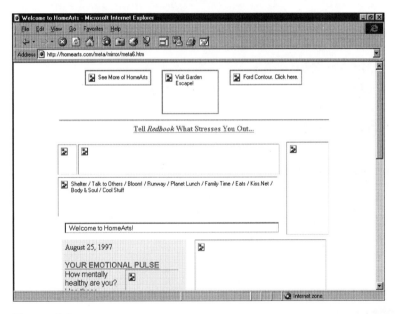

Figure 6-3

Placeholders appear instead of graphics after switching off multimedia.

Selectively Viewing Graphics

If you would like to see one of the pictures on a page, move the pointer to the placeholder, click the right mouse button, and choose Show Picture from the pop-up menu. You'll see just this one picture; the rest of the placeholders aren't affected (Figure 6-4).

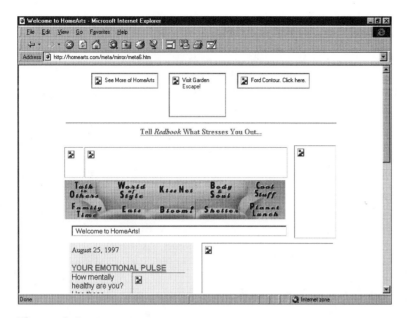

Figure 6-4

This graphic has been displayed with the Show Picture command.

Restoring Multimedia

To view pictures and movies and hear sounds again, choose Internet Options from the View menu, click Advanced, and select all the multimedia options that you turned off earlier. This action won't affect the page you're viewing until you click Refresh on the toolbar.

Increasing the Cache Size

Like all good browsers, Internet Explorer keeps copies of previously accessed documents—including graphics, sounds, videos, and animations—in a cache. Remember, a cache is a special section of your hard disk that's set aside as an extension of a program's memory.

Why Increasing the Cache Size Speeds Browsing

The cache size directly affects your browsing speed. When Internet Explorer encounters a Web site, the program first checks to see whether there's a copy of the site and its various components, including graphics, in the cache. Next it checks to see whether anything on the page has changed since you last accessed it. If not, the program loads the page from your hard disk instead of the network.

6

Now you know why it's so much faster to go back (by clicking the Back button) than it is to access sites you've never visited. When you click Back, Internet Explorer restores the page by loading it from your computer's hard disk. When you access a site you've never visited before, the program must retrieve the page and its components from the network, which is much slower.

The cache speeds Internet Explorer's performance, but it fills up quickly. When it does, the program erases previously visited pages to make room for copies of new ones. If you subsequently return to one of those previously visited pages, the program will not be able to find a copy on your disk, so it must retrieve a fresh copy from the network.

By increasing the size of the cache, you allow more room for storing copies of Web pages. You also increase the chance that the cache will contain a copy of a page that you previously visited. As a result, Internet Explorer will seem to perform more quickly—and that's definitely a good thing.

Where the Cache is Stored

By default, Internet Explorer stores copies of the Web pages you access in a folder called Temporary Internet Files, within the Windows folder. This folder fills up very quickly with all the pages, graphics, sounds, videos, applets, and controls you're downloading.

TIP How much disk space should you set aside for Internet Explorer's use? It depends on how much you have free. If you're using a 1.2-GB (gigabyte) drive and you've only used 220 MB (megabytes), you have lots of free space. You can set aside 15% of your drive (150 MB) and still have plenty of room for new programs and data. If you're really low on disk space, you'll be wise to free up some space before proceeding. You can do this by erasing unwanted programs and moving infrequently accessed data to backup files. Also, consider running DriveSpace 3, the excellent compression program included in the Microsoft Plus! add-on package. On my system, DriveSpace 3 effectively doubled the size of my hard disk without causing noticeable performance loss.

How to Increase the Cache Size

To increase the size of Internet Explorer's cache, choose Internet Options from the View menu and click the General tab. In the Temporary Internet Files area, click Settings. You'll see the Settings dialog box (Figure 6-5). Adjust the disk space slider to increase the percentage of your drive that's set aside for storing temporary Internet files, and click OK.

PART

Figure 6-5

Increasing the cache size is one of the best things you can do to speed up Internet Explorer.

NOTE

If you get low on disk space in the future, remember that you can free up lots of disk space—potentially dozens of megabytes—by reducing the size of the cache. You would return to the Internet Options dialog box and erase all the cache files by clicking Delete Files. Then, in the Settings dialog box, use the space slider to reduce the amount of disk space set aside for temporary files.

Decreasing the Cache Update Frequency

There is another handy speed-improvement trick, but it's risky.

The trick has to do with cache updates, which Internet Explorer performs automatically to see whether a page has changed. (If the page hasn't changed, the program retrieves the page from the cache rather than the network, as you learned in the previous section.)

By default, the program updates pages just once during a session. Suppose it's Monday morning, and you turn on your computer. You access the MSNBC news page, which you last viewed on Friday. Sure enough, Internet Explorer finds that the page has changed, so the program downloads the fresh copy instead of retrieving the Friday page from the cache. Obviously, this is a good thing because you don't want to read Friday's news.

If you choose Internet Options from the View menu, click the General tab, and then select Settings (see Figure 6-5), you'll see that you can

6

choose several update options. If you select Every Visit To The Page, Internet Explorer will always check to see whether a page has changed before retrieving a page from the cache. This process really slows things down. The default setting, Every Time You Start Internet Explorer, performs a check just once in an Internet Explorer session. The third setting, Never, prevents Internet Explorer from ever performing a check.

You can greatly speed Internet Explorer's performance by choosing Never, but here's the risk: You might be looking at old or outdated copies of a page without realizing it. The page might have changed, but you won't know. The change will be pretty obvious, though, if you check out a news page on Tuesday and get news from several days before—the day you chose Never. While we're on the topic of risk, note that there's a small risk with the default setting, too, especially if you leave Internet Explorer running for more than one day at a time. Because the default setting performs updates only once in an Internet Explorer session, you might not realize that a page has changed if you access it more than once during a session.

What do you do about pages that aren't automatically updated? To make sure you're viewing the latest copy of a page, click Refresh on the toolbar. The Refresh command forces Internet Explorer to retrieve a fresh copy.

NOTE

Should you choose Never? For most users, I'd say no. You might forget to click Refresh, and you'll see outdated data without realizing it. A worst-case scenario: You're checking out your mutual fund prices, and you make a sell or buy decision based on incorrect figures! If you're working with time-sensitive data like this, I'd recommend choosing Every Visit To The Page. This setting slows down the program somewhat, but it assures you that you'll never see outdated data.

Escaping the Frame Trap

Sooner or later you'll visit a framed site that falls victim to an evil temptation made possible by frames. This unintended feature of frames enables a Webmaster to trap browsers within their site, so that even external documents appear to be part of the site. You keep browsing the Web, but the framed sites icons and advertising keep blinking away at you. And what's worse, the frame you're browsing in isn't big enough to display the pages you're trying to see. People go to all sorts of absurd lengths to escape from this predicament, including quitting the program, restarting, and typing in the URL manually. But that's not necessary.

PART

There's a quick, handy cure for the frame trap. Point to the link that you want to see, click the right mouse button, and choose Open In New Window. The page breaks free from the frame trap, and you can continue browsing from there without having the framed site encapsulating all the subsequent sites you visit. You can return the compliment to this errant Webmaster by closing the original window.

Coping with Error Messages

You're browsing the Web innocently enough, and everything's going fine—until you see an alert box or encounter an error message. No, this doesn't mean you're a failure with the Internet. It's a big network out there, and all kinds of things can go wrong. Sometimes, try as you might, you just can't get through to a Web site that worked fine just a few days ago. Still, there are some tricks you can try.

Where do you see error messages? If you can't get through to the site at all, you'll see an Internet Explorer message. If you've gotten through to the site but then encounter an error, you'll see a message that's essentially a Web page, generated automatically by the server. Sometimes these are fairly friendly pages that explain what might have gone wrong; sometimes they're just a curt error message containing little more than one of the standard HTTP error codes (such as 401, 403, 404). The following sections help you to piece together what went wrong and suggest strategies for dealing with the problem.

Internet Explorer Can't Open the Site

If you see a message stating that Internet Explorer cannot open a Web page that you're trying to reach, chances are you're not online. If you're using a modem, note that high-speed modems sometimes shut down the connection if there's too much line noise. Try connecting and clicking the link again.

If you get the message again, it's possible that the whole site is down, or it might even have been removed from the Web. Try typing the site's domain name in the Address box and pressing Enter. If you still get this message, then the whole domain's down for some reason. Are you accessing late at night or on a weekend? Some people switch off their systems to perform maintenance when they expect light demand.

Are you getting this message for every site you try to access? There may be a problem with your Internet service provider's Domain Name Service program. A sure sign of this problem is if you can access your e-mail at the ISP's server (see Part II for an explanation of e-mail), but you can't

6

browse the Web. The cure for this situation is a call to the ISP; you'll probably get an apologetic explanation that they're "having problems with their router." This happens a lot, particularly to inexperienced ISP operators who aren't quite sure how to configure all that complicated equipment.

Network Connection Refused by Server

This message indicates that the server is overloaded or, possibly, that the Webmaster is busily making some changes. Try again. If you still can't access the site, try again later.

Too Many Connections

The poor server is overloaded. Try again later.

Bad Request (Error 400)

You just clicked a hyperlink and got this message, right? There's something wrong with the way the Web author wrote the hyperlink. If you're desperate to access this site, move the pointer to the hyperlink and read the URL from the status bar. Chances are there's some kind of mistake in it, such as a space or capital letters where there should be lowercase letters (or the other way around). Try typing the URL manually in all lowercase letters. If this still doesn't work, click the Search button and try searching for the site, using as many pertinent key words as you can think of.

TIP If you've selected the friendly URL option in the Advanced page of the Internet Options dialog box, switch it off. It prevents you from seeing the full URL on the status line. With the friendly URLs on, you can't use the recovery technique suggested above.

Unauthorized (Error 401)

Ha! Tried to get past a password-protected site, did you? In order to access this site, you need to supply a user name and password. Chances are the page you're seeing contains information about how to register or subscribe. Or it might have only a curtly worded message that the site is private and that you should go away.

Forbidden (Error 403)

This one's a shock (Figure 6-6). And it's rude, too, but it's intended to be. This message means you've accessed a document that isn't designed for access outside the organization or regional area that it calls home. It's designed for local consumption only. Too bad. Go away!

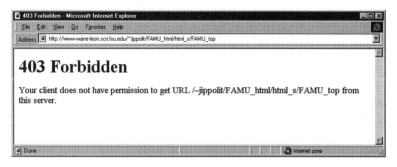

Figure 6-6

You can't access this document from outside its home area.

Not Found (Error 404)

So your screen looks like Figure 6-7, and you weren't even searching for 404, right? Well, there's good news and bad news here. The good news is that part of the Web address you're using is correct. Internet Explorer was able to find the server you're trying to contact. The only problem is that the server couldn't locate a document with the name you supplied.

There are several possible explanations for this message:

🌐 **Did you type the address correctly?** I hate to sound like a broken record, but this is a good possibility. In particular, check to see whether you typed the document's extension correctly. Lots of Web documents use the extension *.html,* but many—dating back to the glory days of Windows 3.1 when three-letter extensions were the order of the day—use *.htm.* If you type *.html* when the server expects *.htm,* it might not retrieve the document.

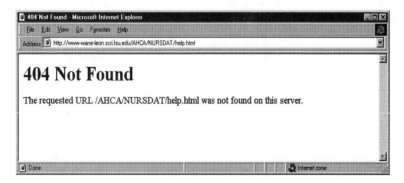

Figure 6-7

You found the server, but the document's missing. Try "backing up the URL."

6

- The document might have moved, and the author didn't have the courtesy to leave a forwarding address. To see whether it's available on some other server or in a different directory location on the same server, try an AltaVista search, as described in the previous chapter.

- The document might have been yanked from the Web. This happens—all too frequently. It even happens when you link to a document from a search service, such as Excite or AltaVista. Sometimes these services take a few days or even a few weeks to discover that a page has disappeared from the Web.

- The author might be right in the middle of updating the page. Try again later.

Internal Error (Error 500)

The server goofed up for some reason. You can generally solve this problem by clicking Back and trying again.

Not Implemented (Error 501)

You tried to use a Web feature that this server doesn't support, such as encryption.

TIP

If you get a Not Found message, try a trick that experienced surfers call "backing up the URL." Suppose you're trying to access the following URL:

www.middle-earth.org/shire/hobbiton/bag-end/frodo.html

You get a Not Found message. Go to the Address box, erase the document name, and press Enter. You'll be using this URL:

www.middle-earth.org/shire/hobbiton/bag-end/

If everything goes well, you'll see the default page for this particular directory. Perhaps you'll find that Bag End has been purchased by a certain Lobelia Sackville-Baggins, and in consequence, the former owner's page—**frodo.html**—has been removed.

Still didn't work? Keep trying:

www.middle-earth.org/shire/hobbiton/

www.middle-earth.org/shire/

www.middle-earth.org/

Eventually, you'll see some sort of welcome page, which may be able to help you find the information you're looking for.

Service Temporarily Overloaded (Error 502)

As they say, try again later.

"This Site Has Moved"

Now here's a thoughtful Web author, with the courtesy to give you a forwarding address (Figure 6-8). If there's a link to the new location, click it.

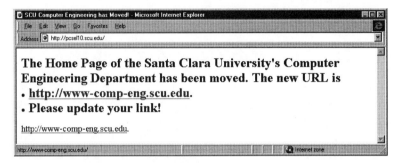

Figure 6-8

When you've been given an updated address, just click the link to go to the site's correct location.

Using Menu Shortcuts

Some menu options have direct keyboard shortcuts. For example, you can start printing a document by pressing Ctrl + P. The table below lists the keyboard equivalents for Internet Explorer menus and commands. If you prefer to use the keyboard rather than the mouse, you'll find these very handy.

Menu	Command	Keyboard Shortcut
File	New Window	Ctrl + N
File	Open	Ctrl + O (the letter)
File	Save	Ctrl + S
File	Print	Ctrl + P
Edit	Cut	Ctrl + X
Edit	Copy	Ctrl + C
Edit	Paste	Ctrl + V
Edit	Select All	Ctrl + A

(continued)

6

continued

Menu	Command	Keyboard Shortcut
Edit	Find (on this page)	Ctrl + F
View	Stop	Esc
View	Refresh	F5
Go	Back	Alt + Left arrow
Go	Forward	Alt + Right arrow

Using Pop-Up Menus (Right-Clicking)

Take a minute or two now to explore a useful and time-saving feature of Internet Explorer: the pop-up menus that appear when you point to something and click the right mouse button. These menus list the things you can do to whatever you clicked. For example, try right-clicking the background of a document. You'll see the menu shown in Figure 6-9. This menu lists all the things you can do when you click within a document text or whitespace. As the following sections discuss, the pop-up menus differ, depending on which part of the screen you right-click.

Figure 6-9

A pop-up menu appears when you click on a document's whitespace or text.

The Title Bar Pop-Up Menu

If you right-click Internet Explorer's title bar, you see a pop-up menu with the following options.

Name	Action
Restore	Restores the window to its previous size. (This command is available only if the window is maximized.)
Move	Enables you to move the window by using the keyboard's arrow keys.
Size	Enables you to size the window by using the keyboard's arrow keys.
Minimize	Minimizes this window.
Maximize	Maximizes this window. (If the window is already maximized, this command is dimmed.)
Close	Closes this window.

The Document Background Pop-Up Menu

If you right-click the document background (or any text that isn't part of a hyperlink), you see a pop-up menu with the following options.

Name	Action
Back	Same as clicking the Back button on the standard toolbar.
Forward	Same as clicking the Forward button on the standard toolbar.
Save Background As	Saves the background graphic to your computer's hard disk.
Set As Wallpaper	Saves the background graphic to your Windows directory and modifies Windows so that this graphic appears as your computer's default wallpaper graphic (cool!).
Copy Background	Copies the background graphic to the Clipboard.
Select All	Selects all the text in the document, but not the graphics.

(continued)

6

continued

Name	Action
Create Shortcut	Creates a shortcut for the current document and places the shortcut on the Windows desktop.
Add To Favorites	Adds the current page to your Favorites folder.
View Source	Displays the source (HTML) code underlying this document.
Language	Chooses the character set to use when displaying this document.
Print	Prints this document.
Refresh	Retrieves a fresh copy of this document from the network.
Properties	Displays the Properties dialog box, which contains information about the document's type, address, size, and creation date. You can also see information about the document's security.

The Hyperlink Pop-Up Menu

The following lists the commands that appear in the pop-up menu when you right-click a hyperlink.

Name	Action
Open	Follows the link and displays the linked document (same as clicking the hyperlink with the left mouse button).
Open In New Window	Follows the link and displays the linked document, but displays the new page in a new Internet Explorer window.
Save Target As	Saves the document that this link would display, but without opening the page.
Print Target	Prints the document referenced in this hyperlink.
Copy Shortcut	Copies the Web address to the Clipboard.
Add To Favorites	Adds this Web address to your Favorites folder.
Properties	Displays general information about the document connected to this link.

PART

Soup

It Up

The Graphic Pop-Up Menu

If you right-click a graphic, the pop-up menu displays the following options.

Name	Action
Open Link	If the graphic contains a hyperlink, follows the link and displays the linked document (same as clicking the hyperlink with the left mouse button). If this option is dimmed, the graphic doesn't contain a hyperlink.
Open Link In New Window	If the graphic contains a link, follows the link and displays the linked document, but displays the new page in a new Internet Explorer window. If this option is dimmed, the graphic doesn't contain a hyperlink.
Save Target As	If the graphic contains a link, saves the document that this link would display, but without opening the page. If this option is dimmed, the graphic doesn't contain a hyperlink.
Print Target	Prints the target referenced in this hyperlink.
Show Picture	If the graphic is merely a placeholder, displays the graphic itself.
Save Picture As	Saves this graphic to your hard disk.
Set As Wallpaper	Saves this graphic to your Windows directory and modifies Windows so that this graphic appears as your computer's default wallpaper graphic.
Copy	Copies the graphic to the Clipboard.
Copy Shortcut	If the graphic contains a link, copies the Web address to the Clipboard. If this option is dimmed, the graphic doesn't contain a hyperlink.
Add To Favorites	If the graphic contains a link, adds the Web address to your Favorites folder.
Properties	Displays a general Properties page about the graphic, including its type, address, size, and creation date.

115

6

From Here

- 🌐 The Internet's a wild place. Learn how to protect your privacy and security while you're online in Chapter 7.

- 🌐 Get out your credit card. Now that you've learned how to log on to commercial sites securely, let's go shopping. Find out how in Chapter 8.

- 🌐 Learn to make your Web pages come alive with hypermedia, including Internet Explorer's cool new NetShow in Chapter 9.

7

Play
It Safe

Thanks in part to many sensationalized articles in the press, some people overestimate the dangers of Internet use. At the same time, other people underestimate the dangers (particularly where kids are concerned). As with most things in life, the truth's somewhere in the middle. The Internet can be secure, safe, and incredibly rewarding—but you've got to inform and protect yourself. That's the goal of this chapter. Once you've read it, you'll be able to use the Internet with confidence.

Let's get started with some basic definitions and concepts, things that every Internet user really needs to understand. The chapter continues with a thorough exploration of all the fantastic things Microsoft Internet Explorer 4 can do to protect your security and privacy while you're online.

Understanding Internet Security and Privacy

To begin, it's important to understand that security and privacy differ, and that sometimes people who are very interested in security aren't interested in privacy—and vice versa.

Security ≠ Privacy

Security and privacy are two different things. *Security* refers to the protection of computer and networking systems against unauthorized intrusion by computer criminals. Although there are security issues in using a PC connected to the Internet (such as computer viruses), security is mainly a concern of Internet service providers and companies trying to do business on the Internet. *Privacy* refers to your ability to keep information about yourself hidden from prying eyes. You should be able to prevent anyone from obtaining information about you, your computer system, your Web site viewing tastes, and other personal data.

Companies and individuals sometimes have common interests when it comes to security and privacy, and sometimes they don't. For example, you and everyone who tries to sell products on the Web would like to ensure the security and privacy of credit card information that you use in ordering on the Web—that's in everyone's interest. However, more than a few firms would love to invade your privacy while you're using the Web, compiling information about your browsing, searching, and shopping choices.

For criminals, the opposite is true. They want total privacy so that they can work out drug deals, terrorist attacks, and other illegal acts without government detection. You can see why governments have mixed feelings about safeguarding the privacy of Internet users. Until something like a digital wiretapping scheme is worked out, which would enable investigators to obtain a warrant and unscramble encrypted messages, don't expect governments to show much enthusiasm for Internet privacy.

The Need for Security and Privacy Protection

It's paranoia time. The following is a rogue's gallery of the various guises that Internet predators can take.

🌐 **Imposters.** Suppose you've decided to order something online. You've accessed a Web site that appears to be the official Web site of a famous West Coast winery. It's a glamorous production.

However, you don't notice that the URL indicates that the site you've accessed is actually located outside the U.S. You upload your credit card data and somebody goes on a shopping spree with it! This is called *spoofing*. Another variation: Somebody logs on to a valid online ordering site with your credit card number, orders a bunch of stuff, has it delivered to a different shipping address, and you get the bill. While this isn't common, it has happened to a few people.

Criminal Hackers. A *sniffer* is a program that runs on a computer connected to the Internet. The program scans all the messages that are routed through the network to which the computer is connected, looking for information that conforms to a certain pattern (such as a Visa card number). Because Internet messages are normally sent in plain text, this is easy to do, and a criminal computer hacker doesn't even need to monitor the program manually. When the pattern is found, the information is displayed on-screen, enabling the criminal to read it. Sniffers are frequently programmed to look for credit card numbers and passwords uploaded in cleartext (unencrypted text).

Saboteurs. If you're not careful about where you obtain computer programs on the Internet, you could infect your system with a computer virus. The Internet is the greatest thing that ever happened to virus authors. It enables them to make trouble for many more people than they could prior to the Internet's explosive growth.

Snoops. Some servers, mainly commercial ones, write data to your hard drive in files called *cookies*. In most cases, this practice is quite legitimate and in your own interest. The cookie files contain information about your preferences, customization choices, and previous page selections. Cookies make Web sites much more functional and easier to use. However, there is a major push underway to use cookies to collect marketing data. At some sites, cookies can be used to compile a dossier about your searching, browsing, and online ordering preferences. Maybe you don't mind—but maybe you do.

7

🌐 **Predators.** Are your kids using the Internet? You'd best be aware that there are adults out there who would love to hit on them, and they know that the Internet is a perfect way to do it. Before the Internet, there was always the danger of a parent intercepting a call or letter. Now, with lots of Internet-savvy kids and Internet-clueless parents, a whole new avenue of communication has opened up that allows sexual predators to get past parents. How common is this? Unfortunately, very common. Let me be perfectly clear: You're out of your mind if you let your kids use the Internet without protection and supervision. Kids might try to snoop around on porn sites, as well as porn-related newsgroups and chat rooms—and that's where the predators find them.

Internet Explorer offers many solutions to security and privacy protection on the Internet. But as you'll see, there are some remaining problems, especially with respect to predators. The following sections indicate how the program gives you good protection against criminal hackers, imposters, saboteurs, and snoops.

Public-Key Cryptography

The answer to these problems may not lie in more legislation but in technology. Most people do not realize that there has been a major technical revolution in cryptography, the science of encrypting or coding messages so that they cannot be read by anyone except the intended recipient. *Public-key cryptography* is a new method of sending super-secret messages between two parties *who have never communicated before.*

Why is this such a major new discovery? Encryption, scrambling a message so that nobody can read it except its intended recipient, has been around since the time of Julius Caesar, but it's always had an Achilles' heel. Somehow you had to convey the *key*—which tells how to decode the message—to the recipient. This could be done by means of a courier, but as you can imagine, conveying the key this way is dangerous. What if the courier is disloyal?

Public-key cryptography solves this problem by using two keys, a public key and a private key. To engage in a secure transaction, you send your public key to somebody, and that person uses your public key to encrypt the message. Nobody can decode the message en route. Only you can decode it, using your private key. As long as the public key is carefully designed, it's practically impossible to break the code by deriving the private key from the public key.

When you use Internet Explorer to contact a secure server, the program and server exchange public keys, and a secure channel of communication is established. Both the data sent by you and by the server are transferred in encrypted form so that nobody—not even a criminal armed with a sniffer—can intercept it.

How will public-key encryption affect you? By making online commerce possible. (Although, as you'll learn elsewhere in this chapter, there's still a problem with protection against pilferers.) What's troubling about public-key encryption is the perfect cover it provides for illegal activity, such as drug dealing, money laundering, and terrorism. The U.S. Federal Bureau of Investigation (FBI) is deeply concerned that, in an encryption-driven future, the electronic equivalent of wiretapping will become impossible, creating unparalleled opportunities for organized crime. At this time, it's far from clear how these issues will develop and how they're going to be balanced against the legitimate privacy concerns of citizens and Internet users.

Public and Private Keys

In order to use public-key cryptography, users must have a program that enables them to generate two keys, the public key and the private key. Together, these are called a *key pair*. Microsoft Internet Explorer can create these for you.

Once you have a key pair, you can exchange secret messages with somebody you've never met. Let's say you want to bid $1 million on an exclusive Caribbean resort that's for sale, but you want to make sure that nobody else finds out what you've bid. The bids are supposed to go to a certain Mr. Smith in the Bahamas, who has published his public key. You encrypt your bid, using Mr. Smith's public key, and send it to Mr. Smith. You also enclose your public key so that Mr. Smith can respond secretly to you. When Mr. Smith gets your message, he uses his private key to decode it. Then he replies ("It's yours"), encrypting this message with your public key. You use your private key to decode the message.

Digital Certificates

What's wrong with the Mr. Smith story? I mean, besides the fact that you don't have a million bucks to burn on a Bahamas investment? The secrecy part's OK. The messages are encrypted, and they cannot be intercepted and read while they're en route. But how do you know you are really communicating with Mr. Smith in the Bahamas? For that matter, what about you? Are you an imposter?

7

Digital certificates provide safeguards against imposters. A digital certificate is essentially a means of countersigning public keys with a "digital ID," the computer equivalent of your driver's license. Digital certificates are supplied by certification authorities (CA), which provide the certificates for free or for a small fee. When you send your public key, you include your certificate. By inspecting your certificate, people can see that the message is really from you.

Digital Signatures

But is it really from you? What if somebody has intercepted and tampered with your certificate and is using it to fake an identity? That's where *digital signatures* come in. Your computer creates the digital signature for each message you send by using a *hash*. A hash is a one-way mathematical function that reduces the content of your message to a short *message digest*. The cool thing about the message digest is that it's a sort of mathematical fingerprint of your message. Also, it's impossible to derive the message from the digest, even if the hash formula is known. All you can do with the hash function is make a new message digest.

Here's how the message digest works. When the receiving computer gets your message, it takes the message and runs the same hash function that you used. Then it compares the two message digests, the one you sent and the one it computed. If they don't agree, there's trouble. Something happened to the message—maybe just a data transmission error, or maybe somebody got hold of the message and altered it in some way. Either way, the message is rejected.

Understanding and Using Certificates

Get started by understanding the types of certificates you can use and getting your own personal certificate. Internet Explorer uses three kinds of certificates.

 Site Certificates. A *site certificate* is issued and validated by an independent, third-party agency. When your browser accesses a secure Web site, your browser examines the site's security certificate. If the security certificate is valid, you know that the server you've accessed is really located at the company you want to do business with. If the security certificate isn't valid, it means that something in the certificate doesn't match up, for example, the site's name or e-mail address isn't what it's supposed to be. This problem might be due to sloppy record-keeping, or it might be due to criminal activity. In either case, you'd be well advised to skip ordering from this site.

- **Publisher Certificates.** These certificates are presented by software publishers when you download software from the Internet. The certificate attests that the software really is from the software publisher (not some imposter) and that you can presume it's trustworthy. However, be aware that the certification authority does not personally inspect every program for viruses.

- **Personal Certificates.** Companies selling goods on the Web have their own concerns about imposters. What if someone has stolen your credit card and is trying to use it to order goods illegally? *Personal certificates* identify you as the person you say you are. A personal certificate is like showing your identification when you use your credit card. It's in your interest as well as the merchants' and banks' interests to make sure that no one is using your card illegally. There are different levels of personal certificates. A Class 1 certificate reflects the lowest level of demanded identification; the only way the CA checks on your identity is to mail the identification to your e-mail account. Stronger identification is provided by Class 2 certificates, which are issued only after your identity has been verified by means of an online consumer database.

Obtaining a Certificate

Get your own digital certificate now. At this writing, VeriSign, Inc., a leading Certificate Authority, was making free trial certificates available to Internet Explorer users. As with everything on the Web, this offer is subject to change and might not be valid by the time you read this.

NOTE In order to obtain your digital ID, you need to set up your e-mail with Outlook Express. If you haven't done so yet, please read Chapter 13 before continuing.

7

To get a free Class 1 digital ID from VeriSign, follow this procedure:

1. Access VeriSign's Digital ID Center at **digitalid.verisign.com**.

2. Look for a button or link labeled Enroll (Request An ID), and click it. You'll see a page asking you what type of digital signature you want and which browser you're using. You want an individual identification (ID), and you're using Microsoft Internet Explorer.

3. Click the link that gives you an individual ID for Internet Explorer. You'll see a page explaining the difference between Class 1 and Class 2 digital IDs.

4. Click Class 1. You'll see a page asking you to supply information, including your name, e-mail address, and the password you want to use for your digital ID.

5. Type the requested information, and follow all the instructions to submit your request.

6. You'll see Internet Explorer's key generation wizard (Figure 7-1). Choose the default options, and click Next until you come to Finish.

7. After a few minutes, check your e-mail. You'll find a message from VeriSign indicating your personal identification number (PIN).

8. Switch back to the VeriSign page in Internet Explorer, and click the link that takes you to the Web page at which you get your ID.

9. On this page, type your PIN and click Submit. Internet Explorer installs the certificate on your system.

Figure 7-1

Internet Explorer's key generation wizard guides you through getting a digital identification.

One drawback to current digital certificate technology is that you can't use your certificate unless you're sitting at the computer where it was downloaded. In the future, computers will be accessed by means of *smart cards,* which are credit-card–sized IDs that contain their own processing circuitry. They will contain your certificate, enabling you to establish your identity no matter which computer you're using.

Safeguarding Online Transactions (Solving the Criminal Hacker Problem)

The key to safeguarding your data from criminal hackers is to *encrypt* it, to scramble it so that it can't be read on any computer while en route. When the data arrives at its correct destination, the receiving computer decrypts it.

On the World Wide Web, encryption becomes possible with *secure browsers* and *secure servers*. A secure browser, such as Internet Explorer, can encrypt the data that you send, while a secure server can decrypt the data at the other end. All this is done automatically, almost instantly. And along the way, it is virtually impossible to decode and read the encrypted data.

Understanding Security Protocols

For Internet browsers and servers to exchange encrypted data, both must be able to work with the same security protocol. A *security protocol* is a set of standards that specify how two computers can communicate by means of a secure (encrypted) channel. So that you can order safely from most of the secure sites on the Web, Internet Explorer recognizes and works with the security protocols listed below. You don't have to choose a protocol when you access a secure site; everything is automatic.

- 🌐 **Secure Sockets Layer (SSL).** This protocol, originally developed by Netscape, is the one used in most secure Web sites. SSL version 3.0, supported by Microsoft Internet Explorer 4, enables Web users and Web sites to exchange certificates for authenticating identity.

- 🌐 **Private Communication Technology (PCT).** This Microsoft-developed protocol builds on SSL and introduces additional features that can help give a greater margin of security.

7

Accessing a Secure Site

Accessing a secure Web site is no different from accessing any other site on the Web: You click a hyperlink or type the URL directly. The site's welcome page often isn't secure. After all, many people are still using browsers that lack security features. Look for a link that enables you to access the secure version of the service.

After you've logged on to the secure service, look for a lock icon on the status bar. The lock icon tells you that you have accessed a secure server and that the information you upload is safe from prying eyes. It's that simple!

Viewing Security Information

Once you've logged on to a secure Web page, you can view the security information, although it's not necessary unless you want to satisfy yourself that the transaction really is secure. To view security information, follow these steps:

1. Choose Properties from the File menu. You'll see the Properties dialog box.

2. Click the Certificates button. You'll see another Properties dialog box; this one shows the security certificate information (Figure 7-2).

3. Click OK to exit the certificate Properties dialog box, and click OK to close the document Properties dialog box.

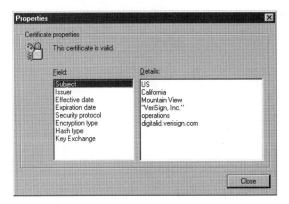

Figure 7-2
You can quickly look up certificate information about the Web page you are viewing.

Choosing Security Options

If you would like to adjust Internet Explorer's privacy and security settings, go to the View menu and select Internet Options; click the Advanced tab. Scroll down to see the Security options. You'll see the options that affect online transactions (Figure 7-3). The following list explains the function of each option; the default setting for each is given in parentheses.

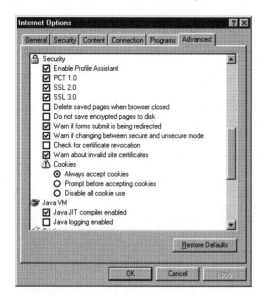

Figure 7-3

You can choose security options in the Advanced page of the Options dialog box.

🌐 **Enable Profile Assistant.** (On) The Profile Assistant allows you to respond to a Web site's request for personal information with a click of the mouse. If you don't plan to use Profile Assistant, you can turn it off here.

🌐 **PCT 1.0.** (On) Enable this option so that you can engage in secure transactions with PCT secure servers.

🌐 **SSL 2.0.** (On) Enable this option so that you can engage in secure transactions with SSL 2.0 secure servers.

🌐 **SSL 3.0.** (On) Enable this option so that you can engage in secure transactions with SSL 3.0 secure servers.

🌐 **Do not save encrypted pages to disk.** (Off) If you're worried that somebody might snoop around in your computer to see secure pages you've visited, you can click this option.

7

- 🌐 **Warn if forms submit is being redirected.** (On) This option warns you if a Web form that you've filled out is about to be sent to a site other than the site you're currently viewing. This helps protect you against spoofing. Leave it on.

- 🌐 **Warn if changing between secure and unsecure mode.** (Off) This option shows a warning box when you move from an unsecure to a secure connection, and vice versa. It's a pain—leave it off.

- 🌐 **Check for certificate revocation.** (Off) This service, not yet complete, will enable you to check to see whether someone's certificate has been revoked.

- 🌐 **Warn about invalid site certificates.** (On) With this option, Internet Explorer will display a warning if the program detects a discrepancy between the security certificate and the particulars (such as the Internet address or e-mail address) of the site you've accessed. This could be a minor error on the server's part, but it could also mean that somebody has tried to set up a bogus site to collect credit card numbers. If you're sure the site is what it says it is, click OK. If you have any doubts or you're not sure, click Cancel. I recommend that you enable this option.

- 🌐 **Cookies.** (Always accept cookies) Cookies are small text files that servers store in your computer. They are often used for purposes that benefit the user, such as storing passwords and other login information. However, they raise privacy issues. You'll learn more about cookies later in this chapter.

Setting Security Levels (Solving the Sabotage Problem)

To prevent your system from rogue programs, including computer viruses, be sure to set the correct security level. You can choose from High (excludes any content that isn't backed by a certificate), Medium (warns you if there's a possibility of damaging content but doesn't exclude it), Low (doesn't warn you), and Custom (for expert users only).

To choose a security level, choose Internet Options from the View menu and click Security. You'll see the Security page shown in Figure 7-4.

You can also set up *security zones,* with different settings for each. These zones offer four possibilities.

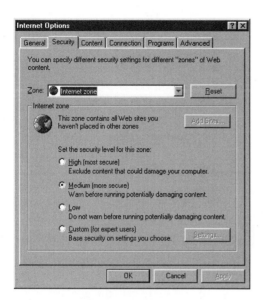

Figure 7-4

Consider choosing the Medium security level for the Internet zone.

- 🌐 **Local Intranet Zone.** If you're using an intranet (an internal corporate Web), you can use Low security. Internet Explorer can automatically detect when you're browsing within the intranet.

- 🌐 **Trusted Sites Zone.** You can set up a trusted sites zone for Low security, as long as you're sure you can really trust the sites. You need to set this up by adding sites to a list. (Select Trusted Sites Zone and click Add Sites.)

- 🌐 **Internet Zone.** This zone is the open, external Internet. Be sure to use Medium or High security.

- 🌐 **Restricted Sites Zone.** If you plan to visit sites that you're nervous about, you can assign these High security. You need to set this up by adding sites to a list. (Select Restricted Sites Zone and click Add Sites.)

TIP

To be on the safe side, you can use High security, but a lot of legitimate content won't work with this setting. If you're browsing sites that you feel you can trust, try switching to Medium. You'll see warnings when doubtful content appears, and you can decide whether to accept it or reject it. (You can still read the text on the page.)

7

Approving Cookie Downloading (Solving the Snooper Problem)

Many Web users are under the impression that you can browse the Internet in perfect anonymity, without anyone knowing which sites you've visited. This impression is false. Every time you visit a Web site, you risk leaving a great deal of information about yourself, including the organization or company with which you're affiliated, your geographical location, the type of computer and operating system you're running, the browser you're using, the Internet address of the computer you're using, the exact time and date of your visit, and the pages you've looked at and how long you looked at them.

The means to collect, store, and analyze this information is your own computer, used without your consent or knowledge. Many servers write files to your hard disk—cookies—that compile additional information about you.

At many sites, the use of cookies is innocent enough; the goal is simply to tailor the site to your benefit. Cookies were introduced by Netscape Communications to get around a problem in Web access—namely, that it's difficult for one page to pass information to another page without adding lots of incomprehensible codes to the URL. Cookies provide a way for one page to leave information for another page. At many sites, this information is used to record your preferences. For example, Microsoft uses cookies to record your start page and MSNBC preferences. That's why it's possible to customize these pages.

TIP If you're concerned about your privacy while you're surfing the Web, start your surfing sessions at The Anonymizer (**www.anonymizer.com**). When you use The Anonymizer as your starting point, subsequent sites cannot determine where you're browsing from. You can still make use of virtually all of the Web's features, including Java programs and password-based authentication.

But not all cookies are used so innocently. A New York-based advertising firm has figured out how to use cookies to track your movements through the several dozen commercial sites with which the company contracts. This advertising firm is building a database about you that monitors your browsing behavior. The purpose of the database is to assist Web advertisers in targeting their markets more effectively. If you've visited any of the sites that contract with this firm, there is a cookie on your hard drive that gives you a unique identification number. This number is used to create a profile about your browsing habits and interests. When you access a site that has contracted with this firm to provide ads, the site sends your number to the marketing firm, which sends back ads tailored to your specific interests.

Is this activity in your best interest? After all, you'll see ads tailored to your preferences. Privacy advocates worry that this monitoring activity goes far beyond the transaction monitoring common in the retail world; it amounts to surveillance concerning which store windows you've looked into. Worse, they say, it's done without the user's knowledge or consent. And to add insult to injury, it employs your own hard drive. Cookie files, incidentally, can consume up to 1.2 MB of your disk space!

TIP

Like to see your cookies? Look for a directory named Cookies somewhere in your Windows directory. (Depending on your version of Windows, it might be buried a few levels down.) There they are! Don't think that you can prevent new ones from being written by deleting the entire Cookies directory; Internet Explorer will simply write a new one. You can, however, choose an Internet Explorer option that lets you selectively decide whether or not to download a specific cookie.

If you wish, Internet Explorer will warn you every time a server attempts to write a cookie to your hard drive. You can inspect the cookie and prevent the server from sending it. To turn on cookie approval, choose Internet Options from the View menu and click the Advanced tab. Under Cookies, choose the option named Prompt Before Accepting Cookies.

After choosing this option, you'll see a dialog box whenever a server tries to send you a cookie. You'll be able to see the cookie's contents, or at least the first dozen or so characters. Cookies are coded, so it's hard to tell what's intended. You can also look at the cookie's expiration date. In general, it's a good sign if the cookie expires in a few days or weeks, a bad one if it's semipermanent. To accept the cookie, click Yes; to reject it, click No.

If you reject the cookie, you can still access the site. But you might find that you're being besieged with cookie after cookie, requiring you to go through a whole series of these dialog boxes. Check to see whether the server is trying to send you the same cookie over and over, the intent being (presumably) to wear you down until you give in and click Yes. Another option (the preferred one) is to leave the site and not come back.

7

Blocking Porn

If children are using your computer, consider setting up the Microsoft Internet Explorer ratings system, which is based on the one created by the Recreational Software Advisory Council (RSAC). Thus far, RSAC has rated more than 35,500 Web sites.

You can set up Internet Explorer so that the program permits access to any Web site except those blocked by an RSAC rating that you select. For smaller kids, you can also set up the program so that it blocks any site that doesn't have an acceptable RSAC rating. (That's pretty inconvenient, though, since so few sites are rated.)

To use RSAC ratings with Internet Explorer, follow these steps:

1. Choose Internet Options from the View menu, and select the Content tab. You will see the Content options shown in Figure 7-5.

2. In the Ratings area, click Settings. You'll see a password dialog box that asks you to type a password twice. Make sure this is something your kids won't figure out or find written down.

3. Click OK to confirm your password. (You'll type this password each subsequent time you access your ratings settings; nobody else will be able to get into them.) You'll see the Content Advisor dialog box (Figure 7-6).

4. Click a rating category and move the slider to the level you're willing to permit.

5. Repeat Step 4 until you've chosen levels for all the categories.

6. Click the General tab to see the User Options (Figure 7-7). Consider whether you want to prohibit all sites that have no ratings—which is most of the Web—or to enable the supervisor to type the password to access restricted sites that have no rating. That's the default setting, and it's the only realistic choice.

7. Click OK. Back in the Content page, note that you can click Disable to disable the ratings, but you'll have to supply the password to do this. Don't forget it!

8. Click OK to confirm.

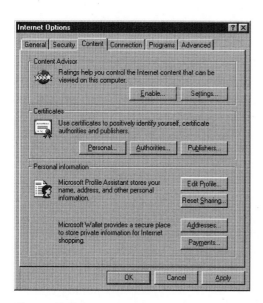

Figure 7-5

From the Content tab, choose Settings to set ratings.

Figure 7-6

In the Content Advisor, choose rating levels for language, nudity, sex, and violence.

7

The Recreational Software Advisory Council Ratings

RSAC uses the following numerical ratings to describe the violence, profanity, nudity, and sex in a rated Web site. To compare these to familiar movie ratings, 1 equals PG and 2 resembles PG-13. A rating of 3 is close to R, and 4 gets into the NC-17 area. In my opinion, the RSAC's system is more informative than movie ratings because it goes into detail about the exact nature of the offending content.

Violence

1. Creatures injured or killed, damage to realistic objects, fighting with no injuries
2. Humans or creatures injured or killed, rewards injuring non-threatening creatures
3. Blood and gore, rewards injuring nonthreatening humans, rewards killing nonthreatening creatures, accidental injury with blood and gore
4. Wanton and gratuitous violence, rape

Language

1. Mild expletives
2. Expletives, nonsexual anatomical references
3. Strong or vulgar language, obscene gestures
4. Extreme hate speech, crude language, explicit sexual references

Nudity

1. Revealing attire
2. Partial nudity
3. Nonsexual frontal nudity
4. Provocative frontal nudity

Sex

1. Passionate kissing
2. Clothed sexual touching
3. Nonexplicit sexual activity, sexual touching
4. Explicit sexual activity

For more information on RSAC, see www.rsac.org/.

If you try to access a site that doesn't have a rating, you'll see the dialog box shown in Figure 7-8. This dialog box comes up often, since only a tiny fraction of the Web's sites are rated. You'll probably get tired of this pretty quick, so go to the View menu, select Internet Options again, click Content, and click Disable.

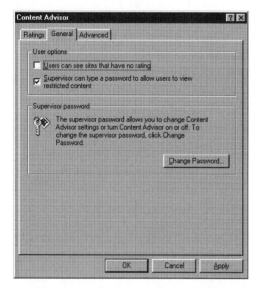

Figure 7-7

You can choose to prohibit all sites that don't have ratings, but you will block most of the Web.

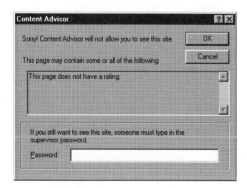

Figure 7-8

A dialog box appears when you try to access a site with no rating.

7

TIP

It's nice that this ratings feature is included. It can be so restrictive that you can enable it while you're out and feel pretty secure that your kids won't be able to access porn sites (or much of anything else, for that matter). But it's really not a complete solution. It doesn't provide much protection against the sexual predators who are trying to get to our children. I prefer "net nanny" programs, such as CyberPatrol, that block incoming and outgoing data at the network level. These put restrictions in place for every Internet application that your kids use, including newsgroups, e-mail, FTP, Internet Relay Chat (IRC), and other browsers. There's another great protection against predators: CyberPatrol can be configured to prevent kids from uploading personal data about themselves, such as their phone numbers and addresses.

From Here

- 🌐 Shop 'til you drop! It's safe, as this chapter has explained, and in the next chapter, you'll find it's convenient, too. Microsoft Wallet, a cool new feature of Internet Explorer 4, enables you to upload credit card and shipping information with absolutely no hassle on your part—and the whole transaction is encrypted.

- 🌐 Make the Web rock in Chapter 9, which covers the multimedia aspects of Internet Explorer, including Microsoft's new NetShow utility.

- 🌐 Like to save or print some of that cool stuff you're finding? Learn how in Chapter 11.

PART

8 Charge It

Now that you know how to protect yourself while you're online, consider doing some online shopping. With Microsoft Internet Explorer's security features, it's much safer than ordering over the telephone. As you'll see in this chapter, online commerce is already growing very rapidly. Once you give it a try, you'll understand why.

With Microsoft Wallet, online shopping is even easier. This ActiveX control enables you to enter and store your personal information and credit card number so that these can be conveniently uploaded to vendors—no more filling out lengthy forms and typing your credit card numbers over and over. And it's safe. Your personal credit card information is stored in encrypted form on your computer, and only you can access it. The data is uploaded using SSL security, so you can be sure that it can't be intercepted en route.

Deciding Whether Web Commerce Is for Real

A few decades ago, hardly anybody ordered things over the phone using a credit card. It was practically unheard of. "Give somebody my credit card number over the phone? Are you crazy?" My, how times have changed. Today credit card ordering is one of the cornerstones of the retail economy. Now people are saying, "Upload my credit card number over the Internet? Are you crazy?" Sounds like a repeat cycle, doesn't it?

A repeat cycle is what most business experts believe is happening. Internet commerce has been slow to develop mostly because it takes time for people to get used to the idea. But online commerce makes sense for many reasons: convenience and privacy for the customers, less expense and wider distribution for businesses. (Just think about the environmental effect of offering catalogs over the Web instead of mailing them by the millions.) And with the encryption technologies now available, ordering over the Internet is as safe as, and possibly even safer than, ordering by phone. The market is certainly there. By the year 2000, nearly 200 million people are expected to be using the Internet.

Already several thousand companies have opened up shop on the 'Net. It's a mixed bag, with people selling everything from hot sauce to lingerie, but some patterns seem to be emerging. In general, the businesses that succeed on the Web are those that offer products of particular interest to Web users or that take special advantage of the Internet's potential as a shopping medium. One example is Amazon.com Books (**www.amazon.com**), where database and Web technology are joined to offer something you can't get in just any neighborhood bookstore. Amazon.com offers more than 2.5 million titles online. The largest chain bookstores offer only about 170,000 titles, while the average mall bookstore stocks just 25,000.

After you've shopped around a bit, you'll see that certain types of products and services seem to be doing better online than others. Here's a snapshot of the current market:

- 🌐 **Books and compact discs.** These are naturals for online ordering. A store can put its entire catalog (perhaps containing as many as 150,000 items) online with a searchable interface.

- 🌐 **Cars.** Internet-based automobile buying services, such as Microsoft CarPoint, are making inroads into the traditional world of dealerships. You can understand why; it's so pleasant to order a car via the Internet, with no bargaining, hassles, or games with dealers.

PART

138

Clothing. You won't find everyday items on the Web. The action here is strictly in specialty items, such as exotic lingerie, bizarre T-shirts, funny ties and hats, and specialty shoes.

 Computer equipment. It makes sense that computer people would feel comfortable ordering computer equipment online. Several excellent online vendors offer great prices on selected equipment.

 Gifts. Flowers and specialty gift shops are prevalent on the Web, indicating that this is another popular area for online orders.

 Specialty foods and wine. You'll find hot sauces, Zinfandels, designer beers, spices, and sweets. All that surfing makes you hungry!

 Sports and recreation gear. There are plenty of online stores that sell specialty gear for golfers, sailors, backpackers, and other sports enthusiasts.

TIP

To keep on top of the Web's fast-breaking commercial developments, check out The All-Internet Shopping Directory (**www.all-internet.com/**). This site lists Web vendors whose sites meet stringent guidelines for quality and service. You'll find lists of the Web's top shopping sites and plenty of links to the newest credit card burners on the Web. This very cool site is updated bi-weekly.

Ordering Online

To see what online shopping is like, take a look at Amazon.com, which bills itself as "Earth's Biggest Bookstore". (And justifiably so, considering that more than 2.5 million books are available and most will reach your doorstep within two or three days of your order.) Amazon.com is worth exploring for another reason besides seeing what electronic commerce is all about. Far more than an online book ordering site, Amazon.com is a community of authors, readers, publishers—anyone who loves books. You can submit your own reviews of any of the books listed in the voluminous catalog at Amazon.com. What's more, you'll find links to Internet-accessible book reviews, author biographies, and publisher sites. If you love books and reading, Amazon.com will quickly become one of your favorite sites on the Web.

8

Searching Amazon.com

To access Amazon.com, type www.amazon.com in the Address box. You'll see the latest version of Amazon.com's home page (Figure 8-1). The home page contains interesting news and offers, but let's search.

Suppose you're curious to see what one of the greatest science fiction writers of all time, Robert Silverberg, has been up to lately. Let's try an author search. Find the search options, and click the option that enables you to search by author. You'll see a page like the one in Figure 8-2. Follow the search instructions, and you'll see a list such as the one shown in Figure 8-3. If you click one of the listed books (they're organized in reverse chronological order and also by availability), you'll see a page describing the book (Figure 8-4). You may also see a synopsis, links to published literary reviews, customer reviews, and even the author's own comments. You can even contribute your own review, if you wish.

Selected Secure Shopping Sites

Here are some places to start your Internet shopping spree. Load up with the latest CDs, a brand-new Walkman, and some gourmet snacks before you hop on the plane to Hawaii.

- **CDWorld** (www.cdworld.com/). One of the best CD stores on the Internet, this site offers a convenient search engine that lets you scan more than 100,000 discs by artist's name, title, or recording label.

- **iMALL** (www.imall.com/). Here's an Internet shopping mall that's beautifully organized on a familiar plan—a real shopping mall! Among the goods you'll find ·for sale are housewares, arts and collectibles, specialty items, electronics, gourmet foods, computer gear, gifts, books, and more.

- **Internet Shopping Network** (www.internet.net/). If you're skeptical about Internet shopping, this is the place to start. You'll find very hot deals on computer and electronics equipment (some of the best deals around). You can see a picture of what you're buying and get full technical information; you generally get much more than you'd find in a print-based catalog.

- **Travel Now** (www.travelnow.com/). This secure site offers hotel and airline reservations, tours, cruises, and travel packages. An excellent feature is the hotel search page that enables you to search for the best rate.

Figure 8-1

Amazon.com bills itself as "Earth's Biggest Bookstore."

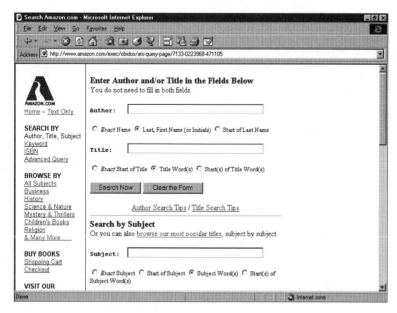

Figure 8-2

You can search Amazon.com by author, title, subject, keyword, ISBN, and combinations of these.

8

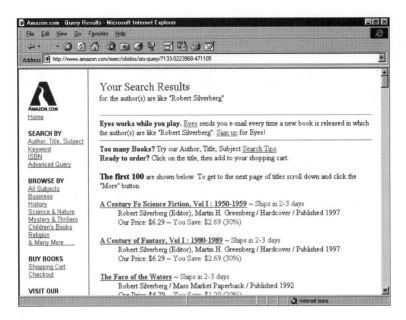

Figure 8-3

A search for "Robert Silverberg" found more than 100 items.

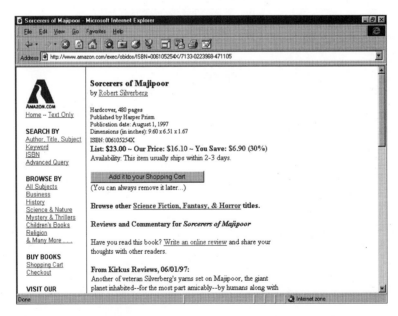

Figure 8-4

Pages describing books contain basic information and pricing and may also contain synopses and reviews.

PART

142

Adding Items to Your Shopping Cart

If you find something you like, add it to your virtual shopping cart by clicking the button. (Adding items doesn't commit you; you can remove them later.) If you'd like to find more books, click Continue Shopping. If you're ready to check out, click Proceed To Checkout.

Checking Out

When you proceed to checkout, you'll have the option of selecting the Amazon.com secure server. By all means, do so; it isn't safe to upload your credit card information in cleartext. When you're connected to the secure server, you'll see a lock icon in Internet Explorer's status bar (lower right corner in Figure 8-5).

You can tell you're connected to a secure server in other ways, too:

🌐 **Look at the URL.** When you're connected to a secure server, you see *https://* instead of *http://* in the Address bar.

🌐 **Choose Properties from the File menu.** Click the Certificates button to see security information for this document. You'll see the site certificate.

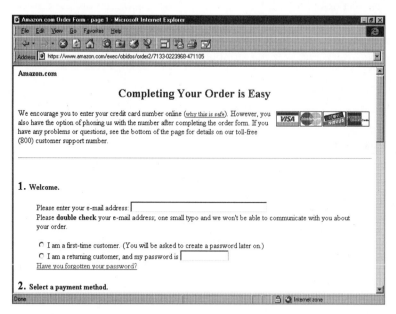

Figure 8-5

When you're connected to a secure server, you see a lock icon in the program's status bar.

8

To complete your order, continue filling out the on-screen forms. You can choose gift wrapping, payment methods, and delivery options. When you finish your order, you'll see a confirmation screen; you'll also receive notification by e-mail when your order is processed and again when it's shipped. This is truly a class act.

Using Microsoft Wallet

Internet Explorer 4 comes with a neat new feature that's designed to make online shopping much more convenient, and in time, even more secure: Microsoft Wallet. In brief, Microsoft Wallet enables you to store and access your payment and address information easily. You don't have to repeatedly type this information into forms. And don't worry about somebody finding your credit card information by snooping around on your computer. The Payment Selector control ensures secure storage of the various payment methods you store.

For secure online submission of your information, Microsoft Wallet uses SSL security. What's more, Wallet includes programming "hooks" that will enable Internet vendors to implement the industry-wide Secure Electronic Transaction (SET) standards, as well as a number of additional electronic links to financial institutions, including electronic checks. (To understand why SET is so important, see the sidebar, "The Pilferage Problem.")

Configuring Microsoft Wallet

Microsoft Wallet is conveniently built into Internet Explorer. To store information in your Microsoft Wallet, choose Internet Options from the View menu and then click the Content tab. Follow these steps to add your address:

1. In the Personal Information area of the Internet Options dialog box, click Addresses. You'll see the Address Options dialog box.

2. Click the Add button to display the Add A New Address dialog box, shown in Figure 8-6.

3. Type your information in the Add A New Address dialog box. You can specify whether this is home or business information by selecting the Home or Business button.

4. When you're done, click OK.

TIP   If you've already added your name and address to the Windows Address Book, just click Address Book to select this information instead of retyping it.

PART

The Pilferage Problem

With Microsoft Internet Explorer, you can send your credit card information through the Internet so securely that even the world's top spy agencies couldn't crack it. But once it gets to the vendor, what happens? It's decoded into cleartext (plain, readable text), and the vendor must manually process the information. Unfortunately, this means that your credit card information is visible to the firm's employees.

That visibility is the last remaining security hole in Internet commerce, and it's serious. Pilferage at the vendor level costs credit card holders and issuers millions of dollars annually. You take exactly the same risk when you order over the telephone. In fact, you take an even greater risk because you are telling people your number over an insecure phone line, which is easily intercepted by anyone with a modicum of knowledge and a few inexpensive snooping devices. If you use a portable phone, you might be broadcasting this information to your neighbors! So pilferage isn't a problem that's unique to Internet commerce. It's characteristic of mail order/telephone order (MOTO) transactions, too. In fact, with the Secure Electronic Transaction (SET) mechanisms, ordering over the Internet will soon become the most secure way you can do business.

Here's why. The SET standards create a three-way connection between you, the vendor, and the credit card issuer. That's great for the vendor because the authorization process becomes automatic; employees don't have to spend time obtaining the authorization manually. And it's even greater for you: No one from the vendor sees your credit card information. You submit your information via Microsoft Wallet, and it remains encrypted as it passes through the vendor's computer and on to the authorization process. All the vendor sees is an authorization code.

SET was jointly developed by a consortium of credit card issuers (including Visa and MasterCard) and industry practitioners (including Microsoft Corporation). Once the implications of this technology ripple through the economy and people realize how safe Internet ordering will become, Internet commerce will gain momentum and grow very quickly. For now, SET is just being implemented, so don't expect many sites to give you this protection. By 1998, SET-supported sites should become much more numerous.

8

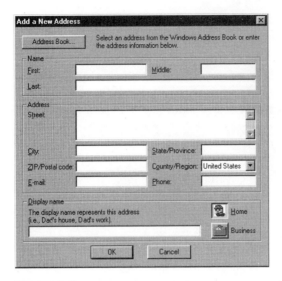

Figure 8-6

Adding a new address is simple.

Now add your credit card information by following these steps:

1. In the Internet Options dialog box, click Payments. You'll see the Payment Options dialog box.

2. Click Add (Figure 8-7) and select the type of credit card you want to add. The Add A New Credit Card wizard appears. Read the introductory page and click Next.

3. Enter your credit card information and a display name (Figure 8-8). The display name lets you quickly identify your credit cards. Choose a name that is meaningful to you, such as Bryan's Corporate AmEx or Chelle's Seafirst Visa. Click Next.

4. You can choose the billing address for your credit card from the addresses you've already entered, or you can enter a new address. After you've specified the address, click Next.

5. The final page of the wizard requires you to select a password (Figure 8-9). This is important. The password is the key to your credit card information, so select it carefully and then enter it into both boxes. Click Finish, and you're done.

PART

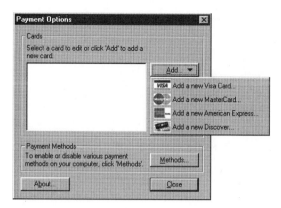

Figure 8-7

Adding a new credit card is just as easy. The Microsoft Wallet will also let you use other forms of payment as they are introduced.

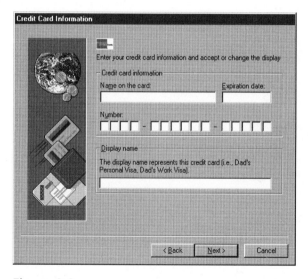

Figure 8-8

Be sure to enter your credit card information exactly as it appears on your card.

8

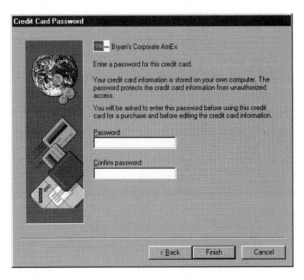

Figure 8-9

The password is the key to your credit card information.

If you need to change any of this information, return to the Address Options or Payment Options dialog box, select the address or card to change, supply your password, and click Edit.

From Here

- 🌐 Make the Web come alive with sounds, movies, NetShow audio and video, Java, and ActiveX! Find out how in the next chapter.

- 🌐 Found some keepers? You can download fantastic shareware programs, as well as print (even in framed documents), copy, and save documents. Chapter 11 shows you how.

- 🌐 You've learned all kinds of super skills browsing the Internet. Chapter 12 tells you how to bring them home to the desktop.

9 Make It Rock

What's the coolest thing about the World Wide Web? Many people would say it's the multimedia capability: sound, graphics, video, and animation. With the right tools, multimedia can become something even richer— *hypermedia,* which employs these media, separately and in combination, as an integral part of a Web presentation. With the introduction of Java, a programming language that enables you to download mini-programs to run, and Microsoft's new ActiveX technology, hypermedia comes alive with eye-popping special effects, such as rotating graphics, scrolling banners, and much more. If you've thought of the Web as a static medium, hold on to your seat.

In this chapter, you'll learn how to take full advantage of all the types of multimedia that the Web can sling at you, including the streaming video and audio capabilities of Microsoft NetShow. In addition, you'll learn how Microsoft Internet Explorer can work with Netscape plug-in programs, which greatly enhance the program's ability to deal with rich data on the Internet.

You'll also learn how Internet Explorer deals with the Java programs you've heard so much about, and you'll visit some cool Java sites. Finally, you'll take a closer look at Microsoft's exciting new ActiveX technology, which can make the Web come alive with safe, secure programs that Internet Explorer automatically downloads from the Internet.

There's one other thing about this chapter that you need to know: you're about to see the future of computing. That's no exaggeration, since it's clear that tomorrow's computers will make use of software obtained from the Internet in addition to software that's already present on the user's hard disk. Internet Explorer's ActiveX technology allows you to begin the process now—without the threat of computer viruses.

Understanding the Difference Between Multimedia and Hypermedia

You've surely heard about multimedia, one of the most hyped concepts in contemporary computing. In brief, *multimedia* involves using more than one medium—for example, text supplemented by animations—to get your point across. There's plenty of multimedia on the Web. In fact, a basic Web page is generally a multimedia effort, blending graphics with text.

So what's hypermedia? It's the use of multimedia as an integral part of a Web presentation, not as a mere sideshow. This distinction isn't understood by all Web authors. Too many of them think they're doing hypermedia by including a few graphics or a sound or two. In a well-conceived hypermedia presentation, the graphics, sounds, and videos stand equal to the text, both as a means of understanding the material and of navigating the site.

Puzzled by what all this means? Take a look at the Internet Public Library's Reference Center at www.ipl.org/ref/ (Figure 9-1). You're in a library's reference room. To see more information about something, click on it. This format works because the image is actually a clickable map (also called an *imagemap*), as you can see by moving the pointer over the graphic and watching as the shape changes.

So what's so great about hypermedia? It's engaging. Whether you're looking for education or entertainment, multimedia provides a much richer experience than mere text. When multimedia is blended with text in a focused, high-quality presentation, the result is doubly interesting.

PART

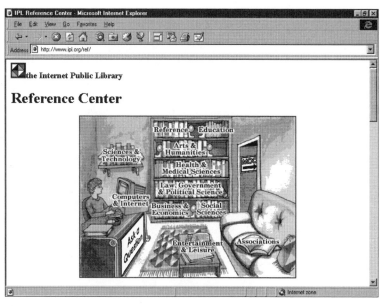

Figure 9-1

*The Internet Public Library uses graphics to improve information accessibility—
not as mere window dressing.*

What Equipment Do You Need?

To enjoy the sounds you can access on the Web, you need to
equip your system with the following:

🌐 **A stereo sound card.** You have a choice of three kinds of
sound cards: non-MIDI capable, FM synthesis, and wavetable synthesis. (MIDI stands for Musical Instrument Digital
Interface.) A non-MIDI capable sound card will do a good
job of reproducing the wave sounds you'll download from
the Web. A *wave sound* is an exact digital reproduction of
an actual sound, such as music or a voice, that is made using
recording techniques similar to those used in making audio
CDs. However, if you want to download and listen to MIDI
files, your sound card must have FM synthesis capability. I'd
recommend, however, that you spend the extra money it
takes to get a wavetable synthesis sound card. MIDI files
do not contain recorded sounds; they contain instructions

(continued)

9

> **What Equipment Do You Need?** *continued*
>
> that tell a sound card how to synthesize a particular sound. Wavetable cards do a much better job of playing MIDI files than do FM synthesis cards. It still doesn't sound like real music, but it's closer.
>
> **Self-powered stereo speakers.** If you plan to put your speakers next to your monitor, be sure they are shielded speakers so that their electromagnetic fields don't distort the image on your monitor.
>
> You don't need any additional equipment to view video with Windows 95, but Microsoft ActiveMovie will automatically take advantage of any hardware that supports Motion Picture Experts' Group (MPEG) that's installed in your computer. With this support, you will be able to view MPEG movies with better resolution and larger display sizes.

Introducing ActiveMovie

Internet Explorer's facility with sounds and movies is due to ActiveMovie, an add-on program that you can download free from Microsoft. In brief, ActiveMovie replaces all the previous Windows utilities for playing back sounds and movies. If you've used previous versions of Internet Explorer or some other browser, you had to link multimedia file types (such as Windows or MPEG movies) with specific players. That's no longer necessary. After you install ActiveMovie, it's all automatic.

Downloading Sounds and Movies with ActiveMovie

There's nothing simpler than playing sounds and movies with ActiveMovie: simply click the link that leads to the sound or movie. You'll see the first page of the File Download dialog box shown in Figure 9-2.

You might be concerned about file safety. If you're downloading a file from a trustworthy location, there's probably not too much to worry about. Also, multimedia files such as sounds and movies aren't dangerous at present; the only files that can contain viruses are executable files (those with the *.exe* extension). Still, virus authors are working overtime to try to figure out how to include harmful information in multimedia files, so it's best to be cautious. The bottom line: Do *you* trust this site? If it's a well-known commercial site, it's probably OK. If it's some weird site at a service provider you've never heard of or at a university (watch out for the *.edu* domain), you need to be more cautious.

PART

To download the file, follow these steps:

1. Decide how to handle the file. If you feel confident that the file is trustworthy, click Open This File From Its Current Location. If you have doubts about the site you're downloading from, click Save This File To Disk (which is the default option). Put the file on a floppy disk, and run it on a computer that doesn't contain any valuable data.

2. Click OK.

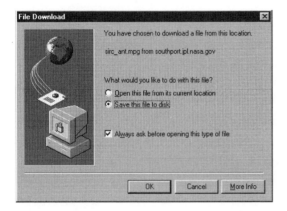

Figure 9-2

This dialog box appears when you download a sound or movie file.

After you click OK, ActiveMovie starts downloading the file. You'll see a progress bar that tells you how much of the file has been downloaded (Figure 9-3).

Figure 9-3

ActiveMovie's progress bar lets you know how much of the file has been downloaded.

9

NOTE

ActiveMovie supports *progressive playback* of sounds and movies. This feature allows you to start playing the sound or movie before it finishes downloading. Although you can't hear the complete sound or see the whole movie until downloading is complete, progressive playback enables you to determine whether it's worth downloading the entire file. If it sounds or looks good, you can keep downloading so you can hear the whole thing. (Note that this feature differs from streaming audio and video, which starts playing immediately and keeps playing.)

Playing a Sound or Movie

Embedded within the page you're viewing, or sometimes within a new page, you'll see a set of VCR-like controls that enable you to control the sound or movie: begin playing (click the Play button), stop playing (click the Stop button), or rewind (drag the slider control back). You can also pause while the sound or movie is running by clicking the Run button, which becomes Pause during play.

Using Keyboard Controls

When playing a sound or a movie, you can also use keyboard controls. Press Ctrl + R to run, press Ctrl + P to pause, and press Ctrl + S to stop.

Using the ActiveMovie Pop-Up Menu

You can also control movies and sounds by moving the pointer within the movie or sound control panel and clicking the right mouse button. The pop-up menu (Figure 9-4) contains the Run, Pause, and Stop controls. From this menu, you can also access the Properties dialog box, discussed in the next section.

Figure 9-4

If you click the right mouse button on the ActiveMovie window, you see this pop-up menu.

PART

Multimedia File Formats

Multimedia resources, such as sounds or movies, are stored using a number of differing compression and storage methods called *file formats*. Each has its own identifying extension. For example, Windows movies are stored in .avi files. There are well over one dozen multimedia file formats in use on the Internet.

Before ActiveMovie, you needed to know a lot about these file formats, but that's no longer true. Still, you may want to know what kinds of sounds and movies ActiveMovie can handle. It's an impressive list.

- **Sun/NeXT sounds (.au)** Commonly found on the Web, these are low-quality monaural sounds, but they don't take up much disk space (which means they download faster). This format is suitable for music, but only to give you an idea of what something will sound like when it's played back properly. It's fine for voice. Often, you'll see two versions of a sound: an .au version, which enables you to see whether the sound is interesting to you, and a higher-quality .mpeg version, which takes up more disk space (and takes correspondingly longer to download).

- **Apple/Silicon Graphics sounds (.aiff)** Not frequently encountered, these are monaural sounds that have somewhat better quality than Sun/NeXT sounds.

- **Windows WAV sounds (.wav)** These are native Windows sounds. They offer excellent quality, and even stereo, but the WAV format requires lots of disk storage space.

- **QuickTime movies (.mov)** This is Apple's movie format, and it's a winner. QuickTime movies offer a good frame rate, relatively compact files, and optional sound.

- **Windows AVI movies (.avi)** These are native Windows movies. Like WAV sounds, they offer good quality, but they require lots of storage space and lengthy downloads.

- **MPEG movies (.mpg, .mpeg)** These movies conform to the MPEG standard. They offer good compression and quality on systems that have built-in MPEG support.

- **MPEG audio (.mp2, .mp3)** MPEG sounds provide impressive near–CD-quality sound, including stereo. If you find one of these sounds, try downloading it. Compression is good, but these sounds still take lots of disk space.

9

Controlling Sound and Movie Properties

If you would like to gain more control over the playback of sounds and movies, display the ActiveMovie pop-up menu by right-clicking the ActiveMovie control and choosing Properties. You'll see the Properties dialog box, shown in Figure 9-5. The Playback page, shown in the figure, enables you to adjust the sound volume and balance, view the timing, choose a play count, turn on auto repeat, and enable auto rewind. The following table sums up the options you can choose on this and the other tabbed pages of the Properties dialog box.

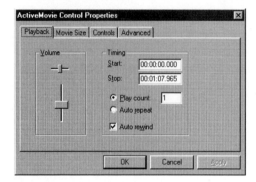

Figure 9-5

ActiveMovie's Properties dialog box enables you to specify advanced settings for the sound or movie you're viewing.

To accomplish this:	Click this:	And do this:
Adjust the volume	Playback	Adjust the volume (vertical) slider.
Adjust the balance	Playback	Adjust the balance (horizontal) slider.
Change the start and stop timing	Playback	Type new start and stop times in the Start and Stop text boxes. By default, playing starts with the beginning of the sound and ends with the end of the sound.
Specify the number of times to play the sound	Playback	Type a number in the Play Count box (default is 1).
Repeat the sound automatically	Playback	Select the Auto Repeat option.

To accomplish this:	Click this:	And do this:
Rewind the sound automatically when it finishes playing	Playback	Select the Auto Rewind option (on by default).
Select the movie size	Movie Size	Choose Original Size, Double Original Size, 1/16 Of Screen Size, 1/4 Of Screen Size, 1/2 Of Screen Size, or Maximized.
Zoom the movie to the full size of the screen	Movie Size	Select Run Full Screen.
View a digital display panel showing timing and tracks	Controls	Select Display Panel.
View the control panel	Controls	Select Control Panel (on by default).
Add position controls to the control panel	Controls	Select Position Controls.
Add selection controls to the control panel	Controls	Select Selection Controls.
Add the trackbar slider to the control panel	Controls	Select Trackbar (on by default).
Change the control panel's foreground color	Controls	Click Foreground, and choose a color.
Change the control panel's background color	Controls	Click Background, and choose a color.

Getting into the Stream of Things

It's called *streaming multimedia*. Compared to the ordinary audio and video that you can download from the Internet, it's far superior in one very important way. The content begins playing almost immediately. Presentations arrive in data "streams." You don't have to wait for the whole thing to download before play begins.

9

Is there a downside to streaming multimedia? Yes, the quality isn't as good as in other audio and video files. In order to deliver streaming multimedia over slow modem connections, it's necessary to use extreme, state-of-the-art compression techniques. Although these techniques result in loss of quality, most users find this trade-off acceptable. Streaming audio is used mainly for delivering voice, which doesn't require CD-quality audio to be worthwhile and enjoyable. It's also used to provide full-length, sample versions of recorded music; since the quality's not that great, record companies figure that you'll run out and buy the CD rather than continue to listen to the sample (and they're right).

What about video? On a modem connection, streaming video isn't anything to write home about. You get jerky motion in a little window, and your first reaction is to laugh. But remember, you'd probably have felt that way looking at one of the first experimental televisions. Years from now, when millions of households have super-fast cable modem connections, we might be watching streaming movies, chosen from a database of hundreds of thousands of films. For now, streaming video is more suited to corporate networks, which deliver data very quickly.

Despite the shortcomings of streaming video, streaming multimedia is worth a try. With Internet Explorer 4, you can take your pick of the two best players around: NetShow and RealAudio. Why two? Recognizing that streaming multimedia deserved support and standardization, Microsoft made an arrangement with Progressive Networks, the makers of the popular RealAudio streaming audio/video player. The deal calls for Microsoft to include RealAudio compatibility in NetShow, while Progressive Networks would reciprocally support NetShow in its products. Until Microsoft can incorporate RealAudio into its own clients and servers, you get both products—RealAudio's RealPlayer 4.0 and NetShow—with Internet Explorer. Let's start with NetShow.

Using NetShow

NetShow is a new streaming multimedia technology developed by Microsoft specifically to complement Microsoft NetMeeting, the Internet telephony and collaboration program discussed in Chapter 17. With the NetShow server, which runs on Microsoft Windows NT, content producers can draw from a wide variety of input sources, including recorded or live video and audio as well as still graphics. (Producers can create a NetShow presentation with live audio and synchronized still screens.) You don't have to worry about all that, though. If you see a link to a NetShow presentation, just click it. You'll see the NetShow player, which displays video along with the rest of the Web page (Figure 9-6).

Figure 9-6

NetShow plays the streaming presentation right on the Web page you're viewing.

Using NetShow's Controls

What you see depends on what type of data you're downloading. Sometimes you'll see an in-line video, with no controls, like the one that's shown in the center of Figure 9-6. Others display the NetShow controls, such as the presentation in Figure 9-7.

Figure 9-7

Some presentations appear in a separate window, with controls.

Some NetShow presentations have *markers*, which are like the tracks on an audio compact disk. If the presentation has markers, you can move directly from one marker to the next. You can also go back to previous markers. When a file has markers, you see the markers on the slider control bar and the marker navigation tools become available. These tools enable you to move around a lengthy presentation with ease.

The following overview explains what these VCR-like tools do.

Name	Action
Play/Pause	Starts play or pauses the presentation.
Stop	Stops the presentation and rewinds it to the beginning (unless the content designer has disabled this option).
Previous Marker	Goes back to the previous marker. If this control is dimmed, the presentation has no markers.
Back	Goes back within the current marker. If this control is dimmed, the presentation has no markers.
Forward	Goes forward within the current marker. If this control is dimmed, the presentation has no markers.
Next Marker	Goes forward to the next marker. If this control is dimmed, the presentation has no markers.
Slider	This control enables you to move around the markers in the presentation. If this control is dimmed, the presentation has no markers.

Using NetShow's Pop-Up Menu

While the presentation is playing, you can control it by clicking the right mouse button within the presentation area. You'll see a pop-up menu with the following options:

- **Pause.** Choose here to pause without rewinding. You can resume by right-clicking the presentation again and clicking Play. (Pause changes to Play when the presentation is paused or stopped.)

- **Stop.** Choose this option to stop playing the presentation and rewind it to the beginning. You can play the presentation from the beginning by right-clicking the presentation again and clicking Play.

- 🌐 **Markers.** Some presentations have markers that enable you to select where to begin. If so, you'll see a dialog box that lists the markers and enables you to choose from them.

- 🌐 **Statistics.** This option displays the Statistics tab of the Microsoft NetShow Player Properties dialog box, which displays statistics about the presentation (including what percentage of the presentation has been received and how much data has been lost through transmission errors). There's also a graph that indicates the reception quality. If you're having trouble playing a presentation, you might want to take a look at this page. If the reception quality is poor, the problem is probably attributable to slow network performance; you'll get better results if you try again later.

- 🌐 **Properties.** This option displays the Microsoft NetShow Player Properties dialog box, with the General page opened. This page shows information about the presentation you're viewing, including the title, author, copyright, rating, and description. If you're terribly curious about the technical details, the Details, Codecs, and Settings pages list such things as the protocol, source link, bandwidth, error correction technique, and compression-decompression (codec) technique. You can also choose settings, including how many times the presentation should play, whether it should rewind after playing, and how the NetShow window should appear.

- 🌐 **Error Details.** If you're having trouble receiving a presentation, click this option to find out what type of difficulty you're encountering.

Using RealPlayer

Also included with Microsoft Internet Explorer is Progressive Network's RealPlayer 4.0, which enables you to access RealAudio-compatible audio and video sources on the Internet. There's a lot of fantastic content out there, including the latest NPR and ABC news broadcasts. (To see what's available, check out the RealAudio home page at **www.realaudio.com.**) Despite the RealAudio moniker, the RealPlayer can handle video, too—RealVideo, that is. Let's take a look at RealPlayer.

9

Using RealPlayer's Controls

As with NetShow, exactly what you see depends on what type of data you're downloading. Like NetShow, RealPlayer gives you the basic VCR controls (Play, Pause, and Stop). Unlike NetShow, though, RealPlayer doesn't have markers. You can use the Forward and Back controls, as well as the slider control, to move around in those parts of the presentation that have already been downloaded. Another difference is that you can navigate RealAudio and RealVideo content by clicking News, Tech, Sports, or any of the other buttons on the navigation panel. If you access a RealAudio sound, the player looks exactly the same, except that it doesn't have the video panel.

Using Netscape Plug-Ins

Before Java and ActiveX, the only way browsers could be made truly interesting was by means of *helper applications* (accessories, like ActiveMovie, that jump in whenever an unusual file is encountered), or *plug-ins,* which give the browser new capabilities. The great thing about plug-ins is that they blend with the browser, sort of like a Vulcan mind meld. After installing the plug-in, the browser can cope with the data type of that plug-in without any help from an external application.

When you visit a site that uses a plug-in, you'll see a dialog box that lets you know that a plug-in is needed (Figure 9-8).

Plug-ins have their downside, though. Most of them are big—1 MB or more in size—and take a long time to download. Once they're downloaded, you must install them, and that often means you must restart your computer. This operational stuff really interrupts your surfing! For this reason, most people don't like plug-ins, and very few of them have become popular. Their functions are being replaced by Java applets and ActiveX controls (discussed later in this chapter).

Figure 9-8

If a Web page calls for a plug-in that you don't have, you'll see this dialog box.

If you encounter a Web site that uses a plug-in, click the link that enables you to download the file. You'll see the File Download box, similar to the one that appears when you download a sound or movie (Figure 9-2). If you're confident that the file's source is reliable, click Run This Program From The Internet and then click OK. The File Download dialog box lets you know how much time will be needed for the download.

HELP

It says the download will take 3 hours!

If the file's too big, skip it by clicking the Cancel button. You might want to return later and download it when you won't need to use your computer for a while or when your connection costs are lower.

Once you've finished downloading the file, Internet Explorer detects that you're about to run an executable (.exe) file and warns you that the security of this file can't be guaranteed (Figure 9-9). As you'll see, with ActiveX programs you'll be able to view the software publisher's certificate of authenticity. But this precaution isn't possible with plug-ins.

If you're sure you're downloading the plug-in from a reputable place, such as a major commercial site or an established organization, click Yes. Otherwise, click No to cancel.

After you click Yes, you'll see a Setup program for the plug-in. Follow the on-screen instructions to install the program on your computer.

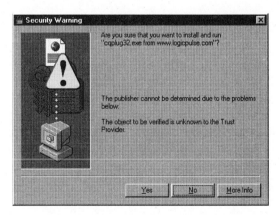

Figure 9-9

A dialog box warns you that the file you're about to download might not be safe for your computer.

9

Running Java Programs

A creation of Internet pioneer Sun Microsystems, the Java programming language enables professional programmers to prepare mini-programs called *applets* that download along with a Web page. After all the Java instructions are downloaded, the Web page you're viewing becomes much more interactive. For example, there are a number of Java-based mortgage calculators on the Web, and each of them enables you to type in numbers (such as the amount you want to finance) and immediately see the result of the computation. What's great about this is its immediacy: You don't have to wait for data to be uploaded to a distant server or for the server's results to be downloaded back to your computer. The software needed to process the data is right there on your computer, and the results display almost immediately. Another way to put this is that Java enables *client-side processing*—the processing occurs on your computer rather than on the server.

To see what I mean, try this example. Go to Fidelity's Fund Evaluator at **personal.fidelity.com/funds/evaluator/evaluator.html** (Figure 9-10). This applet enables you to screen mutual funds using a variety of criteria. The data are supplied by the respected Morningstar mutual fund evaluation service. If you've any doubts about what Java can do, this applet should put them to rest.

Trusted Java Sites

The following sites offer excellent examples of Java applets, and you can be reasonably certain that you won't run into a prank program if you visit them.

- 🌐 **Gamelan** (**www.gamelan.com**). You'll discover over 3,000 applets at this well-organized site.

- 🌐 **Java Center** (**www.java.co.uk/javacentre.html**). There are lots of applets to try, plus information and links.

- 🌐 **Java Applet Rating Service** (**www.jars.com**). Here you'll find ratings of hundreds of popular applets. Check out the top 25.

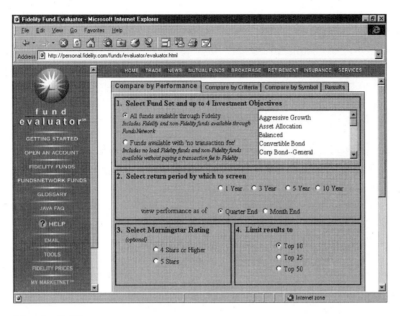

Figure 9-10

See Java in action at Fidelity's Fund Evaluator.

Is it safe to download Java applets?

Good question. By design, Java applets run in a *virtual machine*, a simulated computer that doesn't have access to your computer's file system. Also called a *sandbox*, this virtual machine is supposed to prevent rogue Java applets from doing harmful things. However, some computer experts wonder whether there might be some hidden flaw in Java that would enable a clever prankster to get out of the sandbox and do some damage. Also, the word *sandbox* is well chosen because the limitations placed on Java applets means that they aren't as useful for really serious work that involves storing data on disk. Still, Java is safe enough to use, as long as you're careful about where you download from.

Using ActiveX Controls

Microsoft's new ActiveX technology enables Web authors to prepare programs, called ActiveX controls, which can be downloaded to run on your computer. These programs help bring Web pages to life, with effects such as live audio and scrolling banners. In this sense, ActiveX controls resemble

9

Java applets, but there are at least two major differences. ActiveX offers the security protection that Java lacks, and ActiveX controls can be written in any popular programming language, including Java and Microsoft Visual Basic.

As an Internet Explorer user, you don't need to worry about the sophisticated technology that underlies ActiveX. You just need to devote some thought to whether you should download the control or not.

Deciding Whether to Download an ActiveX Control

If you encounter a site that has an ActiveX control, Internet Explorer checks to see whether the control has been digitally signed. A digitally signed control has been independently certified to be free from computer viruses or destructive effects. If the control has been digitally signed, you'll see the certificate shown in Figure 9-11. It's safe to install this software, and you'll probably want to choose the options (below the certificate) that hide this message for addition controls made by the same company.

When the control doesn't have certification, you see the alert box shown in Figure 9-12. This notice doesn't mean you're about to download a destructive program; it just means that the author hasn't obtained certification. If you're downloading the program from a trusted site, and you're sure you've backed up all your important work, click Yes. If you're rummaging around in college students' home pages, though, or if you have any reason to suspect that the site you're accessing isn't all that it says it is, click No.

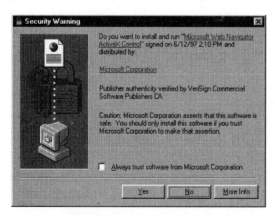

Figure 9-11

An Authenticode certificate identifies controls that have been independently evaluated for safety.

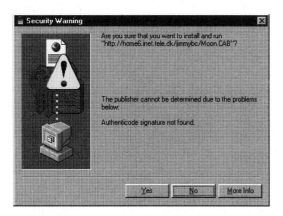

Figure 9-12

If an ActiveX control hasn't been certified, you'll see this message.

From Here

🌐 Begin to explore the Internet world in three dimensions in the next chapter.

🌐 Chapter 11 tells you how to master the art of file downloading.

🌐 Use the Internet browsing skills you've learned to access information on your own computer. Find out how in Chapter 12.

9

10   Go
3-D

When you look at Web pages, you're seeing two dimensions. If you've ever played the computer game Doom or Descent (or any of the many imitators of these games), you'll know how interesting and exciting a three-dimensional computer display can be. Using your mouse or a joystick to navigate, you move *into* the screen, exploring rooms and passages as you please. The presentation of three-dimensional worlds in this way is often called *virtual reality,* because it seems as though you're entering a "real" world that exists entirely within the computer. It's great fun, and thanks to a new computer programming language called VRML, now you can navigate three-dimensional worlds on the Web.

VRML stands for Virtual Reality Modeling Language. It's designed to enable Web authors to embed information about three-dimensional worlds in Web pages. If you're using a VRML-capable Web browser, the three-dimensional world appears *in-line* (that is, within the Web page you're viewing). You can enter this world and explore. In Figure 10-1, you see a VRML world as displayed by Internet Explorer.

169

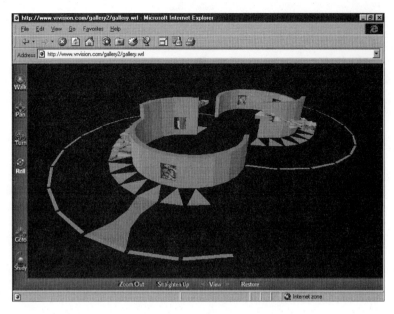

Figure 10-1

VRML enables you to view a three-dimensional world in-line.

Internet Explorer can't view three-dimensional worlds without help; that help is Microsoft VRML Viewer. This add-on program is available on the CD that accompanies this book; it supports version 2.0 of VRML, which offers a number of advanced features, including audio. After installing VRML Viewer, your copy of Internet Explorer takes on new navigation capabilities, but these don't become evident until you access a page containing a VRML world. At that time, a new type of toolbar, called a navigation bar, appears on the left and bottom sides of the VRML window.

Accessing a VRML Site

To get started with the VRML Viewer, you need to access a Web site that includes a three-dimensional world. Connect to the Microsoft VRML site at **www.microsoft.com/vrml/**, and choose the Offworld link. Click one of the worlds to enter three dimensions. You can start navigating this world right away. Just hold down the mouse button, and advance the pointer in the direction you want to travel.

As you access this site, you'll notice that Internet Explorer takes a little longer to download the page than it would normally. That's because it's

PART

downloading the virtual world file. When the downloading is complete, you'll see the VRML navigation bar on the left and bottom of the window (Figure 10-1).

Using the VRML Navigation Bar

The VRML navigation bar appears when you access a page containing a virtual world. You'll see six buttons on the vertical portion.

Click this:	To do this:
Walk	Move forward or backward through the scene, turn to the left, or turn to the right.
Pan	Shift your viewpoint horizontally or vertically—without moving forward, backward, turning, or rolling.
Turn	Turn your viewpoint without moving.
Roll	Spin the virtual world around its center. If this produces unwanted effects, click Straighten Up.
Goto	Go to the place you click.
Study	Rotate objects automatically in front of you so you can see what they are.

You'll see four additional buttons on the horizontal portion of the navigation bar.

Click this:	To do this:
Zoom Out	Go back to get perspective on the whole world.
Straighten Up	Cancel the tilt and straighten your viewpoint with respect to the scene.
View	Go to named viewpoints (if any have been included in this world).
Restore	Go back to the beginning.

HELP

I don't see a toolbar!

VRML authors can control whether the toolbars appear, so you might not see the toolbars if the author has chosen to switch them off. You can still choose navigation options by using the keyboard or pop-up menus.

10

Using Keyboard Shortcuts

You can also use keyboard shortcuts instead of selecting the toolbar items.

To do this:	Press these keys:
Walk	Ctrl + Shift + W
Pan	Ctrl + Shift + P
Turn	Ctrl + Shift + T
Roll	Ctrl + Shift + R
Goto	Ctrl + Shift + G
Study	Ctrl + Shift + S
Zoom Out	Ctrl + Shift + Z
Straighten Up	Ctrl + Shift + U

Understanding the Cursors

When you've chosen a given navigation mode, VRML Viewer displays a cursor showing the navigation option you're using. The following table shows these cursors and explains what they mean.

Cursor	Navigation option
	Walk
	Pan
	Turn
	Roll
	Goto
	Study

TIP If you see curved lines surrounding the cursor, it means you've encountered a special feature that's been built into this world. Click the left mouse button to find out what's up!

Starting Out with Viewpoints

The best way to start exploring a VRML world is to examine the author's predefined viewpoints, if the world you're viewing has any. To see whether any viewpoints exist, click the View button, or click the right mouse button and choose Viewpoints from the pop-up menu. Select a viewpoint from the list.

If more than one viewpoint exists, you can move to the next or previous one by clicking the arrow buttons on either side of the View button. If no viewpoints exist, these arrows are dimmed.

Maneuvering with the Mouse

The best way to learn how to navigate a virtual world is to try it. If you get lost, click the Restore button. As you maneuver, keep the following basic rules in mind:

🌐 The direction in which you drag the mouse affects the direction in which you move.

🌐 The distance you drag the mouse affects the speed with which you move. If you stop moving the mouse but continue pressing the button, you'll continue to move until you release the button.

🌐 If the pointer changes to a hand shape, you've found a hyperlink. Click it to go to the linked document.

Walk

Walking is the way you'll normally move through a virtual world. As you walk, the scene will rotate to accommodate your turns. To walk, click the Walk button, press and hold the left mouse button, and move the mouse in the direction you want to go. Drag straight up to go forward; drag straight down to go back.

Pan

When you pan the scene, it slides past you, as if you had just moved laterally or vertically without changing the way you're facing. To have the scene slide, click the Pan button, press and hold the left mouse button, and move the mouse in the direction you want to go.

Turn

You can turn around in place by clicking the Turn button and dragging left or right. Dragging up or down is similar to tilting your head up or down—except that in a virtual world *you* tilt up or down. Try dragging at an angle

10

for a few moments, and then resume walking forward. Unless you're accustomed to zero gravity, you'll probably find the effect confusing (Figure 10-2). If so, click Straighten Up and the world will right itself.

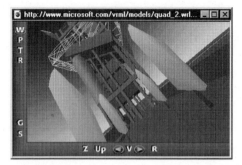

Figure 10-2

This might be a good time to click the Straighten Up button.

Roll

You can tilt the virtual world any way you like. Click the Roll button and drag the mouse to the left or right to tilt the scene. Be aware, though, that if you're looking at a landscape—a scene that's meant to be navigated without a tilt—the effect might not be very pleasant. If you've tried a tilt and you're not too happy with the results, you can "de-tilt" the scene by clicking the Straighten Up button.

Goto

To go to an object quickly, click Goto. The cursor changes to a crosshair, and you can click the place you want to go. To cancel the Goto mode without clicking on an object, press Esc.

Study

To study an object, click Study and then click the object you want to study. Drag the mouse to rotate the object in front of you—or, more properly, to move your virtual self around the object.

Zoom Out

Clicking the Zoom Out button pulls you back from the virtual world until it all fits inside your screen. In some worlds, this feature can make objects extremely tiny, but it's a useful way to get a grasp of the layout of the entire world.

Maneuvering with the Keyboard

If you would prefer to use the keyboard to maneuver through virtual worlds, you can do so. Choose your navigation mode by using one of the keyboard shortcuts. Then use the arrow keys instead of the mouse to drag left, right, up, or down. To straighten up, press Ctrl + Shift + U. To zoom out, press Ctrl + Shift + Z. And to jump between viewpoints, press Page Down and Page Up.

Staying on Course

In case you get lost or confused in the virtual world you've entered, VRML Viewer provides some survival tools:

- 🌐 Is the scene tilted at a crazy angle? Straighten up and fly right by clicking the Straighten Up button.

- 🌐 Can't see where you're going? Turn on the headlight. To do so, click the right mouse button, choose Graphics, and enable the Headlight option.

- 🌐 Hopelessly lost? Return to the world's starting point by clicking the Restore button on the toolbar.

Improving Performance

If the world you're viewing seems to perform sluggishly, you can improve performance by choosing a flat or wireframe image quality. By default, VRML Viewer displays the world with smooth shading, the best that's available. But you can change to flat shading, the medium quality setting, or wireframe, the lowest (Figure 10-3). To do so, click the right mouse button, select Graphics, and choose the image quality setting that you want.

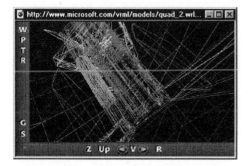

Figure 10-3

This is the same view as in Figure 10-2 with wireframe graphics—ugly but fast.

10

You can also control the speed of apparent movement. By default, this speed is set to medium. To speed up or slow down movement, click the right mouse button, select Speed, and choose the speed you want.

Another way to improve performance is to disable the Full Color option. With Full Color on, you see the best possible color quality, but speed is sacrificed. To turn off Full Color, click the right mouse button, select Graphics, and click Full Color so that the check mark disappears.

You can get a slight improvement in performance by turning off *dithering,* which blends the shaded surface. With dithering turned off, you might see bands instead of smooth gradations in the images, but performance improves. To turn off dithering, click the right mouse button, select Graphics, and click Dithering so that the check mark disappears.

TIP

Does your graphics card have Direct3D graphics acceleration? Take full advantage of it by clicking the right mouse button, choosing Options, and enabling the Hardware Acceleration option.

From Here

 Save or print what you've found on the Web. Find out how in Chapter 11.

🌐 In Chapter 12, use your Internet Explorer skills to browse your Windows desktop. Every folder on your desktop becomes as easy to use as a Web page.

11 Make It Yours

Found something you like? Want to keep it? How you go about making Web content your own depends on what you've found.

- Located some cool software? You can download the program to your computer. Internet Explorer will handle the whole process for you, and you can browse the Web while the download's taking place.

- See a graphic you like? You can copy it to the clipboard or save it to your hard drive. You can even make a Web graphic your default Windows wallpaper.

- Want to have a printout of the site you're viewing? Fire up your printer, because you can print anything you can display (including graphics). There's a very welcome new feature in version 4: You can select and print individual frames in a framed document.

🌐 Found some text you like? You can copy it to the Clipboard, from which you can paste the text into other applications. Or you can save just the text from a document in a plaintext file.

This chapter details all these procedures.

NOTE Please respect the intellectual property rights of Web authors. Many Web pages are copyrighted. If the document you want to use is copyrighted, you should ask the author's permission before copying or saving text or graphics for republication in your own work, whether on the Web or elsewhere. Be aware that under current international copyright regulations, to which the United States is a signatory, it is no longer necessary to place a copyright notice on a work of art. To avoid infringement, you should ask permission to reuse any Web document for commercial purposes. If you're not sure whether a Web document is copyrighted, send e-mail to the document's author. In most Web documents, you'll find a hyperlink to the author's name that makes it easy to do so.

Downloading Software

At last count, some 250,000 freeware or shareware programs were available on the Internet—that's right, a quarter of a million! (The term *freeware* refers to programs that are copyrighted but can be freely redistributed, as long as distribution is not done for commercial gain. *Shareware* refers to programs that require payment of a registration fee if you want to keep using them.) These programs range from the not-very-impressive efforts of beginning programmers to highly professional, full-featured programs.

About Computer Viruses

It isn't much fun to think about, but hundreds—perhaps thousands—of programmers worldwide are busily trying to create rogue programs, called *viruses,* that are capable of harming computer systems and data. A computer virus replicates itself at will, infecting your computer and traveling outward by means of disk and Internet file exchanges. Why do virus authors create these vexing programs? Their motivations vary, but they stem from an inability or unwillingness to put technology in context, that is, to realize that there are people involved in computing. Virus authors focus narrowly on trying to outwit the software

(continued)

About Computer Viruses *continued*

industry, which is doing all it can to prevent your computer from getting infected.

In the past, you could avoid computer viruses by using safe computing practices, but the rise of the Internet has created a new distribution medium for virus authors. In safe computing, you never run programs unless you've obtained them from a reputable source. With so many shareware and freeware programs on the Internet, though, how can you be sure your sources are reputable?

The safest course of action is to avoid downloading software altogether, but this takes away much of the Internet's fun and usefulness. A reasonable compromise is to download with caution. Begin by establishing a regular backup program so that your valuable data is protected if you should encounter a virus, despite all your precautions. If you're searching for a program, use a reputable search service to locate and download software from the Internet, such as CNET's shareware.com. If you know which program you're looking for, search for the software company's home page and download it directly from there. (You'll also be assured of getting the most recent version of the program.) Be careful that the page you're accessing really is the company's home page and not some imposter loaded with rogue programs. Don't ever download executable files from a Usenet newsgroup!

Above all, don't succumb to virus paranoia. I've seen too many users panic when something seems odd about their computer systems. The problem is often just a minor software glitch, which can be cured by a good, healthy restart. Also, remember that there are plenty of virus hoaxes on the Internet; they're all designed to make fools of novices. To avoid getting hoodwinked, bear in mind that viruses can propagate only by means of executable programs. They aren't present in graphics files or e-mail.

If you suspect that you've contracted a virus, check out the AntiVirus Research Center (www.symantec.com/avcenter/index.html). You'll learn about the latest virus and rogue program threats (the real ones, that is). One to watch out for: There's a fake version of PKZIP (PKZIP300.EXE or PKZ300B.EXE), the popular file compression program, that reformats your hard drive. You should also consider purchasing an antivirus program, which scans your computer's drives and memory for viruses.

11

Searching for Software on the Internet

Looking for freeware or shareware? Here are two great places to start:

🌐 **Microsoft Free Product Downloads** (<u>www.microsoft.com/ msdownload</u>). For Microsoft Windows users, this is a computer playground from heaven (Figure 11-1). You'll find free TrueType fonts, games, accessories for Microsoft Internet Explorer and Microsoft Office products, monthly content updates for Cinemania and Music Central, Windows 95 updates and upgrades, and tons more. When you visit, be sure you have lots of free disk space!

🌐 **shareware.com** (<u>www.shareware.com</u>). This outstanding Web site (Figure 11-2) is a production of CNET; it enables you to search a database of more than 190,000 freeware and shareware programs by typing one or more key words. The search engine searches the product description database as well as the filename, so chances are good that you'll find what you're looking for, if it exists at all.

Figure 11-1

The Microsoft Free Product Download site is a treasure chest of goodies for Windows users.

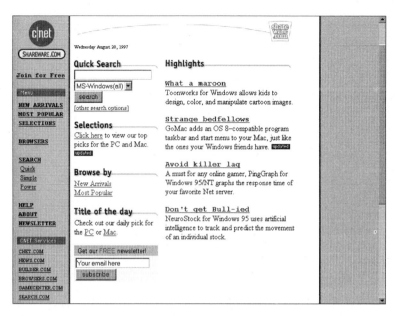

Figure 11-2

At shareware.com, you can search an extensive collection of shareware and freeware.

Deciding Whether to Download Software

If you click a link to a downloadable program, you might see the dialog box shown in Figure 11-3. Are you sure the file is from a trustworthy source, such as Microsoft's Free Product Download page? If so, choose one of the following options:

- **Open it.** If you choose this option, Internet Explorer will download the file and look for an application that can open it. If the file is an executable (.exe) file, Internet Explorer will tell Windows to run it. If it is a compressed (.zip) file, Internet Explorer will look for a decompression program, such as WinZip for Windows 95. If the file is a document (.doc), Internet Explorer will open the document with Word for Windows. As long as you have installed software that can deal with files with the same extension as the one you're downloading, this is the best option.

- **Save it.** If you choose this option, Internet Explorer will download the file to your hard disk. You'll see a Save As dialog box, enabling you to specify where the file should be stored. This is the best option if you don't have a program capable of opening the file. You can open it later after you obtain the necessary program.

181

11

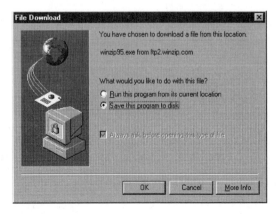

Figure 11-3

When you download a file, you can either open it immediately or save it to a disk.

It's a great tool for Windows computing, but a necessity once you've got your Internet connection: a program that can decompress .zip files. The standard in this area is WinZip for Windows 95, available for downloading from Nico Mak Computing's home page (www.winzip.com/). The program is shareware and requires a registration fee of $29.

About Windows Software Security

If you chose the Open option when you began downloading an executable (.exe) file, you might see the alert box in Figure 11-4 when the download is complete. This alert box appears if you've downloaded an automatic software installation program, which is very common on the Web. The message informs you that the software has not been digitally signed by the publisher. Don't be alarmed; very few of the programs you'll download have been signed in this way. Digital signatures are used mostly for ActiveX controls, described in the previous chapter. As long as you're still sure that you downloaded the software from a reputable source, choose Yes to open the program and let it make changes to your system.

Figure 11-4

When downloading an unsigned program, you might see a security warning.

Downloading the File

While the file is downloading, you'll see a message box that keeps you informed of the download's progress (Figure 11-5). If Internet Explorer is able to determine the size of the file, you'll see a progress indicator that shows visually how much of the file has been downloaded. In addition, you'll see an estimate of how much time is required to complete the download. While downloading is in progress, you can return to the Internet Explorer window and browse other sites.

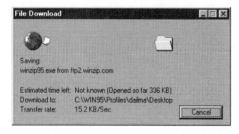

Figure 11-5

Watch your selected file travel through the Internet and into your computer.

If you're using Internet Explorer on a 14.4 or 28.8 Kbps modem line, avoid downloading more than one file at a time. Internet Explorer doesn't prevent you from doing this—you can click file after file, and the program will keep downloading—but your Internet connection will bog down to the point that each of the downloads slows to a crawl. One at a time, please!

11

Accessing FTP Sites Directly

You can download files, as just discussed, by clicking a downloading link on a Web page. But Internet Explorer can also directly access FTP sites. (Remember, FTP is short for File Transfer Protocol. It's a standard protocol for exchanging files on the Internet.)

Using FTP, you can access anything that's stored on the file system of an FTP-accessible computer. In fact, full FTP access lets you get into the file system of another computer and actually control the computer remotely. Yes, it's true. With full FTP access, you can delete files, overwrite them, open and modify them, and generally wreak havoc. I'm sure you can appreciate why most FTP-accessible computers demand a login name and password before such access is granted.

But there's another type of FTP service that isn't so persnickety about access. It's called *anonymous FTP*—"anonymous" because you don't need to supply a user name and password when you access the server. To be sure, the access you get is read-only—you can't erase or modify the files you find—but you can download them, and that's good enough to make anonymous FTP a valuable resource. Organizations make anonymous FTP services available to provide public access to shareware programs, public documents, and freebies of all kinds.

Accessing an Anonymous FTP Server

With Internet Explorer, you can access anonymous FTP sites in two ways:

- 🌐 **Click an FTP hyperlink in a Web page.** Like Gopher hyperlinks, hyperlinks to FTP look the same on-screen as hyperlinks to other Web sites do. If you've enabled the full display of addresses by turning off the Show Friendly URLs option in the Internet Options dialog box, you can see what kind of site you're about to access by moving the pointer over the hyperlink and looking at the status bar. If it's an FTP site, you'll see an address that begins with *ftp* instead of *http*.

- 🌐 **Type the address to an FTP site directly.** You can choose the Open command from the File menu or, even better, type the address in the Address box.

Navigating FTP File Directories

The best thing about FTP is that it lets you directly navigate the file directories of a distant computer. That's also the worst thing. Navigating the directory structure will seem like a step backward into yesteryear's computer interfaces. It will help enormously if you're familiar with the concepts of directories and subdirectories—remember MS-DOS? Actually, most of the computers you'll access with anonymous FTP are UNIX machines. UNIX is a very powerful and not very user-friendly operating system. But don't let that throw you. The directory structure of UNIX is much like that of MS-DOS for the simple reason that MS-DOS (beginning with version 2.0) incorporated UNIX-like directories and subdirectories.

Here's a terminology refresher course, in case Windows has dimmed your recollection of MS-DOS terminology. A *directory* is a list of files (usually in alphabetical order). A *subdirectory* is a directory within a directory. If you select the subdirectory, you see a new directory—a new list of files. But you might want to get back to the *parent directory*, the directory that's one level "above" the subdirectory you're in right now. (With Windows, we now speak of *folders*, and *folders within folders*.)

When you first access an anonymous FTP server, you might find yourself at the top level of the directory tree, at the *root directory* (Figure 11-6). If so, you will want to look for a directory named /pub (Figure 11-7). That's where the goodies usually are. A good FTP hyperlink will land you at the top of the /pub directory.

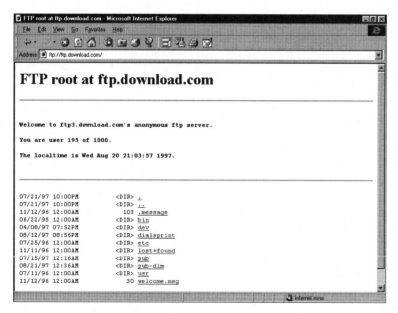

Figure 11-6

The root directory is the top level of the directory tree.

11

Figure 11-7

The /pub directory of an anonymous FTP server shows the files you want to access.

To open a subdirectory, just click it. It's much easier to navigate directories with Internet Explorer than it is with MS-DOS or UNIX. Internet Explorer turns the items in directory lists into hyperlinks, so all you need to do is click the item you want. Presto! You see a new page with yet another directory—unless the item you clicked is a resource, such as a program, graphic, or sound. As with Gopher resources, clicking a hyperlink to a resource produces the appropriate action: programs download, graphics display, and sounds play (assuming you have the correct helper program installed).

To get back to a parent directory, scroll to the top of the page. You'll often find a hyperlink called something like "up to the parent directory" or perhaps "up to higher level directory." (A link that's simply two periods is a UNIXism that means the same thing.) Click this hyperlink to go up to the parent directory.

Downloading Files with Windows Explorer

If you've chosen to view your desktop in Web View, you can access anonymous FTP sites within Windows Explorer. To do this, you'll need the name of a public FTP site, such as <u>ftp://ftp.microsoft.com</u> or <u>ftp://ftp.download.com</u>.

PART

When you've successfully accessed the FTP site, you'll see the FTP directory in Windows Explorer's right panel. You'll also still see your disk in the left panel. Navigate the FTP site's directories by clicking directory names; to go back up one level, simply click the Back button.

When you see a file you'd like to download, click it. You'll see the File Download dialog box, discussed in the previous section. If you're confident the file is safe, click the Open option and continue just as if you'd clicked a download link on a Web page.

TIP If you didn't choose Web View when you installed Internet Explorer, you can do so now. In any Windows Explorer or My Computer window, click View on the menu bar and choose Web. (If you see a check mark next to Web, the Web View is already selected.)

Mailing a Page to Someone

As you're browsing the Web, you'll run across pages that might interest friends or coworkers. You can mail the page to them, and they can see it for themselves. In order to receive the page, your correspondent must have an e-mail program (such as Microsoft Outlook Express or Netscape Messenger) that can display HTML.

Here's how to mail the Web page. Click File on the menu bar, choose Send, and then choose Page by Email from the pop-up menu. Internet Explorer starts Outlook Express and displays a New Message window, showing the Web page. Enter the recipient's e-mail address, and click the Send button.

If your recipient's e-mail program can't read HTML, you can send a link instead. Click File on the menu bar, choose Send, and click Link By Email.

Copying and Saving Graphics

You can copy or save any graphic that you see in a Web document. Once you've copied the graphic, you can paste it into a document that you're creating with another application. If you save the graphic, you can open it later with a graphics program, through which you can display, modify, copy, or print the image.

11

Copying a Graphic

If you see a graphic that you would like to use in one of your documents, you can copy it to the Clipboard. Simply right-click the graphic and choose Copy from the pop-up menu.

To paste the graphic into a document that you're creating with another application, position the cursor where you want the graphic to appear. Then choose the Paste command from the Edit menu, press Ctrl + V, or click Paste on the toolbar.

When you copy a graphic to the Clipboard, Microsoft Windows 95 automatically converts the graphic to the Windows bitmap format. If you want to preserve the original graphics file format of the graphic, you must save the graphic to your hard disk.

Saving a Graphic

Internet Explorer enables you to save a graphic to a disk file so that you can reuse it anytime you want. When you save it, Windows will preserve the graphic's original file format.

To save a graphic, follow these steps:

1. Right-click the graphic.

2. From the pop-up menu, choose Save Picture As. You'll see the Save Picture dialog box. In the File Name box, Internet Explorer displays the document's name. In the Save As Type box, Internet Explorer displays the document's file format. There's no need to change either of these settings.

3. If you want, choose a different location for the saved graphic.

4. Click the Save button.

Copying and Saving a Background Graphic

Some of the documents you'll encounter on the Web have fancy graphic backgrounds, which can range from tasteful to annoying (Figure 11-8). If you'd like to copy or save the background graphic or save it as your default Windows wallpaper, Internet Explorer makes it simple.

Figure 11-8

This Web document contains a seriously annoying background graphic.

Copying a Background Graphic

To copy a background graphic to the Clipboard, right-click the background and choose Copy Background from the pop-up menu.

To paste the graphic into a document that you're creating with another application, position the insertion point where you want the graphic to appear. Choose the Edit Paste command, press Ctrl + V, or click Paste on the toolbar.

Saving a Background Graphic

To save a background graphic, follow these steps:

1. Right-click the background.

2. From the pop-up menu, choose Save Background As. You'll see the Save As dialog box. In the File Name box, Internet Explorer displays the document's name. In the Save As Type box, Internet Explorer displays the document's file format. There's no need to change either of these settings.

3. If you want, choose a different location for the saved image.

4. Click the Save button.

11

Making a Graphic the Default Wallpaper

With Windows 95, you can choose a graphic to serve as *wallpaper,* the image that's displayed on the desktop. If you run across a graphic on the Web that you think you can live with every day, you can quickly make the graphic the default wallpaper. Start by right-clicking the graphic. Then, choose Set As Wallpaper from the pop-up menu.

Viewing the Source HTML

If you're an aspiring Web author and would like to see the HTML code producing the document you're viewing, you can display it using the Notepad utility. From there, you can save or print the HTML code.

1. Right-click the document's background.

2. From the pop-up menu, choose View Source. You'll see the HTML code in a Notepad window, as shown in the following graphic:

3. To print the HTML code, choose the Print command from the File menu in Notepad.

4. To exit Notepad, go to the File menu and choose the Exit command.

You can also save the HTML code to disk by choosing Save As from the File menu in Notepad. This has the same effect as saving a document in HTML from within Internet Explorer.

Copying and Saving Text

If you find some text on the Web that you'd like to reuse in a document you're creating, you can copy it to the Clipboard or save it on your hard disk.

Copying Text to the Clipboard

To copy text from a Web document to the Clipboard, follow these steps:

1. Position the pointer at the beginning of the text you want to copy. The pointer changes from an arrow to an I-beam shape.

2. Drag to select the text.

3. Go to the Edit menu and select the Copy command. Other options are to right-click your selection and choose Copy from the pop-up menu or to press Ctrl + C.

   To select all of the text in the document, choose Select All from the Edit menu or press Ctrl + A. You can also point to any of the document's text and right-click; from the pop-up menu, choose Select All.

Saving Text

You can save any document that Internet Explorer can display in two ways:

🌐 **As Plaintext.** Internet Explorer strips all the HTML code from the document, producing a plaintext document that you can later modify easily with a word processing program such as Notepad or WordPad.

🌐 **As HTML.** Internet Explorer saves the HTML source code, just as you see it when you use the Source command from the View menu. However, Internet Explorer does not save any graphics in the document. If you want to save the graphics, you must use the right-clicking technique (described earlier in this chapter), and you must save each graphic individually. You might decide it's not worthwhile to go to all of this trouble. If you merely want to make sure you can visit a particular site again later, save it as a favorite, as described in Chapter 2. Be aware, however, that the site could change and a particular document may no longer be available.

11

Saving a Document as Plaintext

This option is useful if you want to have a *plaintext* version of the document you're viewing on-screen, without the graphics and HTML codes. (Plaintext is also known as ASCII text, which stands for American Standard Code for Information Interchange; it is a standardized coding method for letters, numbers, and other characters.)

To save a document as plaintext, follow these steps:

1. Choose Save As from the File menu. You'll see the Save HTML Document dialog box. In the File Name box, type a name for the document. In the Save As Type box, choose Text File.

2. Click the Save button. Internet Explorer saves the document in plaintext format.

Saving a Document as HTML

This procedure isn't recommended unless you are an aspiring Web author and want to save the HTML code for later experimentation or inclusion in your own HTML documents. Save a site as a favorite, or make it a desktop shortcut (see Chapter 2) if you just want to make sure you can get back to it.

To save a document as HTML, follow these steps:

1. Choose Save As from the File menu. You'll see the Save HTML Document dialog box. In the File Name box, type a name for the document. In the Save As Type box, choose HTML File.

2. Click the Save button. Internet Explorer saves the document in HTML format.

HTML—The Web's Language for Document Design

HTML is the basis for those cool Web documents you're seeing on-screen. But what is it?

HTML (HyperText Markup Language), as its name indicates, is a *markup language*. In other words, it lets a document designer mark the parts of a document, such as the title, headings, and body text. Marking a document isn't the same as formatting it, as you would format a document with a word processing program. In formatting, you control the document's final appearance (the fonts, font sizes, alignments, emphasis, and spacing). Markup identifies some text as belonging to a certain part of the document; a part is called an *element*. The appearance of the element is left up to the browser. The browser reads the HTML and formats the document on-screen.

(continued)

HTML—The Web's Language for Document Design *continued*

What are the advantages of a markup language? The two biggest advantages are cross-platform compatibility and speed. *Cross-platform compatibility* refers to the ability of people using many different kinds of computers—Sun workstations, Macintoshes, IBM compatibles, and more—to exchange HTML documents. That sharing is possible because HTML documents contain nothing but plain ASCII text, which almost any computer can handle. HTML documents lend themselves to speed because they tend to be compact, and that's because, once again, HTML consists of nothing but text. (Document retrieval slows down noticeably when people load their Web pages with graphics, as you might have noticed.)

HTML is easy to learn. To mark up a document, you can use any word processing program to insert the HTML codes, which are called *tags*. Most tags are paired: a beginning tag and an ending tag. All the tags are enclosed in angle brackets. Here are the tags used to mark a Level 1 heading:

```
<H1>This is a Level 1 Heading</H1>
```

If you want some help creating HTML code, you can obtain a *converter* designed to work with your word processing program. A converter transforms your formatted documents into HTML code (which, you'll find, will almost certainly need some coding by hand before they look just right). You can also use an HTML *editor,* a program that lets you choose the tags from menus.

HTML is changing rapidly, and it's not entirely clear where it's headed. That's because the language is being pulled in two directions. On the one side are HTML purists who want the language to remain a pure markup language, in which the formatting is left up to browsers. On the other side are Web document designers who want more control over the appearance of their Web pages. They want tags that let them specify font sizes, text alignment, and other aspects of document formatting. Stepping into the fray recently was Netscape Communications Corporation, whose Netscape Navigator—the most widely used browser before Internet Explorer—incorporated the Netscape Extensions, a set of nonstandard tags that give greater formatting control. In an effort to restore standards to the HTML community, the World Wide Web Consortium—the closest thing to a standards body that the Web currently has—incorporated some (but not all) of the Netscape Extensions into the current version of HTML.

11

Printing Documents

Printing documents with Internet Explorer is easy, and the results look great, especially if you have a color printer. You can print all or part of a document, and you can also make changes to the default page format.

Printing a Document

To print the document you're currently viewing, follow these steps:

1. Choose Print from the File menu, or press Ctrl + P. You'll see the Print dialog box (Figure 11-9).

2. If you want to print a specific page range, click the Pages option in the Print Range area. Then type the beginning page in the From box, and type the ending page in the To box.

3. If you want to print more than one copy, type a number in the Number Of Copies box, or click the up and down buttons to specify the number of copies you want printed. Click the Collate check box if you want Internet Explorer to collate copies.

4. If you're viewing a framed document, you can choose one of the options in the Print Frames area. You can print the frames as they're laid out on the screen, print only the selected frame, or print each frame on a separate sheet.

5. If you would like Internet Explorer to print a table containing all the Web addresses found in the document, click the Print Table Of Links option.

6. If you would also like to print all the documents that are linked from the current page, click Print All Linked Documents. (Be aware, though, that you might go through several reams of paper if you choose this option!)

7. Click the OK button to initiate printing.

Printing a Selection

If you want to print selected text rather than the whole document, follow these steps:

1. Select the text you want to print.

2. Choose Print from the File menu, or press Ctrl + P. You'll see the Print dialog box (Figure 11-9).

3. In the Print Range area, click the Selection option.

4. Click the OK button to initiate printing.

PART

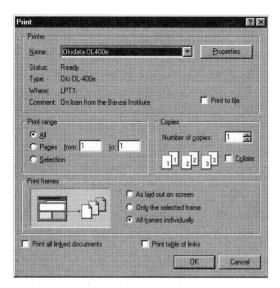

Figure 11-9

The Print dialog box lists several options for printing Web documents.

Setting Up the Page Format

By default, Internet Explorer formats your printout with 0.75-inch margins on all four sides of the page. In addition, the program prints a header with the document's title positioned flush left and the page number positioned flush right. It also prints a footer with the current date positioned flush left and the current time positioned flush right.

As the following sections explain, you can change the paper size, paper tray, print orientation, margins, and headers. To change these settings, choose Page Setup from the File menu. You'll see the Page Setup dialog box (Figure 11-10). From there, you can select and change the printing options described below.

Choosing paper size

If your printer can print with more than one size of paper, you can choose the paper size that you want Internet Explorer to use. From the Page Setup dialog box, select the Size list box and choose the paper size you want to use. (The options you see depend on your printer's capabilities.) Click OK.

Remember that the choices you make in the Page Setup dialog box remain in effect until you change them again. For example, if you choose Landscape printing, Internet Explorer will keep printing with this orientation until you choose Portrait.

11

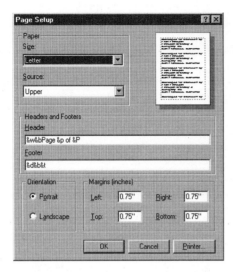

Figure 11-10

From the Page Setup dialog box, you can format how your printed page will look.

Choosing the paper tray

If your printer has two or more paper trays, you can select the tray that you want your printer to use when it prints your Internet Explorer document. From the Page Setup dialog box, select the Source list box and choose the paper tray you want to use. (The options you see depend on your printer's capabilities.) Click OK.

Changing the printing orientation

Some Web pages look best when printed with a portrait orientation (the short side at the top), while others look best when printed with landscape orientation (the long side at the top). Internet Explorer can print Web pages either way. To choose the print orientation, you must first display the document you want to print. In the Orientation area of the Page Setup dialog box, click the orientation you prefer (Portrait or Landscape). Click OK.

Setting margins

By default, Internet Explorer formats your printout with 0.75-inch margins on all four sides of the page. You can change the margins, if you wish. In the Margins area of the Page Setup dialog box, type the margins you want to use. Click OK.

NOTE

Internet Explorer uses the current Windows 95 settings for measurements. For example, copies of Windows 95 that are sold in the U.S. display measurements in inches. If you would like to change the measurement format, click the Start menu, choose Settings, and click Control Panel. In the Control Panel window, double-click Regional Settings. In the Regional Settings Properties dialog box, select the Number tab, if necessary. From the Measurement System list box, choose the number system you want to use, and click OK.

Defining headers and footers

Internet Explorer can print as many as six separate header and footer areas:

- 🌐 **Left header.** The text is flush left at the top of the page. By default, this area contains the document's title.

- 🌐 **Center header.** The text is centered at the top of the page. By default, this area is blank.

- 🌐 **Right header.** The text is flush right at the top of the page. By default, this area contains the page number of the document.

- 🌐 **Left footer.** The text is flush left at the bottom of the page. By default, this area contains the date the document was printed.

- 🌐 **Center footer.** The text is centered at the bottom of the page. By default, this area is blank.

- 🌐 **Right footer.** The text is flush right at the bottom of the page. By default, this area contains the time the document was printed.

You can enter any text in the Header and Footer fields. If you type *Web document* in the Header box of the Headers and Footers area, that's what you'll get on the printouts. If you want to turn off the header or the footer, simply clear the appropriate box.

You can also use special codes to extract current information from the document (such as the page address) or from your computer system (such as the current date and time). Each of these codes begins with an ampersand (&) followed by a single letter. Note that the case of the letters is important. By using these codes, you can customize the headers and footers of the documents you print.

11

Enter:	To Print:
&w	Document title as it appears in the title bar.
&u	Page address (URL).
&d	Current date in the short format specified by the Regional Settings Control Panel.
&D	Current date in the long format specified by the Regional Settings Control Panel.
&t	Current time in the format specified by the Regional Settings Control Panel.
&T	Current time in 24-hour format.
&p	Page number.
&P	Total number of pages.
&&	A single ampersand.
&b	Position specifier.

That last code (&b) lets you specify where a given item should print in the header or the footer. Here's how it works:

- If you use the code only once, the text to the left of *&b* is printed flush left and the text to the right is printed flush right. For example, *&w&b&p* prints the document title flush left and the page number flush right.

- If you use the code twice, the text to the left of the first *&b* is printed flush left, the text between the two *&b* codes is centered, and the text to the right of the second *&b* is printed flush right. For example, *&d&b&p&b&t* prints the current date flush left, centers the page number, and prints the current time flush right. Got all that?

You can also combine text and codes. For example, if you type *Page &p of &P*, Internet Explorer prints the current page number and the total number of pages: Page 7 of 10.

From Here

- Use all the skills you've learned to explore and manage your Windows desktop. Check it out in the next chapter.

- Try e-mail with Outlook Express. Find out how in Chapter 13.

12 Browse the Desktop

Wouldn't it be nice to learn, remember, and use just one set of skills to navigate your own computer system as well as the Internet? Thanks to the Web integrated desktop capability of Microsoft Internet Explorer 4, you can. With the Web view of the desktop, Windows Explorer looks and acts very much like Internet Explorer. For example, file and program names become hyperlinks, which you choose by clicking only once (the way you'd click a hyperlink in a Web page). What's more, every folder on your system becomes a Web page that can display all kinds of cool stuff: backgrounds, graphics, sounds, even active content, such as JavaScripts and ActiveX controls. Internet Explorer 4 installs a few customized folder pages automatically—take a look at the Control Panel or the top-level My Computer window to see the possibilities.

This chapter shows you how to extend your Internet Explorer skills to the Microsoft Windows desktop. You'll learn how to activate the Web integrated desktop (if it's not activated already), how to use the mouse pointer in the Web view, how to run programs from the Address toolbar, and a whole slew of neat tricks that will make Windows more fun to use. I'm assuming you already know how to perform basic file-management tasks with Windows Explorer or My Computer, the two applications affected by the Web integrated desktop. What's covered here are the new, special, and impressive differences that happen once you choose to display your computer's resources using the Web integrated desktop.

NOTE The Web integrated view is not the same thing as the Active Desktop, which enables you to receive "push" content on the desktop. The Web integrated view enables you to browse your computer's resources in much the same way you browse the Web. As you will see, you can turn off the Web integrated desktop and restore the classic Windows interface. If you turn off the Web integrated desktop, you can still subscribe to Web sites and use other Active Desktop features.

Introducing the Web Integrated Desktop

When you install Microsoft Internet Explorer 4, you have the option of enabling the Web integrated desktop. If you've done so, you'll notice some differences right away. Move the pointer over one of the shortcuts on your desktop. You'll see that the caption text changes color and the pointer changes to a hand shape—just like it does on a Web page. You can select the icon by clicking only once. Since you'll need to "unlearn" some Windows mouse techniques (such as double-clicking) in order to use the Web integrated desktop, we'll start by looking at these.

Activating the Web Integrated Desktop

If you didn't enable the Web integrated desktop when you installed Internet Explorer, do it now so that you can try out the tricks and techniques in this chapter. To enable the Web integrated desktop, follow these steps:

1. In any My Computer or Windows Explorer window, click View on the menu bar and choose Folder Options. You'll see the Folder Options dialog box. Click the General tab, if necessary, to display the folder options (Figure 12-1).

2. Click Web Style to enable the Web integrated desktop.

3. Click OK.

If you try out the Web integrated desktop and don't like it, you can restore the normal Windows way of doing things by repeating the above procedure, except choose Classic Style. Note that you can also selectively enable or disable Web integration features by clicking Custom and then Settings. (This chapter covers custom features later.)

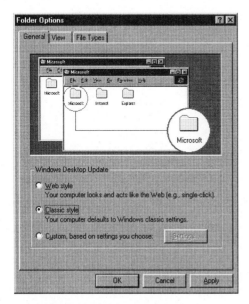

Figure 12-1

Here, you can switch between the Web integrated desktop, the traditional Windows interface, or a hybrid.

Comparing Classic Windows to the Web Integrated Desktop

Using the mouse in the Web integrated desktop differs from the normal Windows way of doing things, and at first you may find the difference a little disconcerting. But stick with it. You'll get used to it quickly, and then you won't want to go back.

The basic operating principle is that for the Web desktop you subtract one mouse click from the classic Windows way of doing things. For example, to select something in the Web integrated desktop view, you don't click at all. You just move the mouse over the item and stop—this is called *hovering*. Differences between the classic Windows interface and the Web integrated desktop are outlined below.

12

To do this:	With the classic Windows interface:	With the Web integrated desktop:
Select	Use single click of the left mouse button.	Don't click at all; move pointer over the item (hover).
Choose (open or run)	Use a double click.	Use a single click.
Select more than one item	Press Ctrl + left mouse button (selects individual items) *or* Press Shift + left mouse button (selects items in a block).	Press Ctrl and hover *or* Press Shift and hover.

Using Windows Explorer

Once you've activated the Web integrated desktop, the Windows Explorer and My Computer windows look different. In fact, they look a lot like Internet Explorer. That's because they *are* Internet Explorer! Just what you see, though, depends on which icon you clicked. If you choose My Computer, you see a single window on whatever folder you're displaying (Figure 12-2). If you choose Windows Explorer, you see a window split into two panes, with a folder Explorer bar visible on the left (Figure 12-3).

Figure 12-2
With the Web integrated desktop, the My Computer window looks just like Internet Explorer, but with a slightly different toolbar.

PART

202

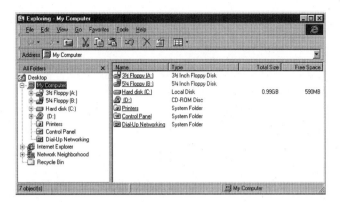

Figure 12-3

The Web integrated desktop version of Windows Explorer closely resembles Internet Explorer, but it displays a folder Explorer bar in the left panel.

Understanding the Windows Explorer Toolbar

When you're browsing your desktop, the Internet Explorer toolbar changes to give you the tools you need for disk-related tasks. It's still very much a browser, as you can see from the Back and Forward buttons, but there's an Up button, too. You need Up to go up one level in the hierarchy of folders on your disk. (You go down by clicking a folder.)

Tool	Action
Back	Display the previous folder.
Forward	Display the folder you went back from.
Up	Go up one level in the folder hierarchy.
Cut	Move the selected item to the Clipboard.
Copy	Copy the selected item to the Clipboard.
Paste	Paste the Clipboard contents into the window.
Undo	Undo the last editing change.
Delete	Delete the current selection.
Properties	View properties for the current selection.
Views	Choose among alternative folder views (As Web Page, Large Icons, Small Icons, List, Details).

12

Choosing Views

When you're displaying a Web page in Windows Explorer or My Computer, you can choose among the following views:

- **As Web Page.** If you choose this option, Explorer displays your folder as a Web page. You see the standard Web view of the folder (Figure 12-4), which has some extremely cool characteristics. You can choose this option independently of the other ones, which are the standard Windows Explorer file display options.

- **Large Icons.** Explorer displays resources (files, folders, and programs) as large icons.

- **Small Icons.** Explorer displays resources (files, folders, and programs) using considerably smaller icons.

- **List.** Explorer lists resources in alphabetical order. By choosing View from the menu bar and selecting the Arrange Icons option, you can choose additional sorting options (Date, Size, and Type).

- **Details.** Explorer shows lots of information (name, size, type, date modified, and, optionally, file attributes).

Viewing Properties

When you've enabled the Web view of a folder by clicking Views and choosing As Web Page, you can take advantage of a rather cunning built-in JavaScript that displays the properties of any resource that you hover over. (In case you've forgotten how to hover, just move the mouse pointer to a resource's name and stop for a moment.) In the left pane of the window, you'll see the name of the file, file type, date of last modification, and size. If you're hovering over a disk's name, you'll see a cool pie chart showing the amount of free space remaining (Figure 12-4).

Customizing Your Folders

Without knowing anything about HTML, you can customize your folders by adding a background picture. The picture you add shows up in the background of the current folder only. This option enables you to add a different graphic to each folder on your disk. Think of the possibilities!

1. Display the folder, click View on the menu bar, and choose Customize This Folder. You'll see the Customize This Folder wizard.

2. Click Choose A Background Picture, and click Next. You'll see the next page of the wizard (Figure 12-5).

PART

Figure 12-4

If you enable the Web Page view of a folder, you can move the pointer over a resource to see its properties.

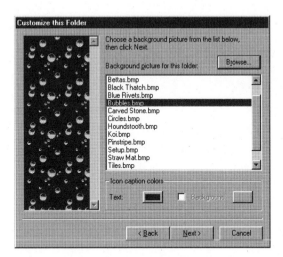

Figure 12-5

The second page of the Customize This Folder wizard shows a list of background pictures from which to choose.

205

3. Select a background picture, or click the Browse button to locate another graphic on your disk. You can choose GIF, JPEG, or Windows bitmap (BMP) files.

4. In the Icon Caption Codes area, choose a text color that will make your icon's text captions stand out against the background graphic you've chosen.

5. Click Next, and then click Finish.

HELP

My background graphic is ugly! I can't read the captions!

Two possible solutions here. Solution 1: Get rid of the graphic. Chances are you've chosen a graphic that has bright and dark areas, so your text won't show up no matter which text color you choose. Solution 2: Try a different background color. If your graphic is predominantly dark, try choosing a light background color. And if your graphic is predominantly light—you guessed it! Try a dark background color. How about deep purple text against a lime background? If everything you try proves as repulsive as the last example, try ditching the whole idea of choosing a background. Click View, choose the Customize This Folder option, click Remove Customization, and click Next until you can click Finish.

Running a Program from the Address Bar

By now you've doubtless typed a URL or two in the Address bar. As you know, this is a fast way to access an Internet site that you've heard or read about. But you can do much more with the address bar because it can tell the difference between Web URLs and local disk stuff. Here's what you can type directly in the address bar:

- 🌐 **Disk and directory names.** Enter the disk (such as c:) or folder name (with path information, such as c:\docs), and press Enter. You'll see the disk directory or folder contents.

- 🌐 **Windows components.** Enter the component name (such as Control Panel or My Computer), and press Enter.

- 🌐 **Program names.** To start a program, enter the pathname (such as c:\Program Files\office\winword.exe), and press Enter.

Playing with Random Cool Stuff

After you've installed Internet Explorer 4, Windows takes on a number of additional capabilities that might not be immediately obvious (unless you spend your free time playing around in your menus just for the heck of it). Here's a quick list of some cool things to try:

- 🌐 **Finding people.** To find people on the Internet, click Start, followed by Find, and then select People from the submenu. You'll see the Find People dialog box, which enables you to type information about the person you're looking for, such as Name, E-mail, Address, and Phone. Type as much information as you know. Then select where to look by choosing an option in the Look In list. You can search the Windows Address Book (which is also used by Outlook Express, as discussed in the next chapter) or any of several Web-based directories. Click Find Now to start the search.

- 🌐 **Adding mini-icons to the taskbar.** You've probably noticed the convenient little Internet Explorer, Outlook Express, and additional icons next to the Start button on the Taskbar. You can add shortcuts to the Taskbar simply by dragging the shortcut to this area and releasing the mouse button. This is a great place to put shortcuts for frequently accessed programs.

- 🌐 **Minimizing all windows quickly.** Click the Show Desktop icon next to the Start menu.

- 🌐 **Customizing the Start and Program menu by dragging and dropping.** This is supremely cool! Drag any item on the Start or Program menus, and drop it where you'd like it to appear. This is a super-fast way to edit and customize these standard menus.

From Here

You've tried just about everything that Internet Explorer's browser can do. Now it's time to communicate. In the next chapter, you get started with Internet e-mail, using Outlook Express.

12

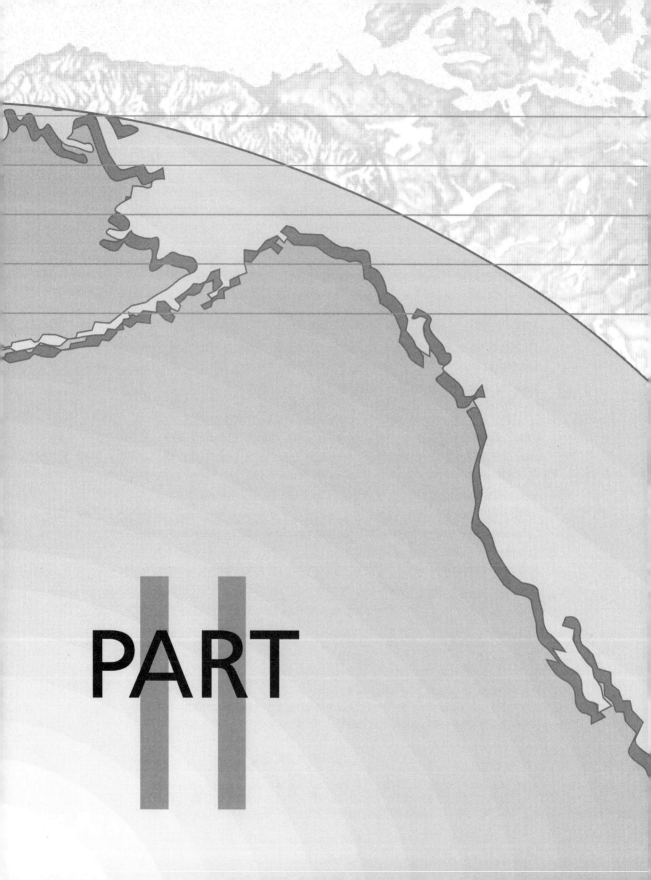

PART

II

Communicate

13 Get in Touch

When asked what they like best about the Internet, most people reply without hesitation, "Internet e-mail." In profession after profession, people soon conclude that they would be at a serious disadvantage if they couldn't communicate via e-mail.

What's so great about e-mail? For one thing, it's faster than snail mail (a.k.a. the U.S. Postal Service), and for many people, that's justification enough for using it. In fact, you can send an e-mail message halfway around the world in less than a minute. (It's not instantaneous because the mail servers need a little time to retrieve and store messages.) It's also free, once you've paid for your Internet connection. This makes an unbeatable combination, and it helps to explain why an estimated 80 to 100 million people are now using it.

There's a downside to e-mail too, as you'll soon discover. Not everyone has e-mail, of course, so it's far from the universal messaging service that the postal service is. What's more, if your recipient doesn't log on to his or her e-mail account, your message isn't received. This makes it tough to stay in touch with people who are on vacation and forget to tell their correspondents that they'll be away from their computers. Still, once you begin using it, you'll soon have many dependable e-mail partners. Although e-mail doesn't replace conventional communications (phone, mail, fax, and express services), it supplements and complements them so nicely that you won't want to give it up.

This chapter introduces Microsoft Outlook Express and covers the program's most useful features. You'll learn how to read and send messages and, what's more, how to use many of Outlook Express's intermediate and advanced options—necessities for productive e-mail usage. For example, you'll learn how to write filters so that you can exclude unwanted mail and sort low-priority mail into named folders. You'll find that Outlook Express is loaded with thoughtful and useful features, and this program will quickly become one of your favorites in the Microsoft Internet Explorer suite. In Chapter 14, you'll learn how to take full advantage of Outlook Express's security features, which enable you to digitally sign your messages and to encrypt them so that they cannot be read while they're en route.

NOTE Outlook Express isn't designed to work with online services, such as The Microsoft Network (MSN) or America Online. To send and receive Internet electronic mail with these services, use the mail software that these services provide.

Understanding Internet E-Mail

E-mail uses the Internet as its transmission medium, which means that it's very fast. But you might not get your messages right away. When somebody sends you an e-mail message, it's stored temporarily in your *electronic mailbox*. This mailbox generally is part of the file storage system of an Internet service provider or an online service such as The Microsoft Network. You don't get your messages until you log on to the service provider and start your e-mail program. The program then checks your electronic mailbox and downloads any new messages to your computer. You can then read them, reply to them, delete them, or forward them. When you finish dealing with your messages, the e-mail program sends any new messages you've created to the service provider, where they're zinged on their way to their destinations.

The service just described is called Post Office Protocol 3 (POP3), and it is the most common service. E-mail access changes slightly if your service provider signs you up to an Internet Message Access Protocol (IMAP) account. With IMAP servers, your messages stay on the server—you don't download them. That's fine, except that you have to be connected to the server while you're reading and composing your messages. For this reason, IMAP isn't really the best choice for dial-up connections; it's more popular for corporate networks. The really cool thing about IMAP is that you can access your mailbox while you're on the road.

Outlook Express can handle both types of mail servers. You'll learn how to configure the program to work with your mail server later in this section.

POP3 and IMAP—What's the Difference?

On the Internet, your incoming mail can be handled in two ways.

POP3 mail servers collect your mail on the mail server's computer. When you access your mailbox, your mail program automatically downloads all your mail onto your hard disk and deletes it from the server. (You can choose an option that enables you to keep your mail on the server, but your service provider won't like this because it takes up too much disk space.) What's nice about POP3 is that your mail is stored on your own computer. You can read it and compose replies while you're offline. That's also the bad thing about POP3. What happens if you're traveling and need to look at some mail you previously received? Your whole mailbox is on your home computer, which you can't access.

Like POP3 servers, IMAP servers collect your incoming mail on the mail server's computer, but that's where the similarity ends. IMAP servers keep your mail there. To be sure, you can download copies of your messages, but the authoritative collection of your mail resides on the server—a real boon for mobile computer users.

13

Interpreting Internet E-Mail Addresses

To get your e-mail message across, you need to know how to use Internet e-mail addresses, which look like this: <u>frodo@bagend.shire.org</u>. Every address has three parts:

- **User name** ("frodo"). This isn't a person's name; it's the name given to a person's electronic mailbox. The user name is often made up of components of the person's name.

- **At sign** ("@"). This symbol is needed to separate the user name from the domain name.

- **Domain name** ("bagend.shire.org"). This name is the Internet address of the computer that contains the person's electronic mailbox. Note that the various parts of the domain name are separated by periods; if you're telling someone your e-mail address, you pronounce the periods by saying "dot," as in "frodo at bagend-dot-shire-dot-org."

TIP

An Internet domain name can give you hints about where a person's mail is coming from. At the end of the name is the *top-level domain,* which is a general category. If the message originates outside the United States, the top-level domain usually indicates the country of origin (For example, *uk* is the United Kingdom, and *fr* is France). Within the United States, messages from universities and colleges use the top-level domain *edu,* government agencies use *gov,* corporations use *com,* and nonprofit organizations use *org.*

Using E-Mail

To use electronic mail, you use your computer to connect to your *mail server,* the computer that stores your incoming mail. When you log on, you supply your user (or account) name and password. The mail server then checks to see whether there's any mail for you. If so, your computer begins downloading the messages.

Once you've downloaded the messages, you can read them, store them in folders, reply to them, forward them to another e-mail address, or delete them. You can also write and send messages of your own. When you've completed downloading and sending your messages, you log off the server.

NOTE

Before using e-mail, you need to understand clearly that U.S. and state governments provide little or no privacy protection for your messages. The Electronic Communications Privacy Act of 1986, the only federal legislation that governs electronic mail, requires U.S. government agencies to obtain search warrants to intercept and read electronic mail messages while they are en route. What the computer-illiterate authors of this bill did not realize, however, is that all mail servers maintain backup tapes, sometimes for years, of all the e-mail messages that pass through their systems. Any investigator can obtain access to these tapes and use them for any purpose whatsoever.

As for e-mail that you send and receive on your employer's computer, the courts have consistently found that employees deserve no privacy protection at all when using their company's computers. Your boss is quite free to read your mail and use it in a termination proceeding, and there's nothing you can do about it.

You'll be very wise to follow this advice: *Never, never, never write anything in e-mail that you wouldn't want to see the next morning on your boss's desk, your mother's coffee table, or the front page of your hometown newspaper.*

Introducing Outlook Express

Outlook Express is an exceptionally capable e-mail program, and it's also very easy to use. That's especially true if you take a few minutes to familiarize yourself with the program's basics.

Getting the Information You Need

To get started with Outlook Express, you'll need to know the following information: your e-mail address, the type of incoming mail server your service provider offers (POP or IMAP), the name of the incoming mail server (POP3 or IMAP server), the name of the outgoing mail server (also called SMTP server), your mail account name (also called login name or user name), the password you use to access your e-mail, and whether your mail server supports Secure Password Authentication (SPA).

Configuring Outlook Express

The first time you run Outlook Express, you'll see a wizard that asks you to supply needed information. Here's how to fill out the various pages you'll see.

13

1. On the Your Name page (Figure 13-1), type your name the way you'd like it to appear in the From field of the outgoing message.

    If you're using e-mail at work, type your real name (first name followed by last name). If you're using Outlook Express for nonbusiness purposes, you might prefer to enter a "handle" (pseudonym) here, such as "Hummer" or "Begonia," but the choice is strictly up to you.

2. Click Next. On the Internet E-Mail Address page, type your e-mail address. Don't include any spaces, and check your typing carefully.

3. Click Next. You'll see the E-Mail Server Names page (Figure 13-2). Choose the type of mail server you're using, and carefully type the addresses of your incoming and outgoing mail servers.

4. Click Next. You'll see the Internet Mail Logon page. Here, you supply your account name and password. Again, type carefully.

5. Click Next. You'll see the Friendly Name page. This page enables you to give your mail account a more readable name than the computer name, but this is optional. If you'd like to supply a friendly name, type it in the Internet mail account name box. (I like to call my account "Barney.")

6. Click Next. You'll see the Choose Connection Type page (Figure 13-3). Choose the type of connection you're planning to use (phone line or local area network).

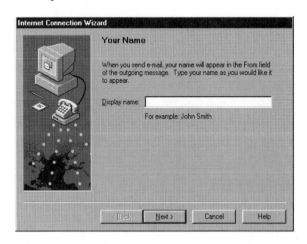

Figure 13-1

The first page of the Internet Connection Wizard asks for your name.

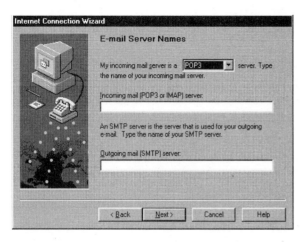

Figure 13-2

Specify the names of your e-mail servers on this page.

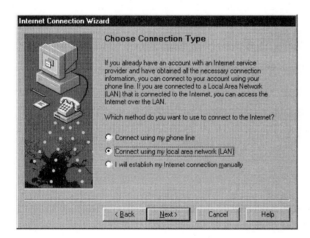

Figure 13-3

Here you can choose the type of connection you will use.

If you're using a modem, I suggest using the manual connection option. With the Connect Using My Phone Line Option, Outlook Express will sever your connection when you quit the program, unless you're also running another Internet application. In spite of the slightly annoying dialog box, I still prefer to log on and log off manually.

7. Click Next, and then click Finish to save your settings.

13

Accessing Multiple Accounts

Do you have more than one e-mail account? Many people do. A very cool thing about Outlook Express is the program's ability to let you work with as many mail accounts as you please. For example, I have a mail account at work, and I use it for work purposes only. I've a different account (with a local service provider) that I pay for and use for my personal messages. But I want to be able to see messages from both accounts in my mailboxes. Outlook Express makes this possible. If you add additional accounts, the program will automatically check all your accounts when it's checking for new mail. This is an excellent feature!

To add an additional e-mail account to Outlook Express, open the Tools menu and choose Accounts. Click Add, and choose Mail from the pop-up menu. You'll see another Internet Connection Wizard, like the one you just filled out. You can use this wizard to add the second or additional accounts in the same way you created the first one.

Understanding What's on the Screen

After you've finished adding your e-mail account information, you'll see Outlook Express's top-level screen (Figure 13-4). By "top-level," I mean the screen you see when you click the top icon in the Outlook Bar, which runs down the left side of the screen. This screen gives you a quick overview of what you can do with Outlook Express.

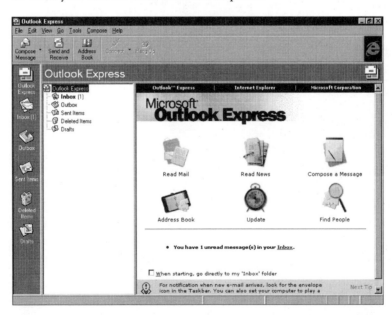

Figure 13-4

The top-level view of Outlook Express offers a quick overview of its functions.

PART
II

TIP This opening page is nice, but it's something of a time-waster after you figure out what you can do with Outlook Express. When I open the program, I want to see my new messages right away. So I prefer to click the option at the bottom of the window that goes directly to the Inbox when the program starts.

Looking at the Window

Outlook Express is designed to look and work like Internet Explorer. There's much that's familiar, such as the program icon and the toolbars. You'll notice, though, that the toolbar buttons differ, and there are two panels within the workspace. These screen areas are dynamically linked. When you select a folder in the folder panel, you see that folder's message list, and the message window shows the message that's currently selected in the message list.

Let's survey the Outlook Express window (Figure 13-4):

- **Title Bar.** To reposition the Outlook Express window, drag the title bar. To maximize the window quickly, double-click the title bar. Double-click again to restore it to the previous size.

- **Menu Bar.** All the Outlook Express commands are on the menu bar, but the most frequently used commands are found on the toolbar.

- **Toolbar.** If the Toolbar isn't visible, choose Toolbar from the View menu. On it you'll find the following buttons: Compose Message, Send And Receive, Address Book, Connect, and Hang Up.

- **Outlook Bar.** The Outlook Bar gives you access to various folders of mail, such as Inbox, Outbox, Deleted Items, and Drafts. You can also return to the main Outlook Express screen by clicking the Outlook Express icon.

- **Folder Bar.** Outlook Express enables you to organize your mail into folders, and the default folders are described in the next section. (By default, Outlook Express is selected.) You can also create your own folders, as you'll learn later in this chapter. The Folder Bar displays the name of the current folder.

- **Main Outlook Express Page.** This area is designed as a sort of launch pad for Outlook Express. From here, you can get to your mail, read newsgroups, or do several other things.

13

- **Status Bar.** In this area, Outlook Express displays messages and information about its status and what it's doing. You can hide the status bar by choosing Status Bar from the View menu, but it's worth keeping it visible because some of the messages are useful or important.

- **Tip of the Day.** The Tip of the Day area is visible only in the introductory screen. Look here for tips on how to make more efficient use of Outlook Express.

Understanding the Default Folders

Outlook Express is set up with the following folders:

- **Inbox.** Here's where your new messages show up—and here they stay unless you move them elsewhere.

- **Deleted Items.** If you delete an unwanted message from the Inbox, Outlook Express puts it here. Think of the Deleted Items folder as the Recycle Bin. To erase a message completely, you must open the Deleted Items folder and delete the message there. If you want to permanently delete all the messages in the Deleted Items folder, right-click the folder's icon and choose Empty Folder.

- **Outbox.** Here's where your messages are temporarily stored until you click Send And Receive; then they're electronically transported to your service provider.

- **Sent Items.** Here's where you'll find copies of messages you've sent.

- **Drafts.** If you're composing a message and need to do something else before finishing the message, simply close the message and tell Outlook Express to save it. Outlook Express places the message in the Drafts folder to await your return.

To view the contents of a folder, click the folder's icon in the Outlook Bar; you can also click the folder's title in the Folder Bar.

Using the Toolbar

The toolbar contains the commands you'll use most often. Here's what they do.

Tool	Action
Compose Message	Displays a blank New Message window, enabling you to write a new message to send to someone.
Send And Receive	Connects with your mail server, automatically downloads any new mail, and sends any outgoing mail that you've written.
Address Book	Displays the Address Book.
Connect	Connects to the Internet, if you're not already connected.
Hang Up	Disconnects from the Internet, if you're currently connected.

Getting Your Mail

To get your e-mail, click Send And Receive. Or you can click Tools on the menu bar and choose Send And Receive. You'll see a dialog box that tells you what's happening. If everything goes right, you'll see your new messages (if any) in the Inbox.

HELP

It says there was an error!

Lots of things can go wrong here, but the most likely cause is that you've typed some of your information incorrectly. (It's easy to do.) Click Tools on the menu bar, choose the Accounts command, and click the Mail tab. Select your mail account, and click Properties. Carefully check all the information to make sure it's correct. If you find a mistake, fix it and try clicking Send And Receive again.

Still didn't work? Click the Details tab to see what's wrong. Perhaps your mail server is down. It happens. If so, you'll see a message stating that the connection to the server has failed. This message appears under the Errors tab, but Outlook Express displays it automatically.

Reading Your Mail

Even if you're totally new to e-mail, you probably already have a message in your Inbox. Chances are it's a sappy welcoming message from your Internet service provider. Outlook Express also has its own welcome message.

13

To read your mail, choose Inbox in the folder list (if necessary) or click the Inbox icon on the Outlook Bar. Unread messages are shown in bold. Next to unread messages, you see an unopened letter icon.

When you select a message, you'll see the text of the message in the preview pane (Figure 13-5). At the top of the preview pane, you see basic information about the message (who it's from, who it's to, and the subject). This information stays put even if you scroll through the message.

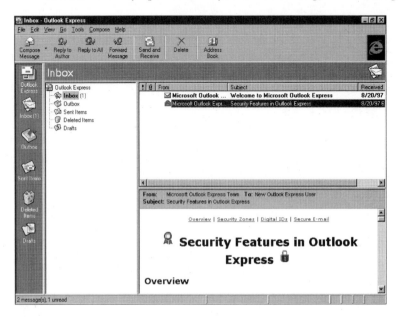

Figure 13-5

When you select a folder to view, the right side of the screen divides into the message list pane and the preview pane.

After five seconds, the bold disappears, and the icon next to the message shows an opened letter, indicating that you've read the message. But five seconds isn't time to read a lengthy message. If you don't have time to read the whole message, you can mark it as unread, which changes the icon back to an unopened letter and again displays the message's name in bold. To do this, click Edit on the menu bar and choose Mark As Unread. If you would like to increase the time it takes to mark a letter as read, go to the Tools menu and select Options, click Read, and increase the time in Message Is Read After Being Previewed For *x* Seconds. Click OK to confirm.

TIP

Got tons of read messages in your Inbox? To see just the unread messages, click View on the menu bar, select Current View, and choose Unread Messages. You'll see only the messages you haven't read. This is a great thing to do occasionally to make sure you've read every important message you've received. You might actually want to work with this view permanently. Just remember that your read messages are still stored and available; you can see them again by clicking View, choosing Current View, and clicking All Messages.

Take a look at the sample message from Microsoft (which might be the only message you'll see at this point, unless there's an automatic message from your service provider). This message, shown in Figure 13-6, gives you a good hint of what you're in for with Outlook Express. Look at the formatting! With Outlook Express, you can send and receive messages formatted with HTML, the same markup language that underlies the appearance of Web documents. You don't even need to know any HTML to do this, as you'll see; formatting your messages is as simple as using a few basic commands that work just like the ones in a word processing program.

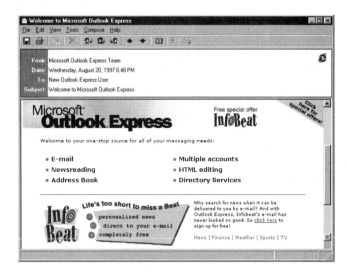

Figure 13-6
This message displays some of the rich formatting available by using HTML.

13

TIP If you don't need to keep a message, click Delete right after reading it. The more unwanted messages you leave in your Inbox, the more time you'll have to spend housecleaning later on.

Using the Message Window

A convenient way to read messages is to use the main Outlook Express window, with its message list and preview pane. The preview pane gives you a quick sense of what's in the letter. You can scroll down to see more, if you wish.

You can also read messages in the message window. To view an entire message in this window, simply double-click the message header in the message list.

One good reason to read your messages in the message window rather than in the preview pane is that you can go through a whole bunch of mail quickly by clicking the Previous and Next buttons on the message window's toolbar. You'll see more of each one's content, too. Another reason is that you can easily add your correspondents' addresses to your Address Book by double-clicking their names. (See "Creating an Address Book" on page 236.)

The message window's toolbar includes convenient tools for your reading purposes. You'll learn more about these tools in the sections to come, but here's what they do.

Tool	Action
Save This Message	Save a copy of this message on disk. Note: You don't really need to do this as long as you don't delete the message; your Inbox folder keeps it for you.
Print	Print the current message.
Copy	Copy the selection to the Clipboard.
Delete	Delete this message.
Reply To Author	Write a reply to the author of this message.
Reply All	Write a reply to all the e-mail addresses listed in the message.
Forward	Forward this message to a third party.
Previous	Display the previous message in the message list.

Tool	Action
Next	Display the next message in the message list.
Address Book	Display the Address Book.
Digitally Sign Message	Sign the message with your digital signature.
Encrypt Message	Encrypt the message for secure transmission.

Navigating in the Message List

To view the next message down in the list: click the message, or press Alt + left arrow, or press Ctrl + >, or choose Next and then Next Message from the View menu.

To view the previous message in the list: click the message, or press Alt + right arrow, or Ctrl + <, or choose Next and then Previous Message from the View menu.

To view the next unread message, press Ctrl + U.

TIP To make messages easier to read, you might want to change the font size. To do so, click View on the menu bar, select Fonts, and choose a relative font size (from Smallest to Largest).

Sorting the Message List

Close the message window for now, and let's take another look at the message list. You'll notice that there's a row of buttons across the top of the message list. Here's what they mean.

Button	Action
Priority (exclamation point)	Sorts message according to priority, with urgent messages first.
Attachment (paper clip icon)	Sorts messages by whether they contain an attached file; these files are shown first.
From	Sorts messages in alphabetical order by the sender's name.
Subject	Sorts messages in alphabetical order by the message's subject.
Received	Sorts messages by the date received.

13

By default, the message list is sorted by the date received, with the most recently dated message at the top. You can change the sort method by clicking the sort bars at the top of the message list. To sort by sender, for example, click From.

Outlook Express can sort the message list in ascending (A to Z) or descending order (Z to A). To change the sort order of the message list, just click the sort button again, choose the View menu, and select the Sort By command. From the submenu, select Ascending so that a check mark appears next to Ascending. To sort in descending order, choose the Ascending command again (so that the check mark disappears).

For most purposes, the best way to display your messages is to sort them by the date you received them and in descending order. You'll see your newest messages at the top of the window.

Displaying Additional Information in the Message List

Outlook Express is configured to display five columns (Priority, Attachment, From, Subject, and Received). If you wish, you can display additional information, and you can configure the columns as you please. This information could include a column indicating the date the message was sent, the name of the person to whom the message was sent, and the size of the message. Since this information really isn't necessary for most purposes, many of you will probably want to stick with the default columns.

To configure the message list columns, choose the View menu and select Columns. You'll see the Columns dialog box (Figure 13-7). In the left panel, you'll see the additional information you can add (Account, Sent, Size, and To). To add this information to the message list, highlight your choice and click Add. To change the position of an item in the Displayed Columns list, select the item and click Move Up or Move Down. If you'd like to remove a column, highlight it and click Remove. To confirm your options, click OK.

If you've done some experimenting with columns and regret doing so, you can quickly restore the defaults. Go to the View menu, choose Columns, click Reset, and click OK.

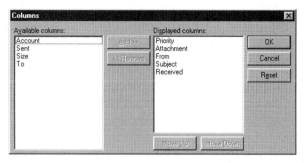

Figure 13-7

The Columns dialog box lets you customize your message list.

Receiving an Attachment

If you receive a message that has an *attachment* (a file sent along with the message), you'll see a paper clip icon next to the envelope icon. To view the attachment, double-click the message. You'll see a message window, just like the one you use when you write a new message, except that there's a special panel at the bottom containing the attachment.

Outlook Express displays the attachment as an icon. To view the attachment, double-click that icon. Windows will attempt to find an application that allows you to view the file. If no application exists that's capable of displaying the file, you'll see a dialog box asking you to associate this type of file with one of your applications.

If somebody wants to send you an attachment, ask that person to send a file that one of your applications can read. For example, if you have Microsoft Word for Windows 95 (version 7), you can read just about any Word file but you won't be able to read a WordPerfect for Macintosh 1.0 file.

Finding a Message

Once you've received and sent many messages, you might find that manual search techniques are too much trouble. To search for a message, choose the Edit menu and select Find Message. (You can also press Ctrl + Shift + F.) You'll see the Find Message dialog box (Figure 13-8).

227

13

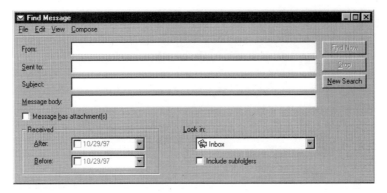

Figure 13-8

Can't remember where you stored a message? Use the Find Message dialog box.

You can then search by sender, recipient, text in the subject line, date received, whether the file has an attachment, or text in the message body. Type the information you want to search for in the appropriate box, and click Find. Outlook Express will try to locate the message you're searching for; if the program finds one or more matches, the Find Message dialog box expands and displays the message headers in its own message list.

Using the Pop-Up Menu

If you click the right mouse button with the pointer positioned within the message list, you'll see the pop-up menu shown in Figure 13-9. This chapter hasn't covered all the items in this list yet, so don't worry if you don't understand what all of them do. For now, just remember that this move is a convenient way to get to some of the most frequently used options in Outlook Express.

Figure 13-9

Right-click in the message list to display this menu.

PART
II

Composing and Sending Messages

You can send messages in three ways: by composing a new message, by replying to a message you've received, and by forwarding a message you've received.

The following sections introduce the fundamentals of sending messages, beginning with a look at the New Message window. Later in this chapter, you'll learn how to get fancy by creating a signature, using an address book, attaching files to your messages, and adding rich formatting.

Understanding the New Message Window

No matter whether you're replying, forwarding, or composing a new message, you'll use the New Message window to address, write, and edit your message (Figure 13-10).

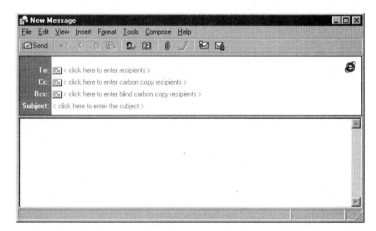

Figure 13-10

The New Message window enables you to compose your message.

The New Message window includes the following parts:

- **Title Bar.** To reposition the window, drag the title bar. To maximize the window quickly, double-click the title bar. Double-click again to restore the window to its previous size.

- **Menu Bar.** All the Outlook Express commands are on the menu bar, but the most frequently used commands are found on the toolbar.

13

- **Toolbar.** The toolbar contains the following buttons, from left to right: Send, Undo, Cut, Copy, Paste, Check Names, Select Recipients, Insert File, Insert Signature, Digitally Sign Message, and Encrypt Message. You'll learn more about these tools later.

- **Header Information.** Here, you type the recipient's e-mail address, the e-mail address for recipients of copies of the message (optional), and a brief subject line.

- **Message Body.** Type your information in this area.

The New Message Window's Toolbar

The New Message window has its own toolbar. You'll learn more about these tools later, but here's what the buttons do.

Tool	Action
Send	Sends the message.
Undo	Undoes the last editing change.
Cut	Cuts the selection to the Clipboard.
Copy	Copies the selection to the Clipboard.
Paste	Pastes the Clipboard contents at the cursor's location.
Check Names	Checks the address aliases you've typed to make sure that the names are in your Address Book.
Select Recipients	Displays your Address Book and enables you to select recipients.
Insert File	Attaches a file to the message.
Insert Signature	Inserts your signature (a text file containing personal information about you).
Digitally Sign Message	Signs the message with your digital signature.
Encrypt Message	Encrypts the message for secure transmission.

Sending a Message

It's easy to use the New Message window to create a message. On the Outlook Express toolbar, click Compose Message. (You can also choose the Compose menu and select New Message, or press Ctrl + N.) When the New Message window appears, type a recipient's e-mail address in the To box, add a brief subject line, and type the message's text.

PART
II

Be sure to check your spelling. Choose the Tools menu and select Spelling, or press F7. If Outlook Express finds a spelling error, the program highlights the error and displays the Spelling dialog box. You can ignore the error, change it by typing the word manually, select a suggested spelling, or add the word to the Office dictionary (if it's correctly spelled). When the spelling check is finished, you see a dialog box that confirms this.

To change the message's priority, choose the Tools menu, select Set Priority, and click High, Normal, or Low. (The default is Normal.)

Want to practice? If you're anxious to send a message to somebody but don't know anyone's e-mail address yet, take a tip from Elvis: You can sit right down and write yourself a letter. Type your own e-mail address in the To box, write a brief subject line, and pour your heart out. After you click Send, click Send And Receive to send your letter, and then click Send And Receive a few moments later to download and read it.

Sending Richly Formatted Messages

If you would like to send your message with rich HTML formatting, choose the Format menu and select Rich Text (HTML) in the New Message window. This toolbar enables you to choose fonts, font sizes, styles, emphases (bold, italic, and underline), font color, numbered lists, bulleted lists, indents, alignments, horizontal lines, hyperlinks, and even images. You simply choose these options and format your letter as you would in a word processing program; Outlook Express takes care of the HTML.

Your message won't come across with intact formatting unless your recipient's e-mail program can decode HTML. If your correspondent is also using Outlook Express, you can be sure that the message will be automatically displayed with the rich formatting. Otherwise, your correspondents will be able to read your message's text, but it will be full of HTML tags. They might not like that.

If you know that one of your recipients can't handle HTML mail, you can modify that person's Address Book entry to make sure that he or she receives plaintext only. For more information, see "Creating an Address Book" on page 236.

13

Using Stationery

If you're thinking about composing rich messages, take a look at the stationery in Outlook Express. These are HTML pages with cool backgrounds and font choices. To compose a message with stationery, open Compose on the menu bar, click New Message Using, and select More Stationery from the pop-up menu. You'll see a dialog box with stationery files. Pick the one you want, and click Open. You'll see the stationery in your New Message window as shown in Figure 13-11.

You can also create your own stationery. Stationery files are nothing more than HTML files, which you'll learn to create in Chapters 18 and 19. You can use Microsoft FrontPage Express to create files with rich backgrounds, images, and even ActiveX controls and JavaScripts. Store your creation in the Stationery folder, which you'll find in Program Files\Common Files\Microsoft Shared.

If you'd like to make a certain stationery file the default for all your outgoing messages, click Tools on the menu bar and choose Stationery. You'll see the Stationery dialog box with the Mail page displayed. Click This Stationery, and select the stationery file you want to use. Click OK to confirm.

Figure 13-11
If your recipient can handle HTML mail, you can use stationery like the one shown here.

Replying to a Message

To reply to a message, you have two options:

🌐 **Reply To Author.** If you choose this option, your reply goes only to the e-mail addresses included in the From line in the header information. (Note that this might include more than one address.) No copies are sent to anyone on the courtesy copy (Cc:) list of the original message.

🌐 **Reply To All.** If you choose this option, your message goes not only to the author but also to everyone on the Cc: list.

HELP

I just sent a private letter to everyone in my company!

You wouldn't believe how often this happens. Many e-mail addresses are actually distribution lists. These look like an e-mail address but actually refer to a lengthy list of e-mail addresses—potentially including everyone in an organization. If you don't notice such an address in the Cc: line and click Reply To All without thinking, you could be sending your message to hundreds or even thousands of people!

Don't make yourself look stupid in front of hundreds of people. Please exercise caution when you click Reply To All. Examine the addresses carefully to make sure you understand who's getting the reply. If you aren't sure or don't feel quite comfortable for some reason, don't choose Reply To All!

To reply to a message, select the message and click Reply To Author. (You can also go to the Compose menu and select Reply To Author, or press Ctrl + R, or choose Reply To Author from the pop-up menu.) If you're certain that you really want to reply to everyone, select the message and click Reply To All. (You can also go to the Compose menu and select Reply To All, or press Ctrl + Shift + R, or choose Reply To All from the pop-up menu.)

You'll see a New Message window. Notice that Outlook Express has included the original text, added the recipient, and positioned the insertion point at the beginning of the letter, above the included text. In addition, the program has added *Re:* before the subject.

Forwarding a Message

Forwarding works exactly like replying, except that Outlook Express doesn't automatically supply the To address. To forward a message, select the message and click Forward Message. (You can also choose the Compose

13

menu and select Forward, or press Ctrl + F, or click Forward on the pop-up menu.) Type an address. You can add some explanatory text in the message box, if you like. Click Send to send your message.

If you wish, you can forward the message as an attachment. An attachment is a separate, closed file that is attached to the message you send. As long as your recipient's e-mail program can handle attachments, this file can be opened, read, saved, printed, or stored. This is the best option to choose if you're forwarding something really lengthy.

To forward a message as an attachment, select the message, choose the Compose menu, and select Forward As Attachment. (You can also click Forward As Attachment on the pop-up menu.) Type an address. Again, you can include text of your own. Click Send to send your message.

Creating a Signature

A signature ("sig," for short) adds a nice touch to your e-mail, as long as it isn't too lengthy. By convention, it's thought best to keep your sig to no more than four lines. That's enough for whatever identifying information you feel comfortable sending.

TIP

There's no need to include your e-mail address in your sig; people get that automatically. But you might want to include your full name, your work number, and your work address. Think long and hard before including personal information such as your home telephone number and address. If you really want to send this information to someone, you can do so in the body of the message.

To create your sig, go to the Tools menu, select Stationery, click the Mail tab, and click the Signature button. You'll see the Signature dialog box (Figure 13-12).

In the Text box, type a brief signature, or click File and use the Browse button to locate a text file containing the sig you want to use. Also on this panel, you'll find two options:

- **Add this signature to all outgoing messages.** When you open the New Message window to start a new message, Mail adds your sig automatically.

- **Don't add signature to Replies and Forwards.** This is a nice touch since replies and forwards can get excessively lengthy with all those repeated sigs.

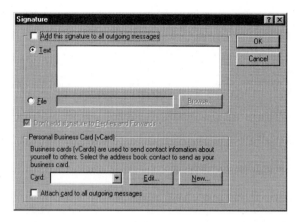

Figure 13-12
From the Signature dialog box, you can create an identifying signature for your e-mail.

If you decide against including the sig in all your outgoing messages automatically, you can still include it selectively by clicking Insert Signature in the New Message window's toolbar.

A cute trick, in which too many Internet users (including myself) indulge themselves, is to include a little ASCII art picture in their signatures. (Mine used to have a sailboat.) As cunning as these works of art might appear to the eyes of those who create them, they come across as gibberish to anyone who's chosen a proportional font to read mail messages. Since that's increasingly common, it's time to bid a fond farewell to these artistic efforts.

Creating a Business Card

Outlook Express enables you to attach a business card to your outgoing messages. A *business card* contains personal information about you and conforms to an unofficial Internet standard called vCard. Some other mail programs can read the vCard format, including Netscape Communicator.

To create a business card, click Tools on the menu bar and choose Stationery. In the Stationery dialog box, click Signature. In the Personal Business Card area, click Card and choose your name from the list. If you haven't entered information about yourself in your Address Book, click New.

13

You'll see an Address Book page, which enables you to enter information about yourself. Enter this information, and click OK.

To automatically attach this card to outgoing messages, click Attach Card To All Outgoing Messages. If you want to attach the card only to some outgoing messages, don't enable Attach Card To All Outgoing Messages. To include it in a message you're sending, click Insert on the New Message window's menu bar and choose Business Card.

Creating an Address Book

It's a bother to type e-mail addresses, and what's more, it invites error. If you make a typing mistake, your message won't get to its destination. To solve the problem (and to organize your e-mail addresses in a convenient way), create an address book. To begin creating your address book, go to the Tools menu and select Address Book. You'll see the Address Book dialog box (Figure 13-13).

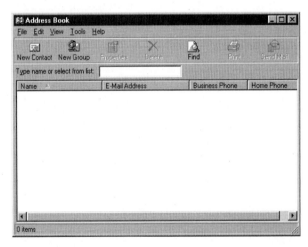

Figure 13-13
The Address Book is the easiest way to organize all your e-mail addresses.

Adding Entries to the Address Book

By far the easiest way to add a person's name and address to your Address Book is to display a message from this person in the message window, right-click the name or e-mail address in the From area, and choose Add To Address Book. You'll see the Properties dialog box. Note that Outlook Express has automatically added the recipient's e-mail address and taken a stab at the name.

PART

II

Although Outlook Express tries to interpret the person's first and last names from the From field's information, it might not succeed, so you might need to edit this information. If you have additional information about this person, you can enter it by clicking Home (for home address and phone), Business (for business address and phone), Other (for your notes about this person), NetMeeting (for Internet conferencing), or Digital IDs. In both the Home and Business pages, there's even a space to put the Web address of the person's personal or business Web page. After you enter the address, you can view the page by clicking the Go button next to the Web Page box.

To add an entry to the Address Book manually, open the Address Book and click New Contact. You'll see the first page of the Properties dialog box. Enter the person's name and e-mail address. If you need to edit a person's information later, highlight the person's name and click Properties.

Creating a Group

Once you've entered two or more names in the Address Book, you can create a group. After you've created the group, you can send a message to the whole group by using the group address instead of individual e-mail addresses. To create a group, click New Group. In the Group dialog box, create a name for your group. Add members by clicking Select Members, selecting names from the Address Book, and clicking OK. Click OK to save your new group. If you later want to add or remove people from this list, find the group name in the address book list—it has a distinctive icon showing two people—and click Properties. To remove a name, highlight the name and click Remove. To add a name, click Select Members, select the name, and click OK. Click OK to close the Properties dialog box.

Importing Address Books

If you created an address book with Eudora Pro or Light, Microsoft Exchange, Microsoft Internet Mail, Netscape version 2 or 3, or Netscape Communicator, you can import your address book into Outlook Express. To do so, go to the File menu and select Import. From the submenu, select Address Book. You'll see the Address Book Import Tool dialog box, which lists all the available import formats. Choose the format of the address book you want to import, and click Import. Depending on which format you are importing, Outlook Express might prompt you with a file location dialog box, or it might ask you to choose a profile from the application the address book is from. Locate the address file or choose the appropriate profile, and click Import.

13

Adding Addresses to Your Messages

Once you've created your Address Book, you can easily add addresses to your messages. In the New Message window, just click the Address Book icon (which looks like a little Rolodex page) next to To or Cc:. (You can also click Select Recipients on the toolbar.) You'll see the Select Recipients dialog box (Figure 13-14).

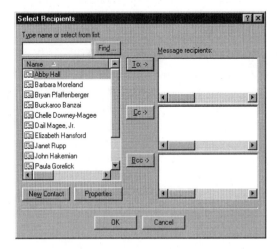

Figure 13-14
Simply point and click to address your e-mail message.

To select the main recipient, highlight the name and click To. (You can add more than one main recipient, but this can complicate things for people if they would like to reply just to you.) To select a recipient for a courtesy copy of the message, highlight the name and click Cc:. You can select as many Cc: names as you want without irritating your recipients.

Adding Attachments (Files) to Your Messages

One of the nicest things about e-mail is that you can send formatted documents over the Internet, including Word, Excel, and Powerpoint files. I don't doubt for a minute that this is going to eat into the profits of express services; all of my publishers (except for a few Luddite-like holdouts) can handle manuscript submissions this way. (That's how this chapter got to Microsoft Press.)

PART

It's easy to include an attachment. Just compose your letter or reply as you would normally, and click Attachment (or go to the Insert menu and select File Attachment). You'll see the Insert Attachment dialog box. Locate the file, and click Attach.

Organizing Your Mail into Folders

Once you've started getting mail, you'll find that it's more convenient to sort your messages into named folders than to keep everything in your Inbox.

Creating a New Folder

To create a new mail folder, go to the File menu and select Folder. From the submenu, select New Folder. You'll see the Create Folder dialog box. Type a name for your folder, select what existing folder you want the new one to appear in, and click OK. You'll then see its name in the Folder list.

Adding Messages to Your New Folder

After you've created a new folder, you can easily add a message to it by selecting the message in the message list and doing one of the following:

- 🌐 Go to the Edit menu, and select either Move To Folder or Copy To Folder. Select the folder to which you'd like to move the message, and click OK.

- 🌐 Right-click the message, choose Move To or Copy To, and select the folder to which you'd like to move the message.

- 🌐 Drag the message to the folder's name in the folder bar or to the folder's icon in the Outlook bar.

Viewing Your Folders

To view the contents of one of the folders you've created, click on the folder name in the folders list. To return to the Inbox, choose Inbox from the Folders list or just click the Inbox icon on the Outlook bar.

Compacting Folders

Mail messages can take up a lot of room. To reduce the space that a folder consumes, navigate to the folder that you want to compact. Go to the File menu, and select Folder. From the submenu, select Compact. If you want to compact all of your folders, select Compact All Folders from the submenu. After you compact the folder, you won't notice any difference

239

13

in the performance of Outlook Express. The program needs a little more time to open messages in these folders, but they take up less disk space.

Deleting Folders

To delete an unwanted folder and all the messages within it, select the folder you want to delete, go to the File menu, select Folder, and select Delete from the submenu. You'll see a confirmation message: Are you really sure that you want to delete all the messages in this folder? If so, click OK.

Routing Incoming Mail to Folders

One of the nicest features of Outlook Express is Inbox Assistant, which can automatically route incoming mail messages to folders of your choice—including Deleted Items. Here's a great way to get rid of junk e-mail!

Inbox Assistant also comes in handy after you subscribe to mailing lists. As you'll quickly discover, once you subscribe to a mailing list, you can get dozens or even hundreds of messages per day, and they get in the way of your personal mail. By automatically routing these messages to a folder rather than sticking them in your face in the Inbox, Inbox Assistant frees you to read them at your convenience.

NOTE   Inbox Assistant shouldn't be used to store any incoming mail that you need to read right away. The mail might go to a folder that you seldom look at. Rather, it's best used to deal with messages that aren't of pressing importance.

Creating Rules

Before you can route incoming messages to folders, you need to create folders to store those messages. If you've subscribed to the Yachting-L mailing list, for example, create a folder called Yachting-L.

Outlook Express relies on *rules* to divert your incoming messages into designated folders. A rule says, in effect, "If an incoming message contains such-and-such in such-and-such an area, move the message to the such-and-such folder." Here's an example, which should be sufficient to illustrate the usefulness of this feature: "If an incoming message is from Arnie Schmuck and contains the text 'I still love you' in the subject line, move it to Deleted Items."

PART

TIP

Plan your rules before trying to create them. Inbox Assistant can match any text in the To, Cc, From, or Subject lines, so think of how you will instruct the program to recognize the correct incoming messages. Browse through your Inbox and display messages that you wish had been automatically diverted. For example, suppose you have subscribed to the Holt stock report, which sends a free daily e-mail newsletter containing stock market results. You want to divert the incoming messages to the Holt Report folder. As you examine the Holt messages, you see that every one contains *GEOHOLT <Geoholt@cris.com>* in the From line. This is good text to use for writing your rule.

It's simple to create rules. Go to the Tools menu, and select Inbox Assistant. You'll see the Inbox Assistant dialog box. Click Add, and you'll see the Properties dialog box (Figure 13-15). Type the criteria you want to match in one of the boxes, and choose the action that you'd like Outlook Express to perform. When you're finished, click OK.

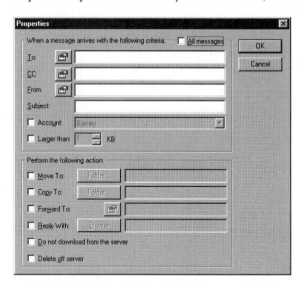

Figure 13-15

Create an Inbox Assistant rule to help you tame your incoming e-mail.

Prioritizing Rules

If you write several rules, it's possible that more than one will apply to a given incoming message. For this reason, you can prioritize your rules. To change a rule's priority, highlight the rule in the Inbox Assistant dialog box and click Move Up or Move Down to move the rule in the list.

13

To illustrate how prioritization solves problems for you, consider this example. Suppose your friend Marvin likes to kid around with silly subject lines such as "Get a life," or "Make money fast." You like Marvin's messages, but you can do without the other "Make money fast" messages, which persistently advertise some kind of Ponzi scheme. So you write a rule that sends Marvin's letters to the Marvin folder, and another rule that sends any message with "Make money fast" to the Deleted Items folder. To make sure Marvin's messages don't get trashed, even if they contain "Make money fast," you place the Marvin rule higher in the priority list.

Printing and Saving Messages

You can print or save a message at any time. To print a message, select the message in the message list, go to the File menu, and select Print (or press Ctrl + P) to see the Print dialog box. From there, you can choose multiple copies, collation options, and print range options. When you've finished selecting your options, click OK.

Outlook Express enables you to save messages to a disk, but there's really no need to do so unless it's something extremely important. Your incoming messages are saved in your Inbox or in your folders, unless you deliberately delete them. (And even then, they're routed to the Deleted Items folder, where you can recover them later.)

Mailing Lists

Mailing lists are one of the most rewarding aspects of the Internet. Imagine being able to find a few dozen or a few hundred people who all share your interest—whether it's collecting Barbie dolls or analyzing the human genome—and entering into daily discussion and resource-sharing with those people. There are thousands of mailing lists on every conceivable subject; many of them are publicly accessible, which means you can join, even if you aren't an expert in a field.

Sounds great, doesn't it? I'm always on three or four mailing lists. But they come at a price. You get many more e-mail messages than you can easily cope with. If you're really interested in a given topic, however, it's worth the effort to plow through dozens of e-mail messages each day.

Before joining a mailing list, you should know what to expect. It isn't all sweetness and light.

⊕ Every once in a while, somebody posts a message that really pushes people's buttons, and you get a regrettable phenomenon called a *flame war*—lots of public name-calling and unpleasantness. Until cooler heads prevail, the mailing list will generate more heat than you might be comfortable with.

⊕ People forget how to unsubscribe—there's a procedure you're supposed to follow—so they post pathetic messages with subjects such as, "Will somebody PLEASE tell me how to get off this list?" Your mailbox is cluttered enough without this.

⊕ Personal and important messages to you alone can get lost amid the dozens or hundreds of messages from lists. Join one mailing list, or maybe two, but take care not to join too many.

Finding a Mailing List in Your Area of Interest

Thanks to the volunteer efforts of Stephanie da Silva, you can access a fantastic index of Internet mailing lists on the World Wide Web. The address is www.neosoft.com/internet/paml/. You'll see the Publicly Accessible Mailing Lists page (Figure 13-16). If you click the Index link, you'll find that you can browse by name or by subject.

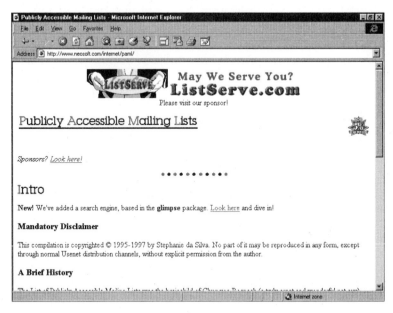

Figure 13-16

The Publicly Accessible Mailing Lists page offers a terrific index of Internet mailing lists.

13

So that mailing list messages don't get in the way of your personal mail, create a folder for the mailing list and write rules to divert messages from the list to this folder. By all means, write a rule that sends messages containing *unsubscribe* to the Deleted Items folder; you'll find it's common for people to forget how to unsubscribe to the list, and you'll get lots of these very annoying messages.

Subscribing to a Mailing List

After you locate information about a mailing list that looks good, try subscribing to it. Please be sure to follow the directions carefully. For example, here are the directions for subscribing to the Wine mailing list, a publicly accessible mailing list for people who appreciate fine wines:

1. Create a new e-mail message addressed to <u>Majordomo@ee.pdx.edu</u>.

2. Leave the Subject box blank.

3. Type *subscribe wine* in the body of the message.

4. Send the message.

You'll soon receive a confirmation plus information about the mailing list. This information includes directions for unsubscribing to the list. *Create a folder named Unsubscribe Info, and save this message—then you can retrieve it if you decide to unsubscribe.*

NOTE These subscribing instructions are good for the Wine mailing list, but they won't necessarily work for other mailing lists. To subscribe to a specific mailing list, you need specific information regarding where to send your e-mail request and what to include in the letter.

Replying to Mailing List Messages

Messages from the mailing list appear like any other e-mail messages; they simply show up in your Inbox. When you reply to a specific message, it goes to the person who created it—not to the list. That's as it should be, because you don't want to post something to the entire list unless you really have something worth saying.

Please don't post *me too* messages or anything else that you'd find irritating if it showed up in your own mailbox.

Unsubscribing to a Mailing List

There's a procedure for unsubscribing to a mailing list, similar to the one you used to subscribe in the first place. After you subscribe, you'll receive an automatic message from the server detailing how to unsubscribe. *Create a folder named Unsubscribe Info, and save this message; that way you'll know how to get off the mailing list later.*

For example, here's the procedure for unsubscribing to the Wine mailing list:

1. Create a new e-mail message addressed to <u>Majordomo@ee.pdx.edu</u>.

2. Leave the Subject box blank.

3. Type *unsubscribe wine* in the body of the message.

4. Send the message.

Unfortunately, it seems that few people save unsubscribe information, so they try to post the unsubscribe message to the mailing list itself. But the unsubscribe message needs to be sent to the server, not to the mailing list, and the server has a different address. The messages these people send don't work, their mailboxes continue to be flooded with unwanted messages, and their messages get increasingly anxious and pathetic-sounding. I know I've said it before, but *please* don't do this. It's really irritating and unfair to people using the mailing list.

From Here

- Learn how to send and receive encrypted e-mail in the next chapter, so you can protect your privacy while using the Internet.

- Explore Outlook Express's news capabilities in Chapter 15.

13

14 Keep It Secret

If you're sending an e-mail message, there's something you should know: That message is about as confidential as an advertisement pasted to the interior wall of a New York City subway. That's right—anyone can read it. It is disturbing that our legal system hasn't kept pace with technology. The privacy protections for first-class correspondence that we've enjoyed for hundreds of years aren't being extended to electronic communication, despite the fact that an estimated 100 million people now prefer to send e-mail messages rather than traditional letters. If you're using the Internet for any sort of personal or business correspondence that you'd prefer to keep away from prying eyes, you'll be wise to explore the powerful new tools for ensuring the confidentiality of your correspondence available in Microsoft Outlook Express.

Outlook Express includes the security features that e-mail users need: digital IDs and encryption. Using a digital ID, you can sign your message so that recipients will be able to verify that it's really from you. Using encryption, you can scramble your message so that nobody except the intended recipient can read it. Taken together, these two measures provide the privacy and confidentiality that e-mail needs to succeed as a public communications medium. You can't do business over the Internet if confidential messages can be intercepted and read by anyone along the way.

Until recently, secure e-mail was very difficult to use; in practice, its use was restricted to the hacker community. Even worse, there were no security standards, which meant that you couldn't exchange secure e-mail with somebody unless that person was using the same e-mail program you were using. Thanks to the new S/MIME protocol, the standards are now in place for the rapid development of secure e-mail. Outlook Express supports this protocol, which means you can exchange secure e-mail with anyone who uses an S/MIME-compatible e-mail program. And as you'll learn in this chapter, Outlook Express has made secure e-mail easy to use.

HELP

But I have nothing to hide!

You don't have to be involved in a multimillion dollar deal for a Bermuda property or be an inventor with a hot new product to have good reason to keep your e-mail secret. No matter what you're talking about, the simple fact of the matter is this: It's nobody's business except the person to whom you're sending your message. How would you like it if, late at night, the staff at your friendly local Internet service provider displayed your e-mail messages and read them out loud, just for a laugh? Technically, it's possible. And from what I've heard from friends who have worked at ISPs, it happens all the time. The answer's simple: seal the envelope.

Introducing S/MIME

In order for electronic mail security to function on the Internet, a standard is needed so that users of different e-mail programs can communicate with each other. In 1996, the Internet Engineering Task Force (IETF) created the S/MIME standard, which defines a comprehensive system for e-mail security. (S/MIME is short for Secure Multipurpose Internet Mail Extensions.)

As long as you're using an e-mail program that conforms to the S/MIME protocol, you can send and receive secure e-mail. You have the following capabilities:

PART
II

- 🌐 You can attach a digital signature (also called a digital ID) to your outgoing messages, so the recipient can verify that the message is really from you and not a forgery.

- 🌐 You can receive mail with digital signatures, so you can verify that the message you've received is really from the person who ostensibly sent it and not an imposter or a forger.

- 🌐 You can send encrypted e-mail that no one can read except the intended recipient.

- 🌐 You can decode and read encrypted messages sent to you.

Using Secure E-Mail

To use secure e-mail, you need a public key, a private key, and a digital ID. The following sections explain how these components work together to ensure your privacy when corresponding via the Internet.

Your Digital Signature

To get going with secure e-mail, you need to obtain a digital ID that supports S/MIME. You must obtain your digital ID from a certificate authority (CA), such as VeriSign; once you've obtained this, Outlook Express will generate your public key and private key.

When somebody receives a message with your digital signature attached, they know that the message is really from you and that it hasn't been tampered with while en route.

Your Public Key

When you add your digital signature to an e-mail message, you are automatically including your public key. Your public key is an encryption formula that people can use to scramble the messages they send you; in other words, it's an encoding key. Once the message has been encrypted with your public key, no one can read it unless he or she holds the private key—and that's something only you possess.

It's to your advantage to make your public key as widely available as possible. That's why you should always digitally sign your outgoing messages (even if you don't encrypt them). Having received your message with your digital key attached, recipients will also possess your public key, and they will be able to use this key to send encrypted mail to you.

14

Your Private Key

Your private key resides on your computer, where you keep it safe by means of password protection. This key enables you to unscramble messages that people have sent to you. Obviously, you don't want to make your private key available to anyone else. If you do, your mail is no longer secure.

HELP

I'm on the road. How can I send secure e-mail?

You can't, unless you've obtained a separate digital ID for the notebook you're using. This is a major shortcoming of secure e-mail at present. In the future, you'll have a smart card that contains your digital ID, and you'll be able to slip this into any computer you use. The card will establish your identity and enable you to send and receive secure e-mail from any computer. But that's a few years off. If you want to use secure e-mail today, you must do so by using the computer on which you installed your digital ID.

Obtaining a Digital ID

To obtain a digital ID for your use, use Internet Explorer to access the Microsoft Outlook Express Digital ID page (<u>www.microsoft.com/ie/ie40/oe/ certpage.htm</u>). Thanks to a special arrangement between Microsoft and VeriSign, you can obtain a free digital ID that's good for six months. Look for the VeriSign link, and click it to begin the enrollment process.

1. Type your first name, middle initial, and last name in the appropriate boxes. Don't add a period after the middle initial.

2. Type your e-mail address in the Email Address box. Check your typing carefully; if the address isn't correct, you won't receive your digital ID.

3. The next item is the challenge phrase. This is a word or a phrase that you can use to ask VeriSign to revoke your digital ID. You don't want anyone else to be able to invalidate your ID, so choose your challenge phrase carefully, type it in the Challenge Phrase box, and be sure to remember it.

4. Some Web sites offer automatic registration if you have a digital ID. If you want to take advantage of this feature, you can supply additional information (such as your country, date of birth, ZIP or postal code, and gender), but this is optional.

PART
II

5. At the bottom of the page, click Next.

6. The next page offers you the choice between a paid digital ID or a trial digital ID that's good for six months. If you choose to pay, enter your credit card and address information.

7. Read through the subscriber agreement, and then click Accept. On the next page, click Submit to send your request to VeriSign.

8. The Credentials Enrollment Wizard appears (Figure 14-1). Read the opening page, and then click Next.

9. If you have more than one cryptographic provider installed in your computer, select one and click Next.

10. Type a name for your new private key. The wizard suggests MyPrivateKey, but you can select any name. Click Finish.

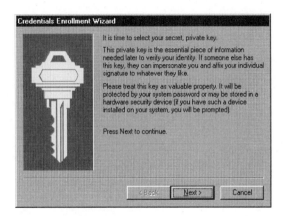

Figure 14-1

The Credentials Enrollment Wizard creates your private key and stores it in your computer.

VeriSign will send an e-mail message to the address you entered in Step 2. In a few minutes, check the Inbox folder in Outlook Express.

1. When the VeriSign message arrives, open it and look for the Next button. Click the button to connect to VeriSign again. You'll see your new digital ID.

2. Below the digital ID, click the Install button. You'll see a tiny message box that says *Digital ID successfully registered.*

3. Click OK to close the message box.

14

Configuring Outlook Express to Use Your Digital ID

Once you've obtained your digital ID and installed it on your system, you need to configure Outlook Express to use this digital ID for outgoing secure messages. To do so, follow these steps:

1. From the Tools menu in Outlook Express, choose Accounts.

2. Click the Mail tab.

3. Click your e-mail account.

4. Click Properties. You'll see the properties page for your mail account.

5. Click Security. You'll see the Security page (Figure 14-2).

6. Click Use A Digital ID When Sending Secure Messages.

7. Click the Digital ID button.

8. Choose your digital ID from the list, and click OK.

9. Click OK, and then click Close.

Now you can send digitally signed and encrypted messages with Outlook Express.

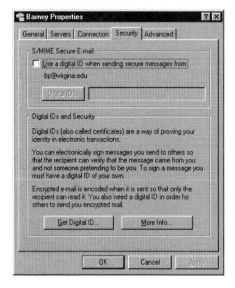

Figure 14-2

On the Security page, you instruct Outlook Express to use your digital ID.

Sending a Digitally Signed Message

After you've obtained the digital ID, it's simple to add it to your messages.

1. Compose your message with Outlook Express.

2. On the toolbar, select Digitally Sign Message. (Or you can choose Tools on the menu bar, and select Digitally Sign.) You'll see a digital ID icon in the message header area.

3. Click Send to send your message.

If you would like to digitally sign all outgoing messages, select Tools on the menu bar and choose Options. Select the Security tab. In the Security page, locate the Secure Mail area and enable Digitally Sign All Outgoing Messages. Click OK to confirm your choice.

Adding a Digital ID to the Address Book

To send an encrypted message, you need your correspondent's digital ID. What's more, the digital ID must be present in your correspondent's Address Book entry. Once you've received your correspondent's digital ID, add it to your Address Book by following these steps:

1. Open the digitally signed message.

2. From the File menu, choose Properties.

3. Select the Security tab. You'll see the security information for this message (Figure 14-3).

4. Select Add Digital ID To Address Book.

5. Click OK.

After you add a digital ID to a correspondent's Address Book card, you'll see a tiny red ribbon on the card icon.

NOTE Sometimes people make their digital IDs available for downloading from their home pages or other sources. If you've downloaded somebody's digital ID in the form of a file, you can add it to your Address Book by following this procedure: Display the individual's Address Book card (or, if necessary, create one), and then choose Digital IDs. Click Import, locate the digital ID file, and click OK.

14

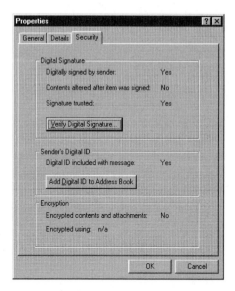

Figure 14-3

Security information for a message appears in the message's Properties dialog box.

Changing the Trust Status of a Digital ID

Is every digital ID trustworthy? In general, yes, as long as the ID has been signed by a recognized certificate authority. But there are other types of digital IDs that are issued by individuals themselves. If you receive a message with such an ID, you'll know that the message hasn't been tampered with, but you don't know whether the message is really from the individual who claims to have sent it. That's the role that's performed by the CA. If there's no CA, then there's no independent corroboration of the individual's identity.

Finding Out Who Signed the Digital ID

To find out whether an individual's digital ID was issued by a CA, select the individual's Address Book entry. From the File menu, choose Properties. Click the Digital IDs tab. In the Digital IDs area, select the individual's e-mail address, and then select the digital ID that you're curious about. Choose Properties. You'll see the Certificate Properties dialog box for this digital ID (Figure 14-4). If the digital ID was signed by a CA, you'll see the CA's name.

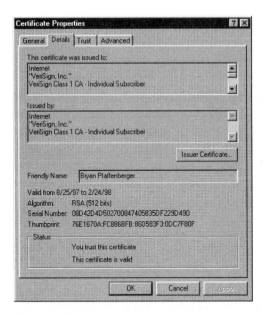

Figure 14-4

You can determine who signed a digital ID by looking at its properties.

Changing the Trust Level

By default, Outlook Express trusts a digital ID if it's been signed by an issuer, which might be a problem if the issuer isn't trustworthy. For digital IDs that individuals issue to themselves, you might want to change the trust level. This way, you'll see a warning whenever you use this digital ID.

1. In the Address Book, select the individual's Address Book entry.

2. From the File menu, choose Properties.

3. Select Digital IDs, and choose the digital ID whose trust level you want to change. Click Properties.

4. Choose Trust tab, and then select one of the following options:

   Inherit trust from issuer. This is the default option. It trusts any signed ID, even if the sender signed it.

   Explicitly trust this certificate. For digital IDs from people you know very well, you can choose this option.

   Explicitly distrust this certificate. Choose this option when you do not trust the digital ID for some reason. This option is better than deleting the ID, because you'll see a warning message when you use it to remind yourself that you have previously expressed misgivings about the ID.

14

Sending and Receiving Encrypted Messages

With Outlook Express, sending encrypted messages is all but automatic. (Be sure the recipient's digital ID is in your Address Book.) To send an encrypted message, click the Encrypt Message button on the New Message window's toolbar.

Receiving encrypted messages is even simpler. The message arrives in your mailbox with a distinctive icon, telling you just what's included—a digital signature, encryption, or both. If the message is signed, you'll know that it's very probably from the person who claims to have sent it. What's more, you'll also know that the message hasn't been altered by somebody during its transmission. If it's encrypted, you'll know that it hasn't been read en route. If it's both signed and encrypted, you have all these measures of confidence that this message is both authentic and confidential.

Here's a quick rundown of the icons you'll see next to signed or encrypted messages. (Note that some icons have more than one possible message.)

Icon	Meaning
	This message is digitally signed, and you haven't read it.
	This message is encrypted, and you haven't read it.
	This message is signed and encrypted, and you haven't read it.
	This message is digitally signed, and you've read it.
	This message is encrypted, and you've read it.
	This message is encrypted and signed, and you've read it.
	There's something wrong with this unread message's signature.
	There's something wrong with this unread message's encryption.
	There's something wrong with both the signature and the encryption in this unread message.
	There's something wrong with this read message's signature.
	There's something wrong with this read message's encryption.
	There's something wrong with both the encryption and the signature of this read message.

PART

II

It says there's something wrong with this message!

So one of your messages has an icon with a warning signal. That's not a good sign. If the message was digitally signed, the warning signal probably indicates that the message was altered in some way while it was en route. If the message was encrypted, the warning signal similarly indicates that the message isn't quite right and might have been damaged or altered. If you see a warning signal of any kind, send a message back to the message's sender, requesting that it be sent again. Most likely, the problem is due to some kind of transmission glitch and won't recur.

From Here

You've mastered all the essentials of electronic mail. Using the Outlook Express skills you've already learned, take a look at Usenet, the subject of the next chapter. Even if you've never used Usenet before, you'll find that Outlook Express makes it easy.

14

15

Join the Fray

Microsoft Outlook Express isn't just an e-mail program. It also enables you to access Usenet newsgroups—using the Outlook Express skills you've already learned. Outlook Express handles your mail and news messages using the same consistent user interface; for instance, the newsgroups to which you've subscribed appear as folders, exactly like your mail folders. Since you've already learned Outlook Express, you'll be able to send and receive Usenet messages in short order. This chapter explains how Outlook Express enables you to use newsgroups, beginning with an introduction to Usenet and an explanation of its peculiarities.

Introducing Usenet

Wide-open, freewheeling, invaluable, shocking. These adjectives spring to mind when Usenet pops up on your screen, and for good reason. For those with access to a computer, Usenet is probably the most open and democratic communication medium ever devised. All kinds of people contribute all kinds of material to Usenet, and its content runs the gamut from garbage to gold.

What Is Usenet?

Imagine a "letters to the editor" page, like the one in your local newspaper. Some of the letters are wise and worth reading, some are amusing, and some are loaded with false or misleading information. Now imagine that every letter to the editor written to every newspaper in North America was automatically reproduced so that every letter appeared in all the newspapers. The daily edition of the newspaper would be roughly 80,000 pages, requiring a serious truck to deliver it to your house. Happily for the trees of this world, Usenet is similar in scope but is distributed electronically.

Don't worry that you'll have to wade through hundreds of thousands of messages to find the ones in which you're interested. Usenet is topically divided into thousands of *newsgroups,* each with its own distinctive name and topical coverage. Just about every conceivable subject is represented, and I can guarantee that there are topics you've never dreamed of.

Is Usenet a Waste of Time?

Is Usenet just so much fluff, the hue and cry of people with nothing better to do than to try to push their ill-considered opinions into other people's faces?

Many people come to this conclusion after a brief Usenet session. There's a lot of hot air on Usenet, to be sure. What's worse, though, is that the network is susceptible to *spamming*—a practice in which inappropriate messages, including self-serving advertisements, are posted to hundreds or even thousands of newsgroups that have nothing to do with the messages' content.

Usenet is also bedeviled by messages from the maturity-impaired, who think they're being cute by posting *trolls* (obviously false statements that are planted in the hope that people will rise to the bait, making fools of themselves in the trollers' eyes), and *flame bait* (deliberately provocative messages that are posted in the hope of starting a *flame war*). There's another recent trend: Usenet has become a happy hunting ground for

PART

260

pyramid scammers and con artists of all stripes, including hucksters pushing penny stocks and perverts peddling pornography.

Unfortunately, so many people abuse Usenet that many formerly interesting newsgroups aren't worth reading anymore. Examples include *alt.internet.media-coverage,* which, at one time, contained intelligent and interesting commentary on the way the media covers the Internet.

Spams, scams, and just plain nonsense aside, there are Usenet jewels, too. The trick is to stay away from anything that sounds controversial; today's Usenet just doesn't handle controversy well. But if there's a Usenet newsgroup that's topically related to a hobby or professional interest of yours, chances are that you'll find Usenet close to indispensable.

In general, the technically oriented newsgroups (especially those in the *comp* hierarchy discussed below) are of the greatest value; there's a real spirit of information exchange and resource sharing. Also of generally high quality are the *moderated newsgroups,* in which every message is submitted to a human moderator, who inspects each one to make sure that it's related to the newsgroup's topic.

NOTE

Please do not post messages to any Usenet newsgroup until you have fully understood the basics of Usenet *netiquette,* discussed later in this chapter. Netiquette isn't mysterious; it's just good manners. Be polite, think of other people's feelings, give credit where credit is due, and don't post anything when you're in the heat of anger. In particular, do not post requests for information that is already in the group's Frequently Asked Questions (FAQ) document.

What Is a Newsgroup?

With more than 7 million people using Usenet on a regular basis and contributing some 80,000 pages of text, sound, graphics, and computer programs daily, it's obvious that some kind of organization is needed to make all this material accessible. This organization is provided by the hierarchical system of newsgroup names.

Here's how this system works. Every newsgroup is part of a *top-level hierarchy,* such as *sci, soc,* or *talk.* The top-level hierarchy indicates the overall topic of the newsgroup; for example, *soc* newsgroups cover the social sciences, social issues, and socializing. Top-level hierarchies fall into three general categories.

15

- **The standard newsgroups.** Every Usenet site is expected to carry these newsgroups. (Examples: *comp, misc, news, rec, sci, soc,* and *talk.*)
- **The alternative newsgroups.** These are optional; Usenet sites don't have to carry these newsgroups, but most do. (Examples: *alt, bionet, biz, clari, K12,* and *relcom.*)
- **Local newsgroups.** These newsgroups are set up to benefit a local community, a university, or an organization, and they are sometimes available to outsiders.

The following is an overview of the general subject matter of the most common newsgroup hierarchies.

Name	Subject area
alt	Newsgroups that anyone can create, on any subject
biz	Business news, marketing, advertising
comp	Computers and computer applications
misc	Stuff that doesn't fit in the other categories
news	Usenet itself
rec	Hobbies and sports
sci	The sciences
soc	Social issues and socializing
talk	Discussion of social issues

Every newsgroup has at least one other part to its name besides the top-level hierarchy, with the parts separated by dots: *misc.test, comp.risks.* This begins the process of narrowing group content.

Many newsgroups have additional parts to their names, which enable an even finer-grained topical focus: *alt.fan.tolkien, alt.fan.woody-allen.*

What Is in a Newsgroup?

When you select a newsgroup to read, you'll see a list of the messages and follow-up messages that people have contributed to that newsgroup. Here's what these terms mean:

- **Message.** Also called a *post,* this is a *message* on a new subject.
- **Follow-up message.** Also called a *follow-up post,* this is a message that someone has contributed in response to someone else's message. Some messages never receive any commentary; others

receive many follow-up messages. When there are many follow-up messages on a particular subject, a *thread* of discussion emerges, rather like a conversation. A good newsgroup reader program enables you to follow such a thread.

🌐 **Binaries.** You can find graphics, videos, sounds, and computer programs on Usenet. Because Usenet can handle only ASCII text, they're coded in a special way that eliminates all but the standard ASCII characters. The resulting files are so large that they're often split into multipart posts. To download and use these files, called *binaries,* your newsreader must decode them. Outlook Express can decode both single- and multipart binaries, as you'll learn later in this chapter.

NOTE

Although you'll find computer programs on Usenet, it's not a good idea to download and run one—at least, not without checking it thoroughly for viruses. It's safe to download graphics and videos (your computer can't get a virus from these), but note that more than a few newsgroups contain pornography, including illegal child pornography and other material that might not be legal in your area.

Introducing Outlook Express's News Features

This section introduces Outlook Express's Usenet capabilities, beginning with an explanation of how to configure the program. You'll also learn how to download the current newsgroup list from the news server and what the news-specific toolbar buttons do.

Getting the Information You Need

To configure Outlook Express to access your news server, you'll need the following information from your Internet service provider:

🌐 The name of the computer that runs the news server. This server uses Network News Transfer Protocol (NNTP), which is analogous to Hypertext Transfer Protocol (HTTP).

🌐 Whether or not you need to log on to gain access to the news server. If so, you'll need to know the user name and password you should use.

15

Configuring Outlook Express

To configure Outlook Express to access your ISP's news server, go to Tools on the menu bar and choose Accounts. Select Add, and choose News from the pop-up menu. You'll see the Internet Connection Wizard, which is very much like the one you used to configure your e-mail account. Here's how to fill out the various pages you'll see.

1. On the Your Name page, type your name the way you'd like it to appear in the From field of the outgoing message. Think twice about supplying your real name here. If you're using serious technical newsgroups, it's probably OK. But if you plan to post to some of the more wide-open alt newsgroups, some degree of anonymity is advisable. However, remember that using a pseudonym does not prevent somebody from figuring out that you sent a message, so don't make the mistake of thinking that the pseudonym gives you full anonymity.

2. Click Next. On the Internet News E-Mail Address page, type your e-mail address (Figure 15-1).

   Spammers—e-mail junk mailers—get addresses by means of automated programs that scan Usenet for e-mail addresses. To prevent these programs from collecting your address, consider modifying your address so that it contains a word or phrase (such as "no spam, thank you") in the midst of the address. Savvy Usenet users will see how to reconstruct your e-mail address, but this trick will foil the spammers.

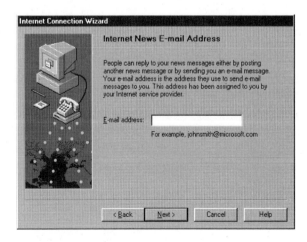

Figure 15-1

Enter your e-mail address on this page—but watch out for spammers.

3. Click Next. You'll see the Internet News Server Name page (Figure 15-2). Carefully type the name of your news server. (Your ISP might call this an NNTP server.) If your news server needs a separate user name and password, click My News Server Requires Me To Log On, click Next, and enter the information requested by the Internet News Server Logon page.

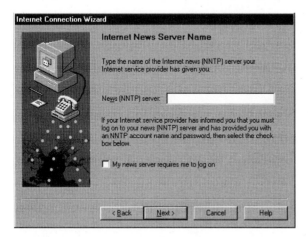

Figure 15-2

Your Internet service provider can give you the name of your news server.

4. Click Next. You'll see the Friendly Name page. This page enables you to give your Usenet account a more readable name than the computer name, but this is optional.

5. Click Next. You'll see the Choose Connection Type page. Choose the type of connection you are planning to use (phone line, local area network, or manual connection).

6. Click Next, and then click Finish. You'll see the new account in the Internet Accounts dialog box. Click Close to return to Outlook Express.

Just as you can create more than one mail account, you can also access more than one Usenet server. To create another news account, repeat the steps above and provide the information concerning the additional server.

15

Using the Newsgroups Window

After you finish creating your account, you'll see a dialog box asking whether you would like to download the newsgroup list. Click Yes. This could take a few minutes. When it's done, you'll see the Newsgroups window (Figure 15-3). Using this window, you can do the following:

- **Search for newsgroups of interest to you.** If you type a word next to Display Newsgroups Which Contain, Outlook Express reduces the lengthy newsgroup list to only those newsgroups that contain this word.

- **Subscribe to newsgroups.** When you subscribe to a newsgroup, you see the newsgroup's name when you click the Subscribed tab. Subscribing to a newsgroup has no effect beyond your own computer; it's simply a way of reducing the huge list of newsgroups to a more manageable size.

- **View a list of new newsgroups.** The next time you log on, there might be new newsgroups. To see a list of new groups, select the New tab.

- **Go to a newsgroup after selecting it from the list.** To read the news in a newsgroup, select it and click Go To.

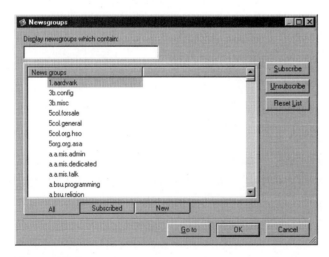

Figure 15-3

The Newsgroups window is your portal to Usenet.

PART
II

In the Display Newsgroups box, try typing the first few letters of a word describing a subject that interests you, such as Microsoft, Internet, hiking, games, or sailing. Select a newsgroup that looks interesting, and click Go To.

Using the News Toolbar

When you've selected a news account, Outlook Express looks just like it does when you're reading mail—with one exception. There's a slightly different toolbar. In the folder bar, click your newsgroup account. You'll notice that the toolbar changes. Some of the tools are the same, but the new ones are news-specific.

Tool	Action
Compose Message	Displays a blank New Message window, enabling you to write a new message and post it to the newsgroup.
Reply to Group	Creates a reply to the selected message, which you can then post to the currently selected newsgroup.
Reply to Author	Replies to the currently selected message by sending e-mail to the author (does not post a copy to the newsgroup).
Forward Message	Forwards a copy of this message to somebody's e-mail address.
Newsgroups	Displays the Newsgroup window, enabling you to subscribe to newsgroups.
Connect	Connects to the Internet.
Hang Up	Terminates the connection.
Stop	Stops downloading the current message or messages.

15

> ## Netiquette: A Primer
>
> Before you post a message to Usenet, learn proper *netiquette*—Internet etiquette. Seasoned Usenet users expect everyone, including *newbies* (beginners), to follow some basic rules. If you break these rules, you could find yourself on the wrong end of a barrage of irate e-mail.
>
> - Be sure to follow a newsgroup's discussion for at least a few days before you post a message. By doing so, you'll learn the types of topics that are appropriate for discussion. You'll also learn what's on peoples' minds, how you can contribute meaningfully, and how to avoid repeating discussions that have been exhausted.
>
> - If the group has a FAQ (list of answers to frequently asked questions), by all means obtain it and read it. You'll find answers to the questions that newbies typically ask, and you're expected to know them. Newsgroup veterans will be annoyed if you ask the same question by posting a message to the group.
>
> - Before posting a reply message to the newsgroup, consider carefully whether your response is really of interest to everyone. If a person asked a question for specific information, chances are that the reply would interest that person and few others. In such a situation, it's best to reply by e-mail. Your reply goes to the person who posted the original message, not to the group.
>
> - Don't post messages that extensively quote somebody's opinion or request, adding only the words "Me too."

Reading the News

Usenet is perhaps the most ephemeral communications system ever invented, next to talk radio. With few exceptions, Usenet newsgroups are not archived. Messages don't linger long, either. At most servers, they stick around for only a day or two before being deleted to make room for the avalanche of new postings. That's why they call it *news*—there's very little on Usenet that can be termed *old*.

When you log on to Usenet and choose a newsgroup, Outlook Express downloads the messages currently found on the server. Chances are you'll see anywhere from a few dozen to a few hundred messages.

When you select a message in the message list, you'll see the text of the message in the preview pane (Figure 15-4). At the top of the preview pane, you see basic information about the message, such as who it's from and the subject.

To view the next message down in the list, click it. (You can also press Ctrl + >, press Alt + left arrow, or go to the View menu and select Next and then Next Message.)

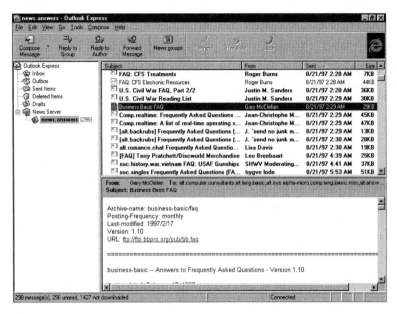

Figure 15-4

Reading newsgroup messages is as easy as reading your e-mail.

To view the previous message in the list, click it. (You can also press Ctrl + <, press Alt + right arrow, or go to the View menu and select Next and then Previous Message.)

Understanding Threading

Like all good Usenet newsreaders, Outlook Express threads messages; that is, messages with the same subject are grouped together. If there's more than one message that pertains to a given subject, you'll see a plus sign next to the message title. If you click the plus sign, all the messages that pertain to this subject will appear.

15

Hey! I can't read this message!

If you encounter a message that seems to be complete gibberish, it's possible that it has been encrypted using the simple ROT-13 scheme, which rotates all characters 13 letters forward in the alphabet. In a more genteel day (that is, five years ago), Usenet posters would sometimes employ this simple encryption technique to prevent innocent minds from coming face-to-face with something outrageous. Should you encounter a ROT-13–encoded message, you can decode it promptly by choosing Unscramble (ROT 13) from the Edit menu.

Frankly, I haven't seen a ROT-13 message since the early 1990s. If you run across what appears to be a ROT-13 message, chances are that it's a binary graphics file that you've downloaded by mistake. It seems the days are long gone when anyone was concerned about the impact a Usenet post might have on its audience. In unwitting testimony to the times, Outlook Express drives this point home by providing facilities for *decoding* ROT-13, but—amazingly—none for *encoding* your outgoing messages.

Unlike some newsreaders that simply group messages by subject, Outlook Express uses true threading. The grouped messages actually refer to each other, and they're listed in the correct order: the third message in a thread is a reply to the second one, and so on.

By default, threads are collapsed. If you would like Outlook Express to expand threads automatically, go to the Tools menu, select Options, click Read, and select Automatically Expand Conversation Threads.

Marking Messages and Threads as Read or Unread

Unread messages appear in bold. When you select a message so that its text appears in the preview pane, or if you double-click a message so that its text appears in the message window, Outlook Express marks the message as read. The message no longer appears in bold and the icon changes.

When a message is opened, by default, Outlook Express allows you five seconds to preview it before marking the message as read. To increase the time you have to look at a message, go to the Tools menu, select Options, and click the Read tab. Increase the time interval in the option called Message Is Read After Being Previewed For x Seconds. Click OK to confirm.

Outlook Express offers several options for managing the volume of messages you can expect from most newsgroups.

○ Hide previously read messages the next time you log on. Go to the View menu, and select Current View. From the submenu, select Unread Messages. The next time you log on, you will see both old and new unread messages.

○ See only new messages the next time you log on. Suppose you didn't read all the messages received, but you want to skip the unread ones and pick up only new messages the next time you log on. You have two options. To mark just the currently selected messages as unread, go to the Edit menu and select Mark As Read (or press Ctrl + Q). To mark the entire collection of messages as unread, go to the Edit menu and choose Mark All As Read (or press Ctrl + T).

○ Mark all messages as read every time you leave any newsgroup. Go to the Tools menu, select Options, and choose the Read tab. Click Mark All Messages As Read When Exiting A Newsgroup. This setting (combined with Unread Messages from the View menu) means any time you log on to any newsgroup, you will see only new messages.

You can override any of these settings at any time and view all messages. To do so, go to the View menu, select Current View, and choose All Messages. (Think of this option as your Refresh button.)

Suppose you have set up Outlook Express to hide read messages and now you've run across a really great message that you don't have time to read. But you've looked at it for a few seconds, and it has been marked as read. Must this message be hidden the next time you log on? No. To mark an individual message as unread, select the message, go to the Edit menu, and choose Mark As Unread.

Using the Message Window

One way to read messages is to use the main Outlook Express window, with its message list and preview pane. You can also read messages in the message window simply by double-clicking the message (Figure 15-5).

15

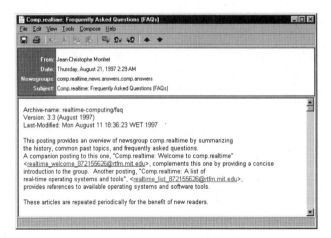

Figure 15-5

You can read messages in the message window.

The message window's toolbar includes convenient tools for your reading. Left to right, they include Save This Message, Print, Undo, Cut, Copy, Paste, Reply To Group, Reply To Author, Forward, Previous, and Next. The Previous and Next buttons give you an easy way of going through the messages in your list.

Using the Pop-Up Menu

If you click the right mouse button with the pointer positioned within the message list, you'll see the pop-up menu shown in Figure 15-6. This chapter hasn't covered all these options yet, so for now, just remember that this pop-up menu is a convenient way to choose some of the most frequently used options in Outlook Express.

Figure 15-6

Right-click in the message list to display this useful menu.

Reading a Different Newsgroup

If you're done reading a newsgroup, it's easy to switch to a different one. To read one of your subscribed newsgroups, simply choose a newsgroup in the folder bar. To read an unsubscribed newsgroup, select Newsgroups. Make your choice from the newsgroups listed, and click Go To.

Adding Your Two Cents' Worth

After reading a Usenet newsgroup for a while, you will doubtless feel the urge to post something. You can send a message in three ways:

- **By replying via e-mail to the message's author.** This is the best way to respond if you have a specific comment or an answer to the author's question, and this information wouldn't be of interest to many people.

- **By posting a reply to the newsgroup.** Do this only if you think that what you have to say would be of interest to many people, not just the author of the message to which you're replying.

- **By posting a new message.** Although valid reasons exist to post messages on a new subject, you should do so only after you fully understand the mission of the newsgroup to which you're posting.

HELP

This search service has a record of everything I've posted—even the stuff to alt.binaries.pictures.erotica.hamsters.duct-tape!

That's right. You need to understand something. When you post a message to Usenet, you're *publishing* your words and whatever else you include in your post— you're making it *public*. Several search services, including AltaVista and Deja News, enable anyone to sit down and put together a portrait of everything you've posted, going back months or even years.

It bears repeating: Don't post *anything* to Usenet that you wouldn't want to see on your boss's desk the next morning.

Understanding the New Message Window

Whether you're replying to a posted message or composing a new message, you'll use the New Message window to address, write, and edit your message (Figure 15-7). The New Message window has five basic parts.

15

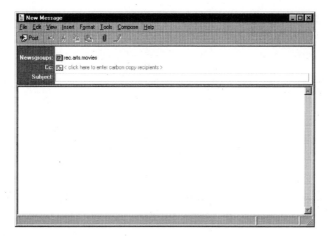

Figure 15-7

The New Message window enables you to create a Usenet message.

- 🌐 **Title Bar.** To reposition the New Message window, drag the title bar. To maximize the window quickly, double-click the title bar. Double-click again to restore the previous size.

- 🌐 **Menu Bar.** Here you'll find all the composition commands, but the most frequently used commands are found on the toolbar.

- 🌐 **Toolbar.** On the toolbar you'll find the following buttons, from left to right: Post Message, Undo, Cut, Copy, Paste, Insert File, and Insert Signature. You'll learn more about what these tools do in later sections.

- 🌐 **Header Information.** Outlook Express automatically supplies the name of the newsgroup. You type a brief subject description.

- 🌐 **Message Body.** Type your information in this section of the window.

Replying by E-Mail

If your reply would be of interest mainly to the author of the original message, reply by e-mail instead of posting a follow-up message. To reply via e-mail, select the message and choose Reply To Author (or go to the Compose menu and select Reply To Author, or press Ctrl + R). You'll see the New Message window.

When the New Message window appears, you'll see that Outlook Express has automatically inserted the author's e-mail address in the To field, and added "Re:" to the message's subject. In addition, the text of the original message is copied, and the insertion point is positioned at the beginning of the message. You're ready to type.

If you think your message is ready (and you've remembered to check your spelling), please read the sidebar, "Don't Post in Anger." If your message passes muster—that is, it wouldn't shock your mother or anger your boss—click Send.

NOTE Outlook Express uses the same Address Book for newsgroups as well as for mail. If you're replying by e-mail, you can capture an e-mail address from the message window and create an Address Book message in exactly the same way you'd do in e-mail. In addition, you can add an address to an outgoing e-mail reply by pasting it from the Address Book. (For more information on creating and using the Address Book, see page 236.)

Don't Post in Anger

You've just finished typing your message. You're ready to click the Send or Post button on the toolbar. Maybe your message is going only to the author. Maybe it's going to the whole newsgroup. Wherever it's going, please hold off just a moment, and do exactly what I say, OK?

If you have composed your message in anger, follow these steps:

1. Move the pointer to the close box, and click the left mouse button. You'll see a message, "Do you want to save changes to this message?"

2. Click No.

Trust me. Now, you're mad at me. Later, you'll thank me.

Creating a Follow-Up Message

You can usefully contribute to Usenet by sending a follow-up message if both the following are true:

1. You actually possess some experience, facts, or ideas that meaningfully contribute to the topic under discussion; *and*

2. What you have to say will prove of interest not just to the original author but to many others who read the newsgroup.

15

If you're satisfied that your prospective follow-up post passes both of these tests, have at it. Highlight the message and choose Reply To Group, or go to the Compose menu and select Reply To Newsgroup, or press Ctrl + G. (Are you posting a follow-up message that's of keen interest to the original author as well as of general interest to the group? Send the message by choosing Reply To Newsgroup And Author from the Compose menu, an option available only on the menu.) You'll see the New Message window, with the newsgroup name, and "Re:" conveniently entered in front of the subject.

As you can see, Outlook Express has copied the entire message. You should edit the quoted text down so that you're including only the part you want to comment on. This step reduces the cost of Usenet transmission—remember, this software will make more than 100,000 copies of your message!—and lightens the cognitive burden on your poor, beleaguered readers.

An ideal follow-up message zeros in on the subject by editing out everything in the original post that's not relevant:

John Smith wrote,

>Where's the best place to find annual reports on the
>Web?

Try Edgar (http://www.sec.gov/). The reports aren't glamorously formatted, but there are thousands of them. Plus, you'll find quarterly reports, which may contain more timely information.

If you genuinely feel that your message is a positive contribution to the group, by all means send it. To do so, simply click the Post button on the toolbar.

 HELP

I just posted my message, but I don't see it in the newsgroup!

Don't panic, and please, don't post your message again. Here's what's going on. The Usenet software has a fairly low priority in the pecking order of the computer systems where it resides—some things are, after all, more important than others. Your message will be processed in due time. In fact, it will be flung hither and yon across the globe. Relax.

Posting a Message on a New Subject

You shouldn't post a new message on a new subject until you've read a newsgroup for a while and grasped the range of acceptable topics.

If you're sure your post is appropriate, select the correct newsgroup, click Compose Message (or go to the Compose menu and select New Message, or press Ctrl + N). In the New Message window, you'll see the name of the newsgroup you selected. You can type more than one newsgroup name, separated by commas, but please don't do so unless you honestly feel that your message pertains perfectly to each newsgroup you list.

Cross-Posting: An Unmitigated Evil?

One reason Usenet's in such bad shape is *cross-posting,* the sending of a message to more than one newsgroup at a time. Unfortunately, Internet abusers try to make money from cross-posting messages to dozens or even thousands of newsgroups, without any regard to fitting their message to the topic at hand. For this reason, cross-posting is viewed with suspicion, especially in the hands of neophytes who don't understand Usenet's traditions and values.

But there's a good argument for a little modest cross-posting now and then. If your message is of genuine interest to more than one newsgroup, then cross-post modestly. No one's going to get irritated at you if you post to two or three obviously germane groups. And there's some storage economy in cross-posting; it takes less disk space to store a message cross-posted to three groups than it does to store three separate messages.

Forwarding a Message

To forward a message to somebody via e-mail, select the message and click Forward Message. (You can also go to the Compose menu and select Forward, press Ctrl + F, or click Forward By Mail on the pop-up menu.) Type an address and add explanatory text, if you like. Click Send to send your message.

If you wish, you can forward the message as an attachment. An attachment is a separate, closed file added to the message you send. As long as your recipient's e-mail program can handle attachments, this file can be opened, read, saved, printed, or stored. This option is best if you're forwarding something really lengthy.

15

To forward a message as an attachment, go to the Compose menu and select Forward As Attachment, or click Forward As Attachment on the pop-up menu. Type an address and add explanatory text, if you like. Click Send to send your message.

Creating a Signature

A signature—a necessity for e-mail—is something of a liability on Usenet. Do you really want your home telephone number to be published in a wide-open public forum, where it could be misused? (You can see for yourself how risky this is. Log on to *misc.invest;* often you'll see posts from people saying, "I just inherited $350,000. Can anyone tell me where I should invest it?" A con artist's dream come true!)

Still, you may want to include some information in a sig. If you're posting professionally to special-interest groups, such as those in the *comp* or *rec* hierarchy, chances are your message is less likely to be scrutinized by crooks or pranksters. You might want to risk including your full name and institutional affiliation.

There's also an old Usenet tradition of including a pithy (and preferably enigmatic or caustic) quote in your sig. One of my favorites, especially after considering recent Congressional legislation concerning the Internet, is from Mark Twain: "Suppose you were an idiot. And suppose you were a member of Congress. But I repeat myself."

To create your sig, go to the Tools menu, select Stationery, and click the Signature button. You'll see the Signature window. In the Text box, type a brief signature, or click File and use the Browse button to locate a text file containing your sig. Also in this panel, you'll find two options regarding where signatures are attached:

- 🌐 **Add this signature to all outgoing messages.** When you open the New Message window to start a new message, Outlook Express will add your sig automatically.

- 🌐 **Don't add signature to Replies and Forwards.** This is a good choice since replies and forwards can get overly lengthy.

Working Offline

For anyone who must pay by the minute for time connected to the Internet, Outlook Express offers an appealing feature. You can download selected messages or entire newsgroups and read the messages offline (after you've logged off).

Marking Messages for Downloading

To mark messages for downloading, hold down the Ctrl key and highlight all the messages you want to download. Then go to the Tools menu and select Mark For Retrieval; from the submenu, choose Mark Message. You can also highlight the threads you want to read. Go to the Tools menu and select Mark For Retrieval; from the submenu, choose Mark Thread. To mark the whole newsgroup for downloading, go to the Tools menu, select Mark For Retrieval, and choose Mark All Messages.

Marking Newsgroups for Downloading

You can also mark entire newsgroups for downloading. Go to the Tools menu, select Mark For Retrieval, and choose This Newsgroup. You'll see the Mark Newsgroups dialog box.

Here you can choose what will be retrieved when Outlook Explorer downloads a newsgroup. First enable the When Downloading This Newsgroup option. Then you can choose between downloading New Headers, New Messages, and All Messages. If you want to browse only the headers of the messages, enable the New Headers option. If only the new messages concern you, select New Messages. If you want to sort and read the entire content of a newsgroup, regardless of whether the information is new, choose the All Messages option.

Choosing Expiration Options

By default, Outlook Express deletes downloaded messages five days after you downloaded them, and it deletes read messages. If you would like to change these options, select Options from the Tools menu and click the Advanced tab. In the Local Message Files area, change the amount of time that Outlook Express will keep stored messages before deleting them.

Cleaning Up Newsgroup Files

If you're downloading entire newsgroups, your newsgroup files can grow to be very large, even if you use the default expiration options. So Outlook Express provides options for compacting, reducing, and erasing these files, options that come in handy if you're low on disk space.

To clean up your newsgroup files, go to the Tools menu, select Options, and click the Advanced tab. Click the Clean Up Now button. You'll see the dialog box shown in Figure 15-8.

15

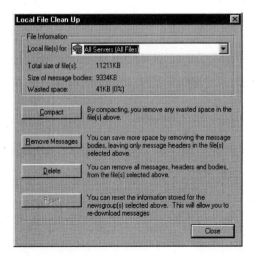

Figure 15-8

Use this dialog box to clean up your newsgroup files.

In the Local Files list box, choose the files you want to work with. (The default option, All Servers (All Files), works with all downloaded files.) To compact your files, click Compact. To remove message bodies but leave the headers, click Remove Messages. (This option isn't recommended because you might not be able to retrieve the message bodies again if they've expired at the server.) If you're sure that you want to get rid of everything you've downloaded, click Delete.

Decoding Binaries

With Outlook Express, you can download and decode binary files, including graphics, sounds, videos, and programs. What's more, you can do so even if they're split up into multiple parts, which is often necessary given the message-length limitations imposed by some portions of the Usenet network.

To decode a binary that's contained in a single message, simply select the message. Outlook Express will automatically download and decode the message, and it will appear as an attachment. Look for the paper clip icon next to the message header in the preview pane or for the shortcut in the message window. To view or execute the binary, click the paper clip or double-click the shortcut.

To decode a multipart binary, select all the parts of the binary, click Tools on the menu bar, and choose Combine And Decode. You'll see a dialog box asking you to place all the parts of the file in the correct order. If necessary, select the parts and change the order, and then click OK. Outlook Express downloads and reconstructs the file. As with a single-part binary, you'll see a paper clip icon or a shortcut. Click the paper clip or double-click the shortcut to view or start the binary.

Searching Usenet

There's a lot of information on Usenet—some bogus, some valuable. But one thing's for sure: You're not going to find it by scrolling manually through thousands of newsgroups, unless you're very lucky.

That's why search services are offering searches of Usenet newsgroups, and they're worth exploring. To access Usenet search services, click the Search button on Internet Explorer's toolbar. Usenet searches are currently offered by AltaVista, Excite, and InfoSeek, among others. If the search service finds a match, you can view the relevant message by clicking the link in the retrieval list.

From Here

You're just getting started in your tour of the Internet. In the next chapter, learn how to use the fabled and funky Internet Relay Chat, with Comic Chat as your none-too-serious guide!

15

16   Chat It Up

Depending on your point of view, Internet Relay Chat (IRC) is either the coolest thing on the Internet or a time-wasting hangout for the maturity impaired. But one thing is certain: You can easily be diverted for a few hours, as you'll quickly discover with Microsoft Chat. Just make sure you don't have any appointments!

In Microsoft Chat, you engage in real-time conversation with other characters in a comic strip, which is generated on the fly as you converse. It may sound sort of silly, but it's better than the text-based interface of most chat systems—and after a while, it grows on you. It's nice to be able to express a range of emotions while you're conversing online. I'm not a huge fan of IRC, but I'm really enjoying Chat; in fact, I've had a heck of a time pulling myself away from the screen to finish this chapter!

NOTE Don't think that the use of comic characters in Microsoft Chat means that this application is for kids—it isn't. IRC discussion groups, called *channels,* often involve flirting, profanity, sexual situations, and aggressive behavior. It's strictly an adult playground.

Understanding Internet Relay Chat

In brief, IRC is a real-time chat system of global dimensions that's made possible by the Internet. With IRC, you can engage in conversations with people from all over the world. On a single IRC server, you can join a conversation channel and get involved in a text-based give-and-take with as many as a couple dozen people. At any given time, there are hundreds of servers in operation worldwide.

IRC can be fun, but it has a well-deserved bad reputation. For one thing, it's a hangout for some of the most malicious and antisocial hackers you'll ever run across, whose common aim is to ruin everyone's fun. If you can manage to steer clear of the misfits, though, IRC provides an interesting diversion to the everyday grind. It's a fun way to spend a lunch break. If you're lucky enough to find a channel visited by like-minded people and you return regularly, you can form lasting relationships that might migrate to other media, including e-mail and Real Life.

In a text-based IRC client, the conversation runs like this:

[Joe-Bob] Where are you from?
[Nikkie] Belgium.
[Joe-Bob] What part?

You can describe actions as well as type text:

[Joe-Bob opens the bar and pours everyone a longneck.]

Understanding Microsoft Chat

Microsoft Chat is a graphics-based IRC client that links the give-and-take of IRC chat with a real-time comic strip. You choose one of several characters, and you see your character on-screen, interacting with others, as if you were living out a cartoon (Figure 16-1). The words you type appear in your character's word balloons in the frames of a comic strip. Microsoft Chat automatically inserts other characters in each cartoon panel and creates new panels as needed. Before long, you'll find yourself in a story. You can even give emotions to your character and choose to "say," "think," or "whisper" words to other characters.

Figure 16-1
Microsoft Chat makes you part of a real-time comic strip.

Getting Started with Microsoft Chat

To start Microsoft Chat, go to Start, select the Programs menu, and choose Microsoft Chat. You'll see the Connect dialog box (Figure 16-2).

Figure 16-2
Before you can chat with anyone, you must connect to a chat server.

16

A Microsoft Chat Romance (A Story from Cyberspace)

"Cleopatra, are you here?" I saw her name on the member list pane. Sure enough, she popped up.

"Hi," she said. But then Brutus walked in, and the rest is Microsoft Chat history.

It was supposed to be a discussion group for pet owners. After the usual round of introductions, we learned that Cleopatra, a nurse, lived in Australia, while Brutus, a musician, lived on the outskirts of London.

Cleopatra asked brightly whether we ought to talk about pets, but I pointed out that we really didn't have to, and Cleopatra beamed. It wasn't long before Cleopatra and Brutus fell to talking; it turned out that he works in an advertising firm during the day but plays bass guitar for a funk band in London at night.

As Brutus beguiled the lovely Cleopatra with compliment after compliment, she paused to ask herself, "Is he coming on to me?"

Seeing her train of thought, I whispered, "Yes, he is."

Cleopatra was thrilled. Not one to ignore a cue, I slipped aside and put some romantic music on the CD player.

In further conversation, Brutus and Cleopatra discovered that they had both visited Bangkok. They discussed the shows, the pollution, the traffic.

Smiling warmly, Brutus said, "I like you, Cleopatra." The happy couple exchanged their real names—and whispered more, but I couldn't quite catch what they said. I think they might have exchanged e-mail addresses.

At that very moment, though, the captivating Latoya arrived. Cleopatra exclaimed furiously, "Another woman!" Ever the gentleman, Brutus invited Latoya to stay, leading to a jealous tirade on Cleopatra's part. Latoya, feeling unwanted and unwelcome, left the room in a huff.

(continued)

A Microsoft Chat Romance (A Story from Cyberspace) *continued*

I was starting to feel the way Latoya did, but I thought I still had a role to play. I was right, too.

"I apologize for getting jealous," Cleopatra said, adding "She is attractive, though," in a none-too-subtle test.

"Not as attractive as you, though," Brutus replied, adroitly.

Cleopatra thought to herself, "He's so sweet."

Brutus chose that very moment to pop the question, "Will you marry me, Cleopatra?"

"Well…," Cleopatra replied.

I whispered to Cleopatra, "You hardly know him."

Cleopatra played for time. "Should I or shouldn't I?" she mused. "He is attractive."

Brutus urged her on, a bit too aggressively, I thought, so I whispered to him, "Don't pressure her! Give her time and be supportive!"

"Thanks," Brutus whispered back.

But Brutus had won me over, too. I found myself whispering to Cleopatra, "Actually he is a very nice guy."

This did the trick. "Well, OK Brutus, let's get married."

I congratulated the happy couple.

Cleopatra turned to me, radiant. "If it wasn't for you convincing me…Thanks."

The couple agreed to live in Bangkok. Brutus asked me to be the best man. Just then Jetboy happened by, and after a quick, whispered exchange, he agreed to perform the nuptials. Just as Brutus slipped the ring on Cleopatra's finger, though, she said, "But…," leading Jetboy to say, a tad testily, "It's a little late now, isn't it?" Cleopatra relaxed and beamed, and before any of us knew what had happened, Brutus and Cleopatra had slipped away.

16

This dialog box connects you to an IRC server. There are many IRC servers in existence, although they tend to come and go. By default, Microsoft Chat hooks you up with Microsoft's chat server, a benefit for you because it's policed against the antisocial behavior rampant on IRC. Before proceeding, though, you need to choose information about yourself, so click the Cancel button.

Choosing a Persona

To choose a character for yourself, go to the View menu and select Options. You'll see the Microsoft Chat Options dialog box, shown in Figure 16-3, with the Personal Info page displayed. In this dialog box, you type information that will be accessible to other IRC users. There's no need to supply your real name and e-mail address. (Frankly, you shouldn't.) If you would like to disclose this information to somebody you meet on IRC, you can do so at your own risk. But please, do so by "whispering" to your online friend, rather than broadcasting your personal information far and wide.

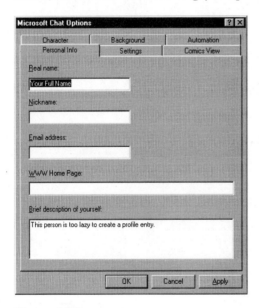

Figure 16-3

On this page, you type the information you want other IRC users to see.

Start by choosing a nickname for yourself that doesn't disclose too much. (Women might want to use non-female-sounding names—unless you think you'll really like having every 13-year-old geek on IRC coming on to you.) If you'd like, type a brief description of yourself, but bear in mind that this is accessible to everyone. You'll find out how to access other peoples' profiles later in this chapter.

Now click the Character tab to choose a character for yourself. You can also test a character's emotions from the emotion wheel (Figure 16-4).

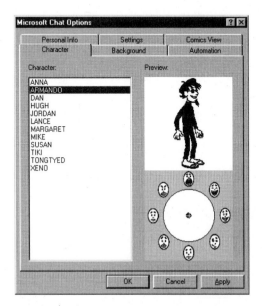

Figure 16-4

On the Character page, you can decide who you will be.

Next click Comics View. The important option here is Page Layout. Choose a panel width (1, 2, 3, or 4 panels) that doesn't cause your screen to scroll horizontally. (If you later find that the screen scrolls, choose this command again and reduce the number of displayed panels.) Try 2 to start.

If you would like to add a degree of automation to Microsoft Chat, click the Automation tab. Here you can enter text strings that you send by pressing a simple key combination. There are two types of macros available. The first enables you to send a message automatically to users that enter the room after you do. This powerful feature even writes in the user's name and the name of the room. The second macro simply enables you to send a string of text with a quick key command.

Finally, click the Background tab and choose the background you prefer. Click OK to confirm your choices.

16

If you're connecting to an IRC server that's not set up to handle Microsoft Chat, go to the Settings page and click Don't Send Microsoft Chat Specific Information. You can still see comic characters on your end of the conversation.

Connecting to the Server

To connect to an IRC server, choose New Connection from the File menu, or press Ctrl + N. You'll see the Connect dialog box. Click Show All Available Chat Rooms, so you'll be able to choose the chat room you want. Click OK to connect to Microsoft's default IRC server.

When you've made the connection to the server, you'll see the Chat Room List (Figure 16-5). If the list is lengthy, you can type a word in the Display Chat Rooms box; click Also Search In Room Topics to help you locate a chat room of interest. Otherwise, look for #Newbies, a good place to start.

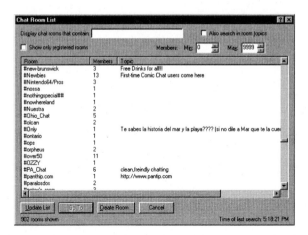

Figure 16-5
Use this window to find a suitable chat room.

Note the number of members in each chat group. More than seven or eight active members may make the conversation complex and difficult to follow, but a room with only one or two participants may be moribund. (Participants sometimes go away from their computers temporarily without logging off.)

When you've found a room that looks good, click Go To. You'll see the main Chat window (Figure 16-6). So you'll be ready to jump into the swing of things, take a moment to learn what the various parts of the window are for.

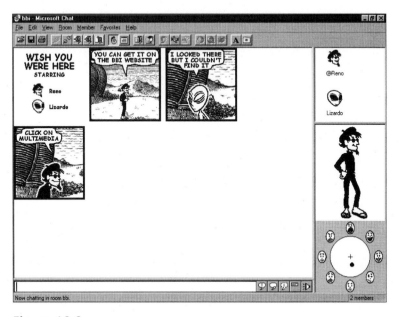

Figure 16-6
Your conversation starts in the Chat window.

Understanding the Chat Window

The Chat window (Figure 16-6) has four panes:

🌐 **Self-View Pane.** Here's your character. To choose emotions, drag around the black dot in the emotion wheel. At the edges, you find the eight extreme emotions: shouting, angry, happy, bored, sad, laughing, scared, coy. As you drag the dot from the edge toward the center, the emotion is less extreme. Take some time to experiment with the emotion wheel. To adopt a neutral pose, drag the dot to the center.

🌐 **Member List Pane.** This pane lists the current characters. You can view the member list as text names or icons. To select one of these options, go to the View menu, select Member List, and then choose List or Icon. You can also click the right mouse button within the member list pane and choose List or Icon.

16

- **Viewing Pane.** Here you see the underlying IRC conversation as a comic strip. If you'd like to see just the text, go to the View menu and select Plain Text. To restore the comic strip, choose Comic Strip.

- **Compose Pane.** In this pane, you type the words that you want to appear in your character's word balloon. You can choose Say (words everyone can read), Think (thoughts everyone can read), Whisper (words only one person can read), and Action (words, prefaced by your nickname, that appear at the top of the cartoon panel).

Using the Chat Toolbar

As with most Internet Explorer modules, you'll find that the most frequently used commands are found on the toolbar. Here's what you'll find on the Chat toolbar:

Tool	Action
Open	Opens a previously saved conversation.
Save	Saves the current conversation.
Print	Prints the current conversation.
Connect	Connects to the chat server.
Disconnect	Disconnects from the chat server.
Enter Room	Displays the Enter Room dialog box, which enables you to type the name of an existing or new room to enter.
Leave Room	Leaves the room you're currently in.
Create Room	Creates a new chat room.
Comics View	View the comic characters.
Text View	Chat using text only.
Chat Room List	View the current list of chat groups.
User List	View the current list of users online. (You can also search for a specific user.)
Get Identity	Displays the identity of the selected character.
Invite	Invites a character to a private chat.
Whisper Box	Lets you carry on more than one whispered conversation at a time.

Tool	Action
Send Email	Sends e-mail to the selected user.
Visit Home Page	Opens the Web page of the selected user.
NetMeeting	Makes a NetMeeting call to the selected user.
Set Font	Changes the font used in Comics View.
Open Favorites	Opens your Favorites folder.

Jumping into the Conversation

You're in. Now you can talk, show a thought balloon, whisper privately to someone, or describe an action you're taking.

Talking to Someone

To say something to another character, click the person you want to talk to and choose an emotion from the emotion wheel. Type the text you want to appear. Don't worry about capital letters, since the text appears in all caps, but do watch your spelling. If you include the word "you," your character will point to the person you're talking to. If you use "I," your character will point to yourself. To send the speech, click Say, press Enter, or use the Ctrl + Y keyboard shortcut.

This guy's really bothering me.

Somebody bugging you? Ignore him. Right-click his icon or nickname in the members list, and click Ignore. You won't see this person's character or messages, although other participants will (unless they choose to ignore him, too).

Thinking Aloud

A thought shows others what you're thinking and can add a fun dimension to your conversation. Choose an emotion from the emotion wheel, and type the text you want to appear. To send the thought, click Think or use the Ctrl + T shortcut.

Whispering to Someone

When you whisper to someone, only that person can see what you said. Click the person you want to whisper to, and choose an emotion from the emotion wheel. Type the text you want to appear in the balloon. To send, click Whisper or use the Ctrl + W shortcut.

16

Performing an Action

You can describe an action you perform. The action begins with your name, and it appears in a panel at the top of the cartoon frame. Type the text that describes your action. Remember that Microsoft Chat will automatically insert your name at the beginning of the action, so plan your text accordingly. ("*Ryouga* sidles up to the bar and orders a tall, cool one.") Click Action, or use the Ctrl + I shortcut.

Viewing a Character's Profile

Did you fill out your profile? No? Maybe somebody else filled out theirs. To find out, click a character's name or icon in the member list pane and click the right mouse button. Choose Get Profile from the pop-up menu. You'll see the character's profile, if any, in a special frame inserted within the comic. (Only you see this frame.)

Chatting Tips and Tricks

Once you've learned how to join in the give-and-take of a Microsoft Chat conversation, you're ready to have fun. (Save this section to read after you've explored a chat channel for a while.)

Adding Favorites

Found a great chat room? Add it to your Favorites by choosing the Favorites menu and selecting Add To Favorites. To return to your favorite chat rooms later, choose Open Favorites, select the favorite from the dialog box, and click Open.

Changing Channels

You'll often find that a conversation degenerates. Sometimes it's because there are just too many people involved, other times because of the juvenile behavior of some participants. To bid them farewell and choose a new channel, go to the Room menu and select Room List. From the Chat Room List dialog box, choose a new chat room, and click Go To.

TIP

If somebody tries to disrupt your channel by *flooding* (typing a single character and pressing Enter repeatedly) or by other means, you can kick them off the channel. To do so, right-click the offender's character and choose Kick. Enter the reason for your action (which will be displayed to everyone else in the room), and click OK.

Creating a New Channel

If you don't find a channel on a subject you like, you can create a new one by following these instructions:

1. Go to the Room menu and select Create Room. When the Create Chat Room dialog box appears, type a new chat room name. (Begin the name with a pound sign, as in #over40.)

2. In the Topic box, type a brief, descriptive topic for your channel. While you're here, you can also set other useful parameters for the room, such as whether users can see it in the room list (hidden) or whether attending the room is by invitation only.

3. Click OK to create the new room.

Saving and Printing

If you've had a great session, you might want to save it and print it. To save the chat session, go to the File menu, select Save, type a filename, and choose OK. To print a conversation, go to the File menu, select Print, choose the settings you want from the Print dialog box, and click OK.

From Here

Chatting is fun, but you can actually talk to people on the Internet almost as if you were talking on the telephone. And it's free—even if you're talking to somebody halfway around the world. Find out how to use Internet telephony in the next chapter.

16

17 Work Together

The Internet will change the way we work—that's certain. E-mail already has become close to indispensable, both for internal communication within companies and with coworkers and colleagues around the world. With Microsoft NetMeeting, there's a new way to collaborate, using the Internet as a communications medium.

Microsoft NetMeeting is a real-time Internet communication tool that enables you to converse with other Internet users, as if you were using a telephone. But it's far more than an Internet telephone. NetMeeting includes the following advanced features:

- **Point-to-point audio and video communication via the Internet.** Think of it as a free long-distance phone call. The audio quality isn't fantastic, and often there's a delay of a second or two—but hey, it's free! If your computer is equipped with a digital video camera, you can also send real-time video images along with your voice. And if you're conversing with somebody who also has a digital video camera, you can see each other while you're talking.

🌍 **A shared whiteboard space.** Everyone participating in the meeting, whether it's just 2 of you or 25, can collaborate within this graphic space. Anyone can draw and type, and everyone sees the results as they're created.

🌍 **A chat area.** Users can type and send text-based messages, which everyone who's connected can see.

🌍 **File transfer.** While you're in a meeting with one or more other people, you can send a file and everyone will receive a copy. Others can send files to you, too.

🌍 **Application sharing.** You can start any Microsoft Windows application on your system, and others can see what you're doing. For example, you can start Excel and show everyone your worksheet. You can even select an option that enables collaborators to make changes to your document.

🌍 **Multipoint communication.** Most other Internet telephony standards support only point-to-point (two people) communications for whiteboarding. With NetMeeting, you can involve three or more people in the shared whiteboard space, the chat area, and application sharing.

🌍 **Standards based.** Unlike many Internet telephony programs, NetMeeting is based on open standards, which are currently supported by more than two dozen companies. This is very important, since the reason Internet telephony hasn't taken off is that the various programs won't work with each other. With NetMeeting, you'll be able to talk with people who use other standards-based programs, including a recent offering from Intel.

Whether or not you've ever tried an Internet telephony application, you'll soon be chatting away happily and collaborating over the Internet with this chapter as your guide.

Understanding Internet Telephony

Let's start off with an important point: The Internet wasn't designed for the real-time delivery of voice, let alone audio or video. It has taken some very clever programming and industrial-strength compression technology to make

Internet telephony possible. Even so, you'll find that voices often sound garbled, and sometimes there are interruptions and delays.

Another drawback of Internet telephony is that it's somewhat inconvenient to use. You have to be near your computer, and you have to be logged on to the Internet. That's fine if you're working in your office or if you've got unlimited Internet access, but it's not so convenient for home users who log on intermittently and have to pay per-hour charges. On balance, the MCIs and AT&Ts of this world don't have much to be concerned about, at least at this point; long-distance telephones aren't going away any time soon.

Still, if you're the type of person who sits in front of a computer all day (like me), you'll find NetMeeting of great value for calling other computer shut-ins.

But it's a mistake to think of Internet telephony as merely a substitute for the telephone or a way around long-distance charges. Rather, it's an opportunity for collaboration. Think of NetMeeting as a telephone plus the tools you need to work with others, even if they're located halfway around the world. Here's an example of what you can do with NetMeeting:

- 🌐 **Go over a proposal with a client.** As you work on the figures and agree on the terms, you can make the changes. When you're done, you can send your client the completed file for further review and printing.

- 🌐 **Write a document collaboratively.** You and your collaborators can jointly compose a Microsoft Word document on-screen.

- 🌐 **Make a presentation.** Using NetMeeting's application-sharing capabilities, you can share a PowerPoint presentation in a meeting involving two or more participants—even if they're scattered all over the world. You can even give them control of the application so they can navigate through the slides as they please.

- 🌐 **Develop a Web page design.** Work interactively with your Webmaster to develop your home page. As you express your preferences, your Webmaster composes the code. With a click of the mouse, you can see the results in Internet Explorer.

These are only some of the potential applications of NetMeeting. Because you can share any Microsoft Windows application using NetMeeting, the possibilities truly are limitless.

17

Understanding the ULS Server

A problem for Internet telephony is that so many people connect to the Internet using modems. With most modem connections, your computer is assigned a temporary Internet address. The next time you log on, you will probably get assigned a different Internet address. That's no problem when you're browsing the Web, but it is a problem if people are trying to call you. It's as if your telephone number changed every time you made a call.

To solve this problem, NetMeeting's designers created a User Location Server (ULS). When you start NetMeeting, the program sends your e-mail address and your current Internet address to the server. By accessing your name through the ULS, people can call you even though your address has changed.

Not all User Location Servers are public. If you're using NetMeeting from within an organization, you might be given the address of an organizational ULS. (An organization can set up a ULS using Microsoft Internet Information Server and Microsoft Windows NT.) To specify a default ULS other than Microsoft's, start NetMeeting, go to the Tools menu, select Options, click Calling, and type a new address in the Server Name box.

Getting Started with NetMeeting

Now that you know what NetMeeting's capabilities are, you're ready to try them yourself. Get started by configuring your audio system and understanding NetMeeting's window.

Running NetMeeting for the First Time

To use NetMeeting for real-time audio communication, you'll need a sound card, speakers or headphones, and a microphone. The first time you run Microsoft NetMeeting, the Audio Tuning Wizard will appear, and you'll be asked to test your microphone. Be sure it's connected and ready to go.

You'll also be asked to provide some information, so have this ready too: your e-mail address, name, city, and country; any comments you would like to make visible on the public server; whether you'd like your name published on the User Location Server; and the user location server you would like to use (default is *ils.microsoft.com*).

To start NetMeeting, choose Microsoft NetMeeting from the Start menu and follow the on-screen instructions.

TIP

If you would rather that NetMeeting not automatically publish your name in the User Location Service, go to the Tools menu and select Options. Click the Calling tab, and enable Do Not List My Name In The Directory. People can still call you if they know your e-mail address. To remove all your information from the listing service, disable the option called Log On To The Directory Server When NetMeeting Starts. Click OK to confirm.

Looking at NetMeeting

After you've finished running the NetMeeting configuration wizard, you'll see NetMeeting on-screen (Figure 17-1). In addition, you'll see the NetMeeting icon on the taskbar.

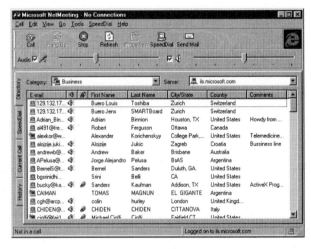

Figure 17-1

With Microsoft NetMeeting, you can talk anywhere the Internet reaches.

The following sections appear in NetMeeting's window.

🌐 **Title Bar.** To reposition the NetMeeting window, drag the title bar. To maximize the window quickly, double-click the title bar. Double-click again to restore the previous size.

🌐 **Menu Bar.** Here you'll find all the NetMeeting commands, but the most frequently used commands are found on the toolbar.

301

17

Toolbar. The toolbar contains the following buttons: Call, Hang Up, Stop, Refresh, Properties, SpeedDial, and Send Mail. To display or hide the Toolbar, select Toolbar from the View menu.

 Audio Controls. From here you can adjust the microphone and speaker volume.

 List Area. In this area, you can view one of four different lists. The Directory, SpeedDial, Current Call, and History lists are all accessible via a set of four tabs that run vertically along the left side of the window.

 Status Bar. In this area, NetMeeting displays messages and information about its status and what it's doing. You can hide the status bar by selecting Status Bar from the View menu, but it's worth keeping it visible because some of the messages are useful or important.

TIP

With the Current Call tab, you can view information about the people connected to you. You'll see the person's name, information about whether sharing is enabled and the type of connection that's been achieved (voice or no voice), and any other information that the person has elected to make public by means of the User Location Service. When you initially make your connection, the first thing you'll want to know is whether audio is enabled, so it's nice to see this information automatically.

The NetMeeting Toolbar

NetMeeting's toolbar contains the most frequently chosen commands. Here's a quick overview of what these tools do.

Tool	Action
Call	Initiates a call.
Hang Up	Hangs up the connection.
Stop	Stops the current download.
Refresh	Refreshes the current window.
Properties	Displays properties for the currently selected item.
SpeedDial	Opens the SpeedDial window.
SendMail	Opens the New Message window in Outlook Express.

Using the List Area

NetMeeting displays four different lists in the list area. To see a list, click the appropriate tab in the tab bar running down the left side of the window.

- **Directory list.** Once you've logged on to a user location service, you'll see the current list of users in the directory list. To call one of these users, select the user's entry and click Call.

- **SpeedDial.** In the SpeedDial list, you'll see the names of people you've put on your SpeedDial list. (If you haven't added any, this list is blank.)

- **Current Call.** This list shows information about the current call. This window also contains the Remote Video window. (If you prefer, you can detach this window by choosing Detach Remote Video from the View menu.)

- **History.** This window shows calls you've placed previously.

NOTE Do you have a video camera mounted on your computer, ready to go? From the Tools menu, select Options, and click the Video tab. Enable the option Automatically Send Video At The Start Of Each Call to automatically start sending video. Note that you can send video even if the person you're talking to doesn't have a camera. If you'd like to receive video automatically, enable the option Automatically Receive Video At The Start Of Each Call.

Making a Call

After you've installed NetMeeting, I'm sure you'll want to try to place a call right away. To get the most out of this experience, spend a few moments reviewing your long-distance phone bills. This step will help enormously in overlooking the audio deficiencies of Internet telephony.

You can call someone on the Internet in three ways: using a User Listing Service, using SpeedDial, or typing an Internet address directly.

Placing a Call with the User Listing Service

To place a call using the User Listing Service, follow these steps:

1. Click the Directory tab. You'll see the Directory list.

2. In the Category list box, choose the category of user that you want to call. Categories include business or personal users, users who

17

have video cameras, users in your country, and others. To see the largest possible list, choose All.

3. In the Server list box, choose the server you want to use.

4. To search for a user, click on the header of the column you would like to search and scroll through the list.

5. When you've found the user you want to call, select the user's information and click Call. If you want to cancel the call, go to the Call menu and select Stop Placing Call.

Placing a Call with SpeedDial

To place a call with SpeedDial, you must first create a SpeedDial entry, as described later in this chapter. When that is done, follow these steps to place your call.

1. Click the SpeedDial tab. NetMeeting will display all the names you have entered into the SpeedDial list.

2. Choose the person you want to call from the SpeedDial list.

3. Click the Call button in the Toolbar; NetMeeting will display a New Call dialog box with the address already in place.

4. Choose the type of connection appropriate for the person you're calling. If this person is registered on a Directory Server, select Call Using Directory Server. If you know this person's permanent IP address, select Network (TCP/IP). If you aren't sure and want NetMeeting to decide, select Automatic.

5. If there is a meeting taking place, enable Join The Meeting and type in the name of the meeting you want to join.

6. Click the Call button.

Placing a Call with an Internet Address

If you know somebody's Internet address (four numbers separated by dots, with no spaces), you can place a call to this person without going through the User Location Service. Users of corporate LANs often have permanent Internet addresses.

1. Go to the Call menu, and select New Call.

2. In the address box, type the person's Internet address. The address will consist of four numbers separated by dots, with no spaces.

3. If you've been notified that there is a meeting taking place, enable Join The Meeting and type in the name of the meeting you want to join.

4. Click the Call button.

Placing a Call with the History Tab

After you've placed a few calls, you can see a list of the most recently used numbers by clicking the History tab. You can also place a call to one of these numbers simply by choosing it and clicking the Call button.

HELP

It says, "The person you called is not able to accept Microsoft NetMeeting calls"!

This message could be caused by several problems. You might have typed the number incorrectly. (Check your typing and try again.) A network error might have prevented the call from getting through. (Try again.) Finally, the person might have quit NetMeeting and closed the NetMeeting icon on the taskbar. In this case, send e-mail or, as a last-ditch act of desperation, place a real telephone call to find out whether you've got the right address and, while you're at it, to ask the person to start NetMeeting. To configure NetMeeting to accept calls even when the NetMeeting window is closed, go to the Tools menu, select Options, and click the General tab. Select the options Show Microsoft NetMeeting Icon On The Taskbar and Run When Windows Starts And Notify Me Of Incoming Calls.

Establishing the Call

If you've successfully made contact with the person you're calling, you'll hear a chiming sound and you'll see two names in the Current Call list (Figure 17-2). Don't be surprised if you can't say "Hello" right away. NetMeeting needs a little time to determine what type of connection is possible.

The icons placed next to each caller's name—for audio, video, and text chatting—indicates the type of connection that's possible with this person. If an icon is dimmed, the current connection doesn't support it.

If you've joined a meeting with more than two callers, you can use audio and video with only one person at a time. To switch audio and video to a different person, click Switch on the toolbar and choose the person's name from the submenu.

17

Figure 17-2

When you've achieved a connection, you see the names of everyone who's involved in the call in the Current Call list.

While you're talking to someone, you have a good opportunity to create a SpeedDial shortcut for this person. In the connections window, right-click the person's name and choose Add SpeedDial. After adding this shortcut, you will see the name in the SpeedDial menu. (For more information, see "Using SpeedDial Shortcuts" later in this chapter.)

If the person you're talking to can't hear you very well, try increasing the microphone volume by moving the slider control. Also, try speaking more directly into the microphone. To adjust the speaker volume, move the slider control next to the speaker icon.

To see information about the person you're talking to, right-click the person's name and choose Properties. You'll see a Properties dialog box, which lists the information that this person has made available to the User Location Service.

Receiving a Call

When a call comes in, you'll hear a ringing sound and see a dialog box asking whether or not you want to accept the call. Click Accept or Ignore. By default, NetMeeting does not answer calls automatically.

You may want to change the default call receiving options. To change these options, go to the Tools menu, select Options, and click the General tab. You can choose the following options for call receiving:

🌐 **Show Microsoft NetMeeting icon on the taskbar.** This icon enables you to display the NetMeeting window quickly. To do so, right-click this icon and choose Open.

🌐 **Run when Windows starts and notify me of incoming calls.** This option automatically starts NetMeeting and enables you to receive calls in the background.

🌐 **Automatically accept incoming calls.** This option configures NetMeeting so that every time someone calls you NetMeeting automatically answers it and establishes communication.

🌐 **Show the SpeedDial tab when NetMeeting starts.** When enabled, this option automatically brings up the SpeedDial list when NetMeeting is opened.

🌐 **Show Intel Connection Advisor icon on the taskbar.** This choice places an icon in the Windows 95 taskbar for the Intel Connection Advisor. The Advisor can help you diagnose connection problems.

Starting a Meeting

When you start a meeting, you don't need to actually place a call. Rather, the people who call you can join or leave, much as they would in a chat room on Microsoft Chat. You can choose to accept callers automatically or to screen them.

To start a meeting, go to the Call menu and select Host Meeting. You'll see an information box explaining how meetings work. Click OK to continue. You'll see your personal icon in the connections list. As others call in, you'll see their names on the list, too. Since only one pair of callers at a time can use audio and video in a meeting, you will use the Chat window to communicate with the people in your meeting.

If you're the host of the meeting, you can disconnect someone, if you wish. Simply right-click the person's name and click Remove From Meeting.

To stop your participation in the meeting, click Hang Up or go to the Call menu and select Hang Up. If you're the host of the meeting, all parties will lose their connections when you hang up.

17

Using Chat

If you're placing a non-audio call, or if network performance degrades so that you can't understand the audio, you will need to communicate using the Chat window. To open the Chat window, go to the Tools menu and select Chat (or use the Ctrl + T shortcut). You'll see the Chat window (Figure 17-3). When you open the Chat window in a meeting, other participants' Chat windows open as well.

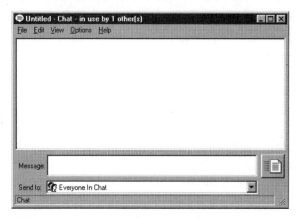

Figure 17-3
The Chat window lets you communicate with text.

Conversing with Chat

Chat works exactly like a text-based Internet Relay Chat client: You type a line of text and press Enter. The program then sends what you've typed to other meeting participants. In the window, you see a running record of what everyone has typed (Figure 17-4).

By default, Chat sends your text to everyone in the call. If you're chatting with two or more people, you can choose to send your text to only one of the participants. (This is analogous to "whispering" in Microsoft Chat.) To send private text, choose the person's name in the Send To list box, type your message, and press Enter.

Choosing the Chat Format

By default, NetMeeting places the person's name at the beginning of each line the person types and wraps lengthy lines so that the line starts next to the person's information. If you go to the Options menu and select Chat Format, you can change the default display. You can display or hide the

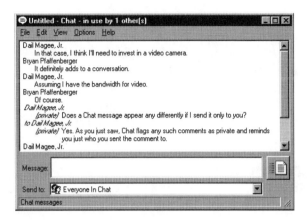

Figure 17-4

Each person in a chat is clearly identified.

person's name, as well as the date and time, in the information automatically inserted with each line of text. You can also format the entire message to be placed on one line instead of wrapping the text. Or you can choose a formatting option that places the information display on the line preceding the text the person types.

Saving, Retrieving, and Printing Chat Files

If you wish, you can save and print a chat conversation the same way you save any text document. To save the conversation, go to the File menu, select Save, type a filename, and click Save. To print a conversation, go to the File menu, select Print, choose the print options you want, and click Print.

If you haven't saved a conversation, you'll see an alert box when you exit the conversation that asks you whether you want to save it. To save it, click Yes. To abandon the conversation, click No. To return to Chat, click Cancel.

Using Whiteboard

Whiteboard provides a shared graphical workspace for generating and sharing ideas. Although Whiteboard appears to resemble the simple Windows Paint accessory, it's a surprisingly full-featured accessory that offers multiple pages, a yellow highlighter for emphasizing text or graphics, and screen capture capabilities that enable you to take a "snapshot" of a window and show it to others in the meeting.

17

Starting Whiteboard

To start Whiteboard, go to the Tools menu and select Whiteboard, use the Ctrl + W shortcut, or click Whiteboard on the toolbar. You'll see the Whiteboard window (Figure 17-5). After you start Whiteboard, all other meeting participants will also see their Whiteboards. Collaboration is automatically enabled so that a change made by any participant will be seen by everyone. To prevent others from making changes, go to the Tools menu and select Lock Contents, or click Lock Contents on the toolbar.

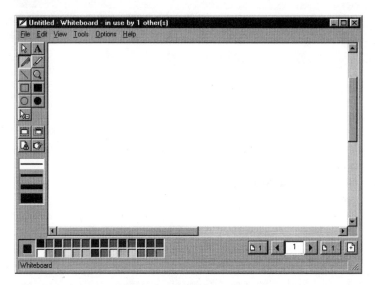

Figure 17-5

The Whiteboard window enables callers to use a shared graphical workspace.

Understanding the Whiteboard Window

The Whiteboard window has the usual window features, including the title bar and menu bar. In addition, you'll find the following:

- **Toolbar.** Click here to use the various tools. To hide or display the toolbar, go to the View menu and select Tool Bar.

- **Color Selector.** Click here to select a color when you're typing or drawing.

- **Page Selector.** These tools are useful when Whiteboard contains more than one page.

- **Status Bar.** The status bar displays Whiteboard's messages. To hide or display the status bar, choose Status Bar from the View menu.

PART
II

When you're working in the Whiteboard window, you can zoom in for a closer look. Simply go to the View menu and select Zoom, or click the Zoom tool. To restore the window to the default magnification, select or click Zoom again.

You will see your own pointer in the window, but others can't see your pointer. If you would like to point at something in your window, select Remote Pointer from the Tools menu, or click the Remote Pointer On tool. A colored hand appears in everyone's Whiteboard windows, which you can then move by dragging it with your mouse pointer.

Although Whiteboard superficially resembles the Paint accessory, it is far superior. Each addition you make can be individually selected, edited, or moved.

Using the Tools

On the toolbar, you'll find the tools that enable you to create text and drawings, highlight text or graphics on-screen, and paste windows into Whiteboard. Here's a quick overview of the tools you can use to add content to the window:

🌐 **Text.** Click here to add text to Whiteboard. After clicking the tool, click the pointer where you want to start entering text. To change the font, font size, or font effects (strikeout or underline), click the Font Options button or go to the Options menu and select Font. Make the choices you want in the Font dialog box, and click OK.

🌐 **Pen.** Click here to draw a freehand line. After clicking the tool, drag within the window to draw shapes.

🌐 **Line.** Click here to draw a straight line. After clicking the tool, hold down the mouse button and drag within the window to draw a straight line. Release the mouse button where you want the line to end.

🌐 **Unfilled Rectangle.** Click here to create a rectangle that doesn't have a background color.

🌐 **Filled Rectangle.** Click here to create a rectangle that's automatically filled with the background color currently selected in the color selector.

🌐 **Unfilled Ellipse.** Click here to create an ellipse that doesn't have a background color.

🌐 **Filled Ellipse.** Click here to create an ellipse that's filled with the background color currently selected in the color selector.

17

For each drawing object you create, you can choose a color and line width. To change the object's color, choose a color from the color selector, or go to the Options menu, select Colors, click a color in the Color dialog box, and click OK. To change the object's line width, click a line width in the Toolbar, or go to the Options menu, select Line Width, and choose a line thickness from the submenu.

Editing and Highlighting

After you create an object with the text or drawing tools, you can move the object by selecting it with the Selector tool and dragging it to its new position. You can send the object to the background—select Send Back from the Edit menu—or bring the object to the foreground—select Bring to Front from the Edit menu. Use the Delete key to delete a selected object.

A nifty feature of Whiteboard is the Highlighter. To highlight text or graphics within the Whiteboard window, click the Highlighter tool. If necessary, click the yellow color in the color selector.

Pasting a Window into Whiteboard

You can show meeting participants a selected part of your screen or all of another window by pasting a graphic "snapshot" of the selected screen area or window into Whiteboard.

To prepare for pasting, minimize Whiteboard and arrange the screen so that the material you want to paste is visible. Then restore Whiteboard.

To paste a portion of the screen into Whiteboard, click Select Area (or go to the Tools menu and choose Select Area). Whiteboard disappears, enabling you to select a screen area by dragging. When you release the mouse button, you see your selection within Whiteboard. Click the Selector tool, and drag the window to position it.

To paste a window into Whiteboard, click Select Window (or go to the Tools menu and choose Select Window). Whiteboard disappears, enabling you to click the window you want to paste into Whiteboard. After you click this window, Whiteboard reappears and you see the window within Whiteboard. Click the Selector tool, and drag the window to position it.

NOTE Unlike a shared application, a window pasted into Whiteboard isn't live. Participants won't see any changes you subsequently make in the original window. However, pasting a window into Whiteboard consumes much less Internet bandwidth than running a live demonstration. If there is no need to show conferees a running application, use the Whiteboard.

Paging Through Whiteboard

You can add more than one page to Whiteboard using the page selector tools: First Page, Previous Page, Page, Next Page, Last Page, and Insert New Page.

To add an additional page to Whiteboard, click Insert New Page. The number in the Last Page box increases to show the total number of pages.

To move to a page, click the Next Page or Previous Page buttons, or type a page number in the Page box and press Enter. You can go to the beginning by clicking First Page or to the end by clicking Last Page.

Sharing Applications

The most advanced feature of NetMeeting is the program's ability to display a shared application on the screens of everyone participating in a meeting. You also have the option of enabling others in a meeting to control the program and work with the data you're displaying.

To share an application, begin by starting it and displaying the information you want to share. From the Tools menu, choose Share Application, and choose the application's name from the list (or click the Share button on the toolbar and choose the application's name.) To give others the ability to choose commands and alter data, click the Collaborate button on the toolbar.

If you're sharing an application, clicking on its window will bring it to the foreground not only in your computer but in the computers of everyone in the meeting. If someone else is sharing a program with you, the program starts automatically and you see the application on-screen. To take control of the program, double-click the program window. (You can do this only if the person sharing the program has enabled collaboration.) To stop collaborating, go to the Tools menu and click Stop Collaborating (or click the Collaborate button again).

Sending and Receiving Files

One of NetMeeting's most useful features is file transfer, which enables you to send and receive files while you're connected with others. (If more than one person is in a meeting with you, you can send the file to everyone in the meeting or choose the person to whom you'd like to send the file.) The file transfer is efficient and relatively quick, depending on the quality of your Internet connection. Best of all, the person receiving the file can verify whether it arrived intact and confirm via audio or the Chat window. For

17

this reason, NetMeeting provides a better way to send files than e-mail attachments (see Chapter 13), which require an exchange of e-mail to verify.

To send a file to everyone in the current meeting, go to the Tools menu, choose File Transfer, and select Send File (or press Ctrl + F). To send a file to just one person in a meeting, right-click the person's name and click Send File. You'll see a file-selection dialog box. Choose the file you want to send, and click Send. NetMeeting then displays a progress indicator that shows how much of the file has been sent. When the file has been received successfully, you'll see a message confirming this.

If you would like to change the directory to which NetMeeting saves files, go to the Tools menu, select Options, click the General tab, and choose a directory by clicking the Change Folder button in the File Transfer area.

Using SpeedDial Shortcuts

SpeedDial shortcuts enable you to establish a call quickly. The easiest way to create one is to do so while you're conferencing with someone. To create the SpeedDial shortcut, right-click the person's name in the connections window and choose Add SpeedDial.

To create a SpeedDial when you're not connected with someone, go to the Call menu and select Create SpeedDial. You'll see the Add SpeedDial dialog box (Figure 17-6).

Figure 17-6
Create SpeedDial shortcuts to save time when you're in a hurry.

In the SpeedDial information area, choose the connection method and type the Internet address, if necessary. In the SpeedDial area, choose Add To SpeedDial List to create a new entry in your SpeedDial list, choose Save

PART
II

On The Desktop to save the shortcut on your computer's desktop, or choose Send To Mail Recipient to mail the shortcut to someone. Click OK to confirm your choices. If you chose Send To Mail Recipient, Windows will start your mail program and place the shortcut in a new, blank message.

TIP To have NetMeeting automatically make SpeedDial entries for the people you call and for those who call you, click Tools on the menu bar and choose Options. In the Options dialog box, click the Calling tab, and select Always. Click OK to confirm your choice.

Hanging Up

To end your conversation, say goodbye and click Hang Up. NetMeeting terminates the connection. The person or persons with whom you've been communicating will see dialog boxes indicating that you've hung up.

From Here

You've accessed plenty of Internet content—now it's time to create your own. In the next part of this book, you'll learn how to create compelling Web content using Microsoft FrontPage Express.

17

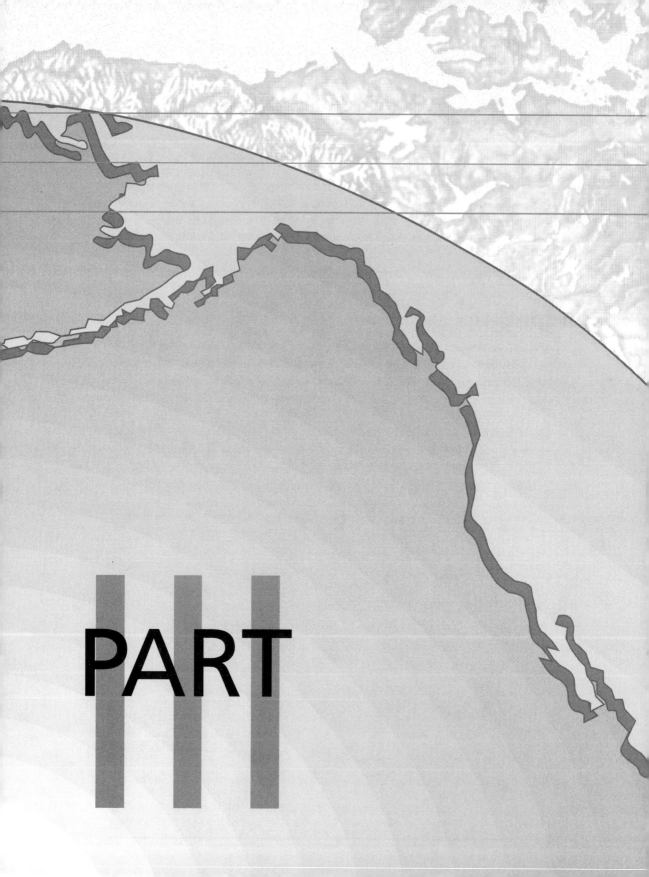

PART III

Publish

18 Sketch It Out

The Web isn't strictly a couch potato's medium; you can create content as well as sit back and groove on it. That's exactly what makes the Web so vibrant and exciting. Sure, it's fun to browse the big commercial sites. But you'll really understand the Web when you find that little page somewhere—a page that few others would find interesting—that contains exactly the information you need. The Web grows richer every time a user decides, "Hey, what I've got to say just might be useful to somebody else."

This chapter introduces Microsoft FrontPage Express, the Internet Explorer module that enables anyone to create compelling Web content. You don't need to learn HTML to create exciting Web pages with FrontPage Express; it's as easy as using a word processing program. In this chapter, you'll learn how to sketch out your Web page. You'll also learn how to publish your page so that others can access it. In the next chapter, you'll learn how to add all kinds of cool features to your pages, including background sounds, background graphics, ActiveX controls, and much more.

319

NOTE Microsoft FrontPage Express is a simplified version of Microsoft FrontPage, but don't let the word *simplified* fool you. FrontPage Express may seem simple on the surface, but there's a world of HTML functions beneath. Three chapters certainly can't cover every feature and capability of FrontPage Express, especially for anyone who knows a little HTML. So this chapter and the next one are designed to serve as an introduction to FrontPage Express, highlighting the features that Web authors use most often—as well as the ones that are the most fun.

Introducing FrontPage Express

The Web becomes richer every time a new page appears. Until recently, though, the difficulty of learning HTML posed a roadblock to widespread Web publishing. HTML, short for Hypertext Markup Language, enables Web authors to prepare documents for publication on the Web. Browsers are programmed to detect HTML markup, and they display documents according to the underlying HTML. You don't normally see the HTML in your browser; if you want to see it, go to the View menu and select Source. Figure 18-1 shows some of the HTML code that underlies a popular Web page.

Actually, HTML isn't all that difficult to learn, but it does require a few days or a couple of weeks of study and experimentation. Worse, it's difficult to edit HTML pages directly. (Frankly, I think that's one reason there are so many outdated pages on the Web.) Take a look at Figure 18-1, and imagine making changes to the text. FrontPage Express removes the roadblock by making it unnecessary to learn HTML. You create and edit your page just the way it appears when viewed by a Web browser.

WYSIWYG Editors

One of the most tedious things about composing in HTML is that you can't see what your page looks like right away. You must save your HTML file (which is a text file with a lot of funny-looking symbols in it), and then open the file with a browser. Chances are you've made some mistakes, so it's back to the text file again for more editing.

PART
III

Figure 18-1

It's a tough job to edit HTML documents directly because the HTML instructions, or tags, get in the way.

Thanks to a new generation of WYSIWYG ("what you see is what you get") HTML editors, the tedium's gone. ("WYSIWYG," by the way, is pronounced "wiss-see-wig.") With a WYSIWYG editor, you create a Web page much the way you'd create a word processing document. You type text and choose formatting commands that affect the text's appearance. A good WYSIWYG editor automatically creates all the HTML code for you. You can also add graphics and other multimedia resources. And all the while, the program shows your document the way it will look when it's displayed by a Web browser. Any changes you make are instantly reflected on the screen. You don't have to switch to your browser to see what your document looks like; you see your document's appearance while you're editing.

You'll find quite a few WYSIWYG editors in today's market, but one of the most impressive is included with Microsoft Internet Explorer: FrontPage Express. Figure 18-2 shows how FrontPage Express displays HTML files in a WYSIWYG environment, enabling you to create and edit Web pages as easily as you would write or modify a word processing document. (Hard to imagine that this is the same document shown in Figure 18-1.) You can even create and edit tables, as Figure 18-2 shows.

18

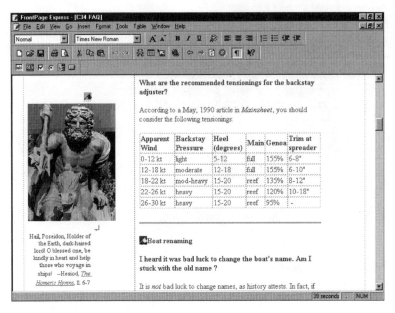

What are the recommended tensionings for the backstay adjuster?

According to a May, 1990 article in *Mainsheet*, you should consider the following tensionings:

Apparent Wind	Backstay Pressure	Heel (degrees)	Main	Genoa	Trim at spreader
0-12 kt	light	5-12	full	155%	6-8"
12-18 kt	moderate	12-18	full	155%	6-10"
18-22 kt	mod-heavy	15-20	reef	135%	8-12"
22-26 kt	heavy	15-20	reef	120%	10-18"
26-30 kt	heavy	15-20	reef	95%	-

Boat renaming

I heard it was bad luck to change the boat's name. Am I stuck with the old name ?

It is *not* bad luck to change names, as history attests. In fact, if

Hail, Poseidon, Holder of the Earth, dark-haired lord! O blessed one, be kindly in heart and help those who voyage in ships! --Hesiod, *The Homeric Hymns*, ll. 6-7

Figure 18-2

FrontPage Express displays HTML files in a "what you see is what you get" environment, enabling you to create and edit Web pages easily.

Why FrontPage Express?

FrontPage Express is easy to use, and it's included with Microsoft Internet Explorer. It is essentially a simplified version of FrontPage Editor, the WYSIWYG editor that's included in Microsoft FrontPage. FrontPage is a professional Web publishing program—and it isn't free. So it's a genuine bargain to get so much of FrontPage Editor's power in this simplified version.

But don't let *simplified* fool you into thinking that FrontPage Express is useful only for simplistic Web pages. FrontPage Express offers more than enough features to help you create highly effective and complex Web pages. To make your page as appealing as possible, you can add fonts, tables, sounds, ActiveX controls, Java applets, and much more.

Moving Up to Microsoft FrontPage

So if FrontPage Express contains virtually all of the tools you need to create and edit high-quality Web pages, why would anyone need the full FrontPage package?

PART
III

FrontPage Express is designed for individuals who prepare their own pages and upload these pages to Web servers that somebody else maintains. Microsoft FrontPage, in contrast, is designed for Web professionals who not only prepare Web content but also administer complex Web sites. Site administrators appreciate the organization and administration features of FrontPage Explorer, one of the two basic components of FrontPage. (The other is FrontPage Editor, which closely resembles FrontPage Express but offers additional features and options.)

Understanding the Web Publishing Process

To make your completed Web pages available for others to see, you need to place them on a computer that's running a Web server. (Remember, a Web server is a program that runs on an Internet-connected computer.) This program waits in the background until someone clicks a hyperlink that's pointed at one of the Web pages stored on the server's computer. The server intercepts this request and sends out a copy of the desired document, along with any associated graphics, multimedia resources, controls, or applets that the page contains. Since publishing your page will involve uploading it to a computer that's running a Web server, this section briefly describes the Web publishing process. Chapter 19 explains in detail how to upload your page once it's finished.

Introducing Web Publishing Wizard

Running a Web server requires a computer with a permanent Internet connection—something most people don't have. Most Internet users access the Internet by means of a dial-up connection and a modem, but this type of connection isn't sufficient for running a Web server. For this reason, most Web authors prefer to *upload* (send) their pages to their Internet service provider's Web server. When the Web pages are placed in an ISP's Web storage space, they become accessible to other Internet users.

When you're ready to publish your page, you can use Web Publishing Wizard, one of the options you can download along with Internet Explorer. You'll learn how to use the wizard later in this chapter.

18

Introducing Personal Web Server

If you access the Internet by means of a dial-up connection, you can't make your Web pages available through a Web server running on your own computer. However, many people use Windows computers connected to corporate local area networks (LANs), and LANs are often hooked up to the Internet. If you access the Internet by means of a LAN, it's possible that your computer has a permanent Internet connection. And if you're also running Windows 95 or Windows 98, you can run Microsoft's Personal Web Server, a free server available on Microsoft's Web site (www.microsoft.com).

Personal Web Server is extremely easy to use. Even if you have no previous experience running a server of any kind, you can set up a Web server easily with this program. Remember, though, that you'll need to leave your computer on 24 hours per day!

Publishing with Microsoft
Internet Information Server (IIS)

If the server you're planning to use happens to be Microsoft Internet Information Server (IIS), you're in luck. You can take advantage of several advanced FrontPage Express features, including these:

- **Page templates and wizards.** FrontPage Express enables you to create Web pages with forms that collect user input, send the user a page acknowledging this input, and store the input in a separate file.

- **WebBots.** Without any programming, you can create *WebBots*, which are hidden scripts you place in your Web page. Included with FrontPage Express are scripts that automatically include another Web page at the script's location, a Search utility that enables users to search all the documents in your site, and a time stamp that automatically displays the day's date and time.

Note that these features work only if you publish your page using Microsoft Internet Information Server. What's terrific about these features is that they automate tasks that formerly could be accomplished only by means of tedious server-side programming using the Common Gateway Interface (CGI) and other programming tools. If you plan to publish using IIS, and you like the page templates, wizards, and WebBots, you've yet another reason to investigate Microsoft FrontPage because it includes many more of these.

Exploring the FrontPage Express Window

FrontPage Express opens in its own window and has its own unique toolbars. Take a couple of minutes to familiarize yourself with the toolbars; they hold the key to many of the neat things that FrontPage Express can do.

TIP If you don't see one or more of the toolbars explained on the following pages, click View on the menu bar and choose the toolbar's name.

The Standard Toolbar

The standard toolbar provides basic commands for creating, opening, saving, and printing files, as well as editing and navigation functions. It also enables you to enter some of FrontPage Express's functions, such as WebBots. The following list connects specific buttons with their functions.

Name	Action
New	Creates a new file.
Open	Opens a page from your local drive or from the network.
Save	Saves the current page.
Print	Prints the current page.
Print Preview	Displays a Print Preview window showing the page's appearance as it will print on your printer.
Cut	Cuts the selection to the Clipboard.
Copy	Copies the selection to the Clipboard.
Paste	Inserts the Clipboard's contents at the cursor's location.
Undo	Cancels the last editing action.
Redo	Repeats an editing action or restores the last action canceled by Undo.
Insert WebBot Component	Inserts a WebBot component at the cursor's location.
Insert Table	Inserts a table at the cursor's location.

(continued)

18

continued

Name	Action
Insert Image	Inserts an inline image at the cursor's location.
Create or Edit Hyperlink	Inserts a hyperlink or edits an existing hyperlink at the cursor's location.
Back	Moves to the previous document.
Forward	Moves to the next document.
Refresh	Retrieves a new copy of the page from the network.
Stop	Stops downloading the current page.
Show/Hide paragraph marks	Displays or hides paragraph marks and table boundaries.
Help	Displays help for the feature you click after pressing this button.

 Like the toolbars in Internet Explorer, the FrontPage Express toolbars can be dragged to new locations. Unlike Internet Explorer's toolbars, though, these toolbars can be repositioned anywhere on the screen. (In this way, they're like Microsoft Office toolbars.) You can detach the toolbar from the FrontPage Express window completely so that the toolbar becomes a separate window that you can drag anywhere on the screen.

The Format Toolbar

The format toolbar enables you to choose paragraph styles, fonts, font sizes, character emphases, character colors, alignments, and indents. You can access these tools in two ways. One way is to click the button and start typing. The text you type will take on the format you've chosen. The second way is to select some text and then click the button. The format you choose will be applied only to the text you've selected. The list that follows details your options in the format toolbar.

Name	Action
Change Style	Assigns a paragraph style for headings and lists.
Change Font	Assigns a font.
Increase Text Size	Increases the font size.
Decrease Text Size	Decreases the font size.

Name	Action
Bold	Creates bold character emphasis.
Italic	Creates italic character emphasis.
Underline	Creates underlining.
Text Color	Chooses a text color.
Align Left	Aligns text flush left.
Center	Centers the text.
Align Right	Aligns text flush right.
Numbered List	Creates a numbered list.
Bulleted List	Creates a bulleted list.
Decrease Indent	Decreases the paragraph indent.
Increase Indent	Increases the paragraph indent.

The Forms Toolbar

You can use the forms toolbar to enter interactive features, such as text boxes, drop-down list boxes, check boxes, and radio buttons. That sounds nice, but bear in mind that these features by themselves won't do anything. In order to accomplish a meaningful task, the output of these interactive features must be linked with a server-side script or program. Most Web authors don't have the necessary technical skills to add these features. They require custom programming on the server side, and the price can be high.

If you're planning to publish your pages with Microsoft Internet Information Server, you can take advantage of the Form Page Wizard, which enables you to create a form—complete with all the programming necessary to work with IIS. The wizard guides you through the process of creating a form and enables you to choose from a number of options. For example, you can choose whether you want to save the results to a Web page or a text file. As you produce the form page, you create each input field by choosing options from the wizard. The result is a form page that's designed to solicit precisely the information you need. You can then modify this page with FrontPage Express by adding backgrounds, graphics, fonts, other formatting, and hyperlinks.

Since forms, the forms toolbar, and the Form Page Wizard require IIS or custom programming, they're beyond the scope of this book. Even so, you can still create Web pages that include interactive features. Later in this chapter, for example, you'll learn how to create mailto links, which bring up a mail composition window for feedback. If you're planning to give your page to a service provider who will provide the scripting and programming necessary to get the forms to work, you can go ahead and create a page with form features such as drop-down list boxes and

327

18

radio buttons. Just keep in mind that these features won't work unless they're linked to a script. (Forms will be discussed further in Chapter 19.)

The forms toolbar enables you to enter interactive form features by clicking one of the buttons. The following list explains what they do.

Name	Action
One-Line Text Box	Enters a one-line text box (no scrolling).
Scrolling Text Box	Enters a text box that enables the user to enter more than one line of text, with scrolling.
Check Box	Enters a check box.
Radio Button	Enters a radio button.
Drop-Down Menu	Enters a drop-down menu.
Push Button	Enters a push button.

Creating a Web Page with FrontPage Express

Using the tools in FrontPage Express, you can create or modify a Web page in the following ways:

- **Use the page wizards.** FrontPage Express comes with several page wizards, including the Personal Home Page Wizard, the New Web View Folder (for customizing your Windows folders), and several wizards for creating pages designed to work with Internet Information Server. To use a page wizard, choose New from the File menu and select a wizard from the New Page dialog box.

- **Create a page from scratch.** When you start FrontPage Express, the program displays a new, blank page. You can use this to create a new Web page. Another way to begin is to click the New button on the standard toolbar or select New from the File menu, and then choose Normal Page from the New Page dialog box.

- **Edit a page on the Web.** You can open any Web page in FrontPage Express by displaying the page in Internet Explorer and then clicking the Edit button or choosing Page from the Edit menu. Any changes you make won't affect the Web page you've downloaded, unless you possess the password that would enable you to upload these changes to the Web server's computer.

Next you'll learn how to create a home page using the Personal Home Page Wizard; then in the sections to come, you'll try creating a page from scratch. Along the way, you'll find out how to edit an existing page.

Creating a Home Page Using Personal Home Page Wizard

What's the first Web page you're likely to publish? I'll bet it's a personal home page, a page that contains information about you, such as contact details, biographical material, current projects, and special interests. In a company, such a page provides other employees with a means of contacting you. More broadly, a personal home page provides a way for people to find out more about you and to get in touch with you. The benefits of having a home page range from opening exciting new career possibilities to getting in touch with friends from long ago.

To create a home page with the Personal Home Page Wizard, follow these steps:

1. From the File menu, choose the New command or press Ctrl + N. You'll see the New Page dialog box (Figure 18-3).

2. Choose Personal Home Page Wizard to see the Personal Home Page Wizard dialog box (Figure 18-4).

3. Select the types of information you want to include, and click Next. You'll see a page asking you to specify the Page URL and the Page Title.

Figure 18-3

Begin your home page by selecting Personal Home Page Wizard from this dialog box.

18

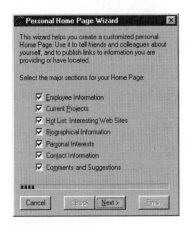

Figure 18-4

You can select the types of information you want to include in your home page.

4. In the Page URL box, type a name for your file. On many servers, a file with the name *index.html* is automatically displayed whenever anyone accesses your public Web directory. For now, name your file *home.html*. You can always rename the file later.

5. In the Page Title box, type a title for your page. The page title is displayed on the browser's title bar, not on the page itself. Still, it's important. Many of the Web's search engines give priority to words found within the title. You should certainly include your name to make it easier for people to find you.

6. Click Next to go to the next page of the wizard. You'll see the page shown in Figure 18-5. If you're creating a page to display on your company's Web server, these options are important. Select the ones that you'd like to include, and click Next.

7. If you selected Current Projects among the items to include, you'll see the projects page (Figure 18-6). Type the names of your current projects, and then select a list option (bulleted list, numbered list, or definition list). Click Next to go to the next page.

8. If you selected Hot List Of Interesting Web Sites among the items to include, you'll see a page asking you how you want your Web sites listed. You can choose from a bulleted list, numbered list, or definition list. You can also import all the links from a specified page, if you wish. When you're finished making your selection, click Next.

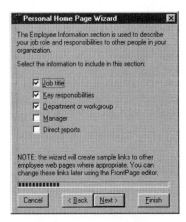

Figure 18-5

In this page of the Personal Home Page wizard, you can select the type of employee information you want to include.

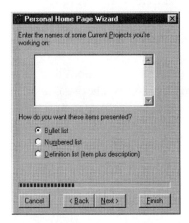

Figure 18-6

You can list the names of your current projects.

9. If you selected Biography among the items to include, you'll see a page asking you to specify the format for your biography section. You can choose from academic, professional, or personal. Choose one of these, and click Next.

10. If you selected Personal Interests among the items to include, you'll see a page asking you to type a list of your personal interests. Type an interest, and press Enter. When you're done, click Next.

18

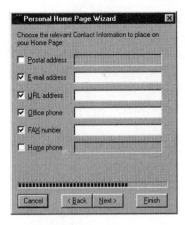

Figure 18-7

Include your contact information so others can find you.

11. If you selected Contact Information among the items to include, you'll see the page shown in Figure 18-7. Add the contact information that you'd like to include, and click Next.

12. If you selected Comments And Suggestions among the items to include, you'll see a page asking how you'd like your comments and suggestions to be solicited and stored. Unless you're publishing your page with Microsoft Internet Information Server, choose Use Link and type your e-mail address in the text box. Click Next to continue.

13. You now see a dialog box showing the items on your home page and asking how you'd like them organized. To move an item, select it and click Up or Down. When you're done, click Next.

14. You'll see a page informing you that you're finished. Click Finish to create your page, which you'll see on-screen (Figure 18-8).

As you can see from Figure 18-8, your home page isn't done. You have raw data, but you need to edit it. Find out how in the next section.

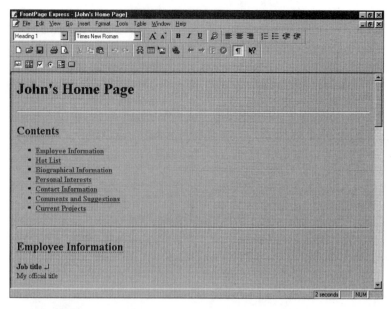

Figure 18-8

Personal Home Page Wizard creates a draft of your home page based on your input.

Learning the Basics of Web Page Editing

Editing Web documents with FrontPage Express is very much like editing a document in a word processing program. However, there are a few peculiarities.

Typing and Editing Text

You can easily add text to your document. Simply place the cursor where you want the text to appear, and start typing. You can use any of the usual Windows editing commands to make corrections or insertions while you're typing.

Finding and Replacing

If you're editing a lengthy document, you can use the Find command to locate specific text in your document. Go to the Edit menu and select Find, or press Ctrl + F. Type the text you want to locate in the Find What box, and press Enter.

18

There's one major difference between word processing and Web publishing that you should bear in mind. Web browsers ignore any additional spaces that you enter. If you try to space text by adding extra spaces, browsers will ignore the extra spaces and your text won't look the way you intended. Also, there's no such thing as a tab in HTML (yet). The only exception to this rule is text formatted with the Formatted style. This format preserves your spaces and line breaks, too.

You can replace text one item at a time or automatically throughout your document. To replace text, choose Replace from the Edit menu or press Ctrl + H. Type the text you want to match in the Find What box, and type the replacement in the Replace With box. To find the next matched item, select Find Next and click Replace to replace the item (or click Find Next to skip this item and search for the next match). To make the replacement throughout your document, click Replace All.

Understanding Paragraph Styles

Whenever you enter text, you're using one of several paragraph styles. To choose a style, select the text and click on a style from the Choose Style list box (in the Format toolbar). Another alternative is to press Enter, choose a style from the Choose Style list box, and start typing. The following list provides an overview of the styles you can use:

 Normal. You should use normal style for entering ordinary text, the kind you place in paragraphs.

 Address. Address style is typically used to type the page creator's name and e-mail address, which appear at the bottom of the page.

 Bulleted List. Use this style to create a bulleted list. To add another item to the list, just press Enter. You can also create a bulleted list by clicking the Bulleted List button in the Format toolbar.

 Defined Term. This style positions the text flush left. To add a definition, just press Enter. FrontPage Express then automatically moves to a definition style for the next line.

 Definition. Used with the Defined Term style, this style formats the selected text with an indent. When you're finished typing the definition, press Enter. FrontPage Express creates a Defined Term style for the next line.

 Directory List. In FrontPage Express, this style creates a bulleted list that's indistinguishable from the Bulleted List style. However, some browsers will format this list differently. Use the Bulleted List style instead.

PART

III

🌐 **Formatted.** This style enables you to format your text using the spacebar; the browser will recognize additional spaces and display your text the way you've typed it.

🌐 **Headings 1 through 6.** To enable you to create headings and subheadings with distinctive formats, FrontPage Express offers six formatted levels. Very few Web authors use more than two headings.

🌐 **Menu List.** In FrontPage Express, this style creates a bulleted list that's indistinguishable from the Bulleted List style. However, some browsers will format this list differently. Use the Bulleted List style instead.

🌐 **Numbered List.** Use this style to create a numbered list. To add another item to the list, just press Enter. You can also create a numbered list by clicking the Numbered List button in the Format toolbar.

Figure 18-9 shows the appearance of most of these styles. Note, though, that most Web authors use only a few of them: normal, bulleted list, numbered list, and two heading styles.

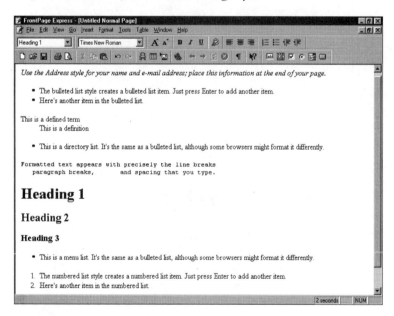

Figure 18-9

You can use any of these styles to enter or format text.

18

To stop typing text in a particular style and return to normal paragraph text, press Enter and choose Normal from the Change Styles list box.

To change a style or select additional options for styles other than lists, select the text that you've formatted with the style, click the right mouse button, and choose Paragraph Properties from the pop-up menu. In the Paragraph Properties dialog box, you can select a different style, and you can also choose alignments for styles (flush left, centered, and flush right).

If you would like to choose options for lists, right-click the list and choose List Properties; you'll see a dialog box that enables you to choose bullet shapes, number formats, and numbering options. You can also use the List Properties dialog box to set the starting number of a numbered list to something other than one.

Controlling Line and Paragraph Breaks

You can enter two kinds of line breaks with FrontPage Express. When you press the Shift + Enter combination, the program starts a new line without adding a blank line. When you press Enter, the program starts a new paragraph with a blank line in front of it. You can create additional blank lines by pressing Shift + Enter or Enter more than once.

If you need to see where you've pressed Shift + Enter, click Show/Hide Paragraph Marks on the format toolbar. You'll see a bent arrow showing where you've started a new line with this command. To remove the line break, delete the bent arrow symbol.

Using Undo and Redo

Did you just perform some editing that you now regret? Go to the Edit menu and select Undo, or press Ctrl + Z, to cancel your last edit. To redo your last edit (or to restore the last change you undid), choose Redo from the Edit menu.

Adding Special Characters and Symbols

The default HTML character set is English-centered. You need to use a special command to enter foreign language characters, as well as symbols such as copyright marks. To enter a special character, choose Symbol from the Insert menu. You'll see the Symbol dialog box (Figure 18-10). Click the character you want to add, and then click Insert. Click Close.

Figure 18-10

The Symbol dialog box lets you add special characters to your page.

Creating a Page from Scratch

If you want to create a page from scratch instead of using the Personal Home Page Wizard, open a new document by clicking the New button on the standard toolbar. You can also select New from the File menu, and choose Normal Page from the New Page dialog box.

Once you've started a new Web page, you need to give it a title. Go to the File menu and choose Page Properties. In the Page Properties dialog box, click the General tab (Figure 18-11). In the Title area, type a title for your document and click Enter.

Don't be surprised when your title doesn't appear in the document. Titles appear on the browser's title bar. Within your document, use the Heading 1 style to repeat the title or some variation on it.

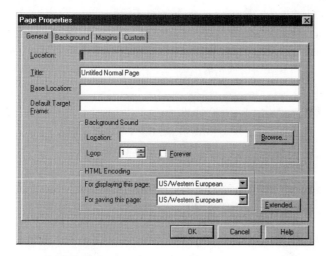

Figure 18-11

You can create a title for your page using this dialog box.

18

Creating Hyperlinks

Most Web pages contain one or more hyperlinks, which users can click to display other pages. FrontPage Express makes it easy to add hyperlinks to your document.

Understanding Hyperlinks

A hyperlink has two parts. The *anchor* is the text that appears in your Web page. Given distinctive formatting (usually colored and underlined), the anchor is clicked to display a different page. The *URL* is the address of the Internet resource to be retrieved when the user clicks the hyperlink. It doesn't have to be a Web page; you can also create links to Usenet newsgroups, files in FTP archives, and many other types of Internet resources.

There's an ultra-cool, ultra-easy way to create hyperlinks quickly. Use Internet Explorer to display a Web page that contains hyperlinks that you'd like to add to your page. Click the mouse button on one of the hyperlinks, and drag it into the FrontPage Express window. When you reach the place you want the hyperlink to appear, release the mouse button. The hyperlink appears in your document, along with the anchor. You can use this quick method to create a lengthy list of hyperlinks.

Inserting a Hyperlink to Another Web Site

To create a hyperlink to a page somewhere on the World Wide Web, note the URL and follow these steps:

1. Position the cursor where you want the hyperlink to appear.

2. Type the text that you want to appear as anchor text (the colored and underlined text that the user clicks). Select the text.

3. Click the Create Or Edit Hyperlink button on the Format toolbar, or press Ctrl + K. You'll see the Create Hyperlink dialog box (Figure 18-12). If necessary, click the World Wide Web tab.

4. On the World Wide Web page, click the Hyperlink Type box, and choose the protocol of the link you're creating. Remember, protocol refers to the type of Internet service that's involved in retrieving the desired information. You can create links using the following protocols: *file* (a file on your local system), *ftp* (a File Transfer Protocol file), *gopher* (a Gopher document), *http* (a page on the World Wide Web), *https* (a secure Web site using Secure

PART

III

Sockets Layer [SSL] security), *mailto* (a mail response link), *news* (a link to a Usenet newsgroup), *telnet* (a link to a telnet [mainframe computer] site), and *wais* (a link to a WAIS—Wide Area Information Server—database).

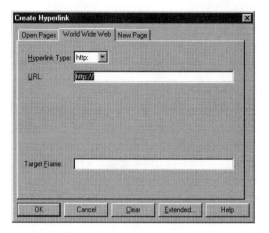

Figure 18-12

Use this dialog box to create a hyperlink.

5. In the URL box, type the rest of the URL.

6. If you're linking to a frame document and you know the name of the frame that you want to link to, type the frame's name in the Target Frame box. Otherwise, just leave this box blank.

7. Click OK to create the hyperlink.

I tried to create a hyperlink, but it put the URL in my document!

You forgot to type and select the anchor before creating the link. Delete what you entered, and start over.

Editing Hyperlinks

If a hyperlink isn't working properly, you might have typed the URL incorrectly. To edit the hyperlink, place the cursor on it and click Create Or Edit Hyperlink on the Format toolbar. You'll see the Edit Hyperlink dialog box, with the current hyperlink information displayed. Check the URL carefully for errors. If you find an error, correct it and click OK.

18

TIP
Be sure to test your hyperlinks. You can do so from within FrontPage Express. Connect to the Internet, if necessary. Point to the hyperlink, and click the right mouse button. Choose Follow Hyperlink. FrontPage Express displays the page for editing in a new window. If you see an error message, something's wrong with the URL. If the page displays, everything's OK. Click the Back button on the Standard toolbar to return to your page.

Soliciting Feedback with a Mailto Hyperlink

Here's a neat trick. Using a *mailto hyperlink* enables you to place a hyperlink in your document that, when clicked, displays an e-mail composition window with your e-mail address already entered. Note that this works only if the person clicking this link is using a mail-capable browser—but these days, almost everyone does. This type of hyperlink works just as well with Netscape Navigator and Netscape Communicator as it does with Microsoft Internet Explorer. To create a mailto hyperlink, follow these steps:

1. Type and select the anchor text that you want to appear in your Web page. (You might want to type your e-mail address so it's visible to people who don't have mail-capable browsers.)

2. Click the Create Or Edit Hyperlink button on the Format toolbar, or press Ctrl + K. You'll see the Create Hyperlink dialog box (Figure 18-12). If necessary, click the World Wide Web tab.

3. In the Hyperlink Type area, choose mailto.

4. In the URL area, carefully type your e-mail address after mailto.

5. Click OK.

Saving Your Page

If your page isn't finished, you can save it locally until you're ready to publish it. Choose Save from the File menu, press Ctrl + S, or click the Save button on the standard toolbar. You'll see the Save As dialog box. Click As File to display the Save As File dialog box. Choose a location for your file, type a name, and click Save.

To continue working on your file later, choose Open from the File menu, press Ctrl + O, or click the Open button on the standard toolbar. You'll see the Open File dialog box. Click From File, and use the Browse button to locate the file. Click Open to resume editing. (The File menu contains the names of the last four documents you've opened, allowing you to open a document quickly by selecting it from this menu.)

Publishing Your Page

If your page is finished and ready to publish, you can save it by uploading it to your Web server storage space. To do so, you must have two pieces of information. First, find the exact location of the computer where you publish your Web pages. This might be an FTP address (such as *ftp://bag-end.hobboton.shire.org/~bilbo/*). Second, you need the user name and the password that enable you to access this directory. Be sure to obtain this information from the person who's running the Web server where you plan to publish. Follow these steps to publish your Web page:

1. If you haven't saved your page before, choose Save from the File menu, click Ctrl + S, or click the Save button on the standard toolbar. If you have saved your page before, choose Save As from the File menu. Either way, you'll see the Save As dialog box (Figure 18-13).

2. In the Page Title box, type the page's title if necessary. (You don't have to do this if you already entered the page's title in the Page Properties dialog box.)

3. In the Page Location box, carefully type the exact storage location of your Web publishing space. This is probably an FTP address, which looks something like this: *ftp://bag-end.hobbiton.shire/~bilbo.* (Here, *bag-end.hobbiton.shire* is the name of the computer that's running the Web server you use to publish your documents, and *~bilbo* is the name of your user directory within this server.)

4. At the end of the address you just typed, type a slash mark (/), if necessary, followed by a file name for the document you're publishing. Use the *.htm* or *.html* extension. If you're publishing a document named *memoirs.html,* for example, the Page Location box would contain the following: *ftp://bag-end.hobbiton.shire/~bilbo/memoirs.html.*

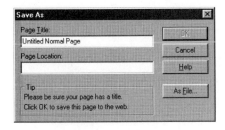

Figure 18-13

In this dialog box, you specify the location for publishing your document.

18

5. Click OK. If you haven't previously published your page on this server, you'll see a dialog box asking for your user name and password. Type these carefully, and click OK.

FrontPage Express now attempts to publish your page. If something goes wrong, you'll see the Web Publishing Wizard; it tries to solve the problem that prevented you from publishing the page.

HELP

I still can't get it to work!

If you're still having trouble publishing your page, click the Help button in the Web Publishing Wizard. You'll see a troubleshooter that walks you through some possible solutions. Also, try contacting the person responsible for the Web server you're using. Make sure you have the exact storage location, user name, and password.

From Here

🌐 You've sketched out your page—but it's sort of boring, isn't it? In the next chapter, you'll learn how to jazz your page up with all kinds of goodies, including background graphics, sounds, marquees, watermarks, ActiveX controls—the works!

🌐 Bring your Web publishing skills home. Anything you can do to a Web page, you can do to a Web folder. Find out how in Chapter 20.

19

Jazz
It Up

In the previous chapter, you learned how to sketch out a Web page, whether you use the Personal Home Page Wizard or create the page from scratch. Either way, with what you've learned so far, your page is basically Early Mosaic, a noted art epoch characterized by plain backgrounds, lots of text, default fonts, no graphics, and precious little zing, unless you're a darned good writer. (Mosaic was the first popular Web browser, and most of the pages available during Mosaic's heyday weren't exactly thrilling from a visual standpoint.) In this chapter, you'll transcend the humdrum by adding all kinds of visual, auditory, and computational excitement to your page.

Continuing the theme that the simplicity of FrontPage Express is deceptive, this chapter shows you how to take your page from humble beginnings to the far reaches of the contemporary Web. Hey, I'm not kidding! When you're done with this chapter, you'll be able to hold your page up against the Cool of the Cool—and look like a Web publishing genius. Of course, you'll have color, backgrounds, and animations, but that's not all.

This chapter also shows you tricks that professional Web authors use all the time, such as combining tables with background graphics to create awesome desktop publishing effects. But why stop there? You'll learn how to add Java applets, JavaScripts, and ActiveX controls to your page, drawing on the incredible free resources that you can download from the Web. Even if you don't know a lick of programming, you can add existing applets, scripts, and controls to your pages through the almost devilishly simple expedient of dragging and dropping, enabling you to create an impressive page in a matter of minutes. As you'll see, FrontPage Express is probably the ideal environment, short of Microsoft FrontPage itself (or several years of HTML coding and knowledge of many programming languages), for adding active content to your pages. Let's rock!

Opening Your Page

Let's begin by opening the very ordinary page that you created in the last chapter. If you published the page, you can open it from the Web. If you saved the file to your disk, you can open it from there, too.

TIP
To open your document the easiest way, click File on the menu bar and choose the document's name from the File menu. The File menu stores the names of the last four documents you opened. You can open documents this way wherever you saved them, either from the Web or from your hard disk.

Opening Your Web Page from the Web

To open your published file from the Web, use Internet Explorer to locate and display the document. Click the Edit button on Internet Explorer's standard toolbar to open the document in FrontPage Express. If you are in FrontPage Express already, choose Open from the File menu or click the Open button on the standard toolbar. You'll see the Open File dialog box. Click From Location, and type the URL of your page in the text box. Click OK to open the document.

Opening a Local Copy of Your Web Page

If you didn't publish your Web page, you can open it from your hard disk. Choose Open from the File menu, or click the Open button on the standard toolbar. You'll see the Open File dialog box. Click From File, and click the Browse button to locate and select your file.

Adding Excitement to the Background

Now that you've displayed your document, it's time to dispense with the ordinary. By the time you're finished with this section, your Early Mosaic document will start showing signs of life. Here's the menu: choose background colors, background graphics, or a background watermark. And how about a background sound that plays when users open your page? If this sounds super-advanced, read on—it's easy with FrontPage Express.

Choosing a Default Color Scheme for Your Document

You can choose a default color scheme for your document. When you do so, you select colors for the following elements:

- 🌐 **Background.** Your choice of a background color affects the browser window background.

- 🌐 **Text.** This color choice affects all the text you enter, with the exception of hyperlinks.

- 🌐 **Hyperlink.** This selection affects hyperlinks that have not yet been visited. (The user's history list keeps track of which sites have been visited.)

- 🌐 **Visited hyperlink.** This selection affects hyperlinks that have been visited.

HELP

I can't read this page!

By now, you've browsed the Web enough that you've probably encountered the Illegible Page, which hits you with some unbelievably ugly and unreadable combination of background and text colors. Please, avoid falling into this trap, and remember that legibility is your main goal. You can assign default colors to text as well as to backgrounds and make the two work together, but bear in mind that contrast is critical. If your background is very dark, your text should be very light—and vice versa. And don't forget the small matter of taste. You get shock value out of purple text on a green background, but not repeat visitors.

19

To choose a default color scheme for your page, follow these steps:

1. Go to the Format menu and select Background. You'll see the Page Properties dialog box, thoughtfully opened to the Background page (Figure 19-1).

2. In the Background area, select a color for your document's background.

3. In the Text area, select a color for the nonhyperlink text in your document.

4. In the Hyperlink area, select a color for the unvisited hyperlink text.

5. In the Visited Hyperlink area, select a color for visited hyperlink text. This should be duller than the hyperlink text color.

6. In the Active Hyperlink area, select a color that appears briefly when the user clicks a hyperlink. This should be brighter than the other two hyperlink colors.

7. To confirm your color choices, choose Enter.

Don't like your color choices? Go back to Format, select Background, and start over.

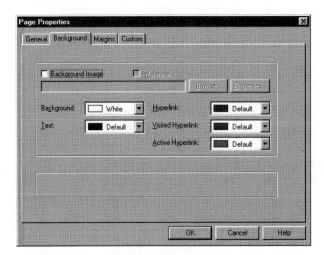

Figure 19-1

In this dialog box, you can choose a background color and default text colors for your document.

Choosing Background Graphics

If a background color doesn't add the zing you're looking for, you can substitute a background graphic. *Background graphics* are relatively small GIF or JPEG files that are tiled so that they fill the entire browser's window, even if the user enlarges the window. But please, don't use a graphic that's too busy. The best background graphics are those that have a consistent, overall tone, like the spacey graphic shown in Figure 19-2; white text is easy to read against the overall dark tone of this background graphic.

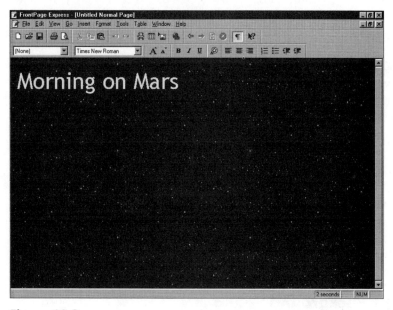

Figure 19-2
Good background graphics enhance your pages; bad ones make them hard to read.

Where can you find background graphics? You'll find many freebie background graphics on the Web. Try an AltaVista search for *"background graphics."* In Internet Explorer, you can also save any background graphic to your system by right-clicking the page background and choosing Save Background As. Please note, though, that the technical ability to do this does not necessarily mean that it's ethical. If you would like to use somebody else's background graphic, ask for permission by e-mailing the page creator. Most people are actually quite happy to grant permission if you only ask. If you don't ask, and you're creating your page for profit-seeking purposes, you're exposing yourself and your company to risk. In other words, don't do it.

19

To add a background graphic to your page, choose Background from the Format menu. You'll see the Page Properties dialog box, opened to the Background page. Click Background Image, and click the Browse button to locate the graphic you want to use. Click OK to confirm.

Although the Page Properties dialog box enables you to specify the URL for a background graphic, please don't use this feature to link your page's background to a graphic that's stored elsewhere on the Web. This is murder on other people's servers, and it needlessly multiplies the amount of data that has to get shuffled back and forth in order to display your page. If you want to use somebody else's background graphic, get permission to do so and use a copy that's stored on your own Web server.

Adding a Background Watermark

What's a watermark? In brief, it's a background graphic that doesn't scroll along with the text. The effect is cool for just about any background graphic—the text seems to float over the graphic—but it's almost essential for large, complex background graphics with abrupt borders. These look terrible if the user sees the tile boundary separating two copies of the graphic. By defining the background graphic as a watermark, you can effectively prevent the tile boundary from coming into view.

To create a watermark, simply click the Watermark check box when you create your background graphic. Note that the Watermark option doesn't become available until you've clicked Background Image. A watermark is a background, after all, and until you've added a background graphic, you can't have a watermark.

Adding a Background Sound

You open a new, strange page on the Web. And new, strange music begins to play through your computer's speakers, even though you didn't click or download anything (at least not deliberately). What's going on? Magic? A computer virus? No, it's called background sound, and you can use the same trick on your pages.

NOTE Not all browsers can display backgrounds as watermarks. But that's no reason not to define your background graphics as watermarks, if you wish. Browsers that don't recognize the watermark coding will still display the background; it's just that the background will scroll along with the text. If the beauty of your page is dependent on the background graphic staying put, it might not look good when viewed with a non-watermark-capable browser.

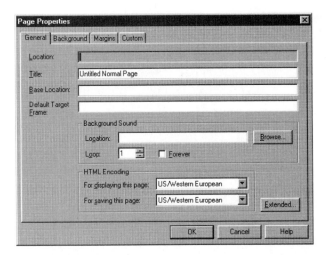

Figure 19-3

In this dialog box, you can add a background sound to your Web page.

To add a background sound to your page, go to the File menu and choose Page Properties. Click the General tab, if necessary, to display the General options (Figure 19-3). Next to the Location box, click Browse to identify the location of the sound. (You can use a sound that's on your system or one located on the Web.) In the Loop box, choose the number of times you want the sound to repeat; click Forever to repeat the sound until the user leaves the page. Click OK to confirm.

You can add many different kinds of sounds as a background sound, including WAV (Windows sounds), AU (Sun/NeXT sounds), AIFF (Apple/ Silicon Graphics sounds), and MIDI (Musical Instrument Digital Interface files). Today's browsers can handle most or all of these sound formats, but the AU format is probably best for reaching the widest possible audience.

NOTE

Not all browsers can play background sounds. If your page is accessed by some-body using a browser that can't play the sound, the user won't hear it. However, your page will still display.

Adding Visual Interest to the Text

You can jazz up your text in a number of ways, including adding colors and emphases, changing fonts and font sizes, varying alignments and in-dents—even using scrolling text (marquee).

19

Adding Character Emphases

You can add the following emphases to the text you type. Either type the text and then select the style, or choose the command and then type the text. To remove formatting from characters, either repeat the formatting command or go to the Format menu and select Remove Formatting.

- **Bold.** Click the Bold button on the Format toolbar, or press Ctrl + B.
- **Italic.** Click the Italic button on the Format toolbar, or press Ctrl + I.
- **Bold Italic.** Choose Font from the Format menu. You'll see the Font dialog box (Figure 19-4). In the Font Style list, choose Bold Italic and click OK.
- **Underline.** Click the Underline button on the Format toolbar, or press Ctrl + U.
- **Strikethrough.** Choose Font from the Format menu. In the Font dialog box, click Strikethrough and click OK.
- **Typewriter.** Choose Font from the Format menu. In the Font dialog box, click Typewriter and click OK.

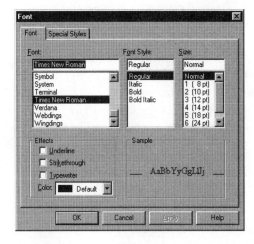

Figure 19-4

Use the Font dialog box to change text fonts, sizes, and styles.

Changing the Font Size

On the Web, font sizes are defined in two different ways: relative and points. You can specify *relative font sizes* using numbers from 1 (smallest) to 7 (largest). The default is size 3. Just what this means in terms of point size depends on the browser. With Microsoft Internet Explorer, size 3 type looks like normal-sized text (about 12 points). Almost all browsers support this means of specifying font size. Also, new HTML standards enable Web authors to specify sizes in *printer's points* (72 points equal 1 inch). However, some older browsers do not support this.

There are two ways to change the size of text in your page. One way is to select the text, go to the Format toolbar, and click the button marked either Increase Text Size or Decrease Text Size. Or, after selecting the text, choose Font from the Format menu (or press Alt + Enter). You'll see the Font dialog box. Select a font size in the Size box, and click OK.

FrontPage Express uses a combination of relative sizes and points, as shown below. This correlation allows you to specify font size in relative terms and still ensure that your choice will appear correctly, even if someone's using an older browser.

Relative font size	Equivalent in points
1	8 pt
2	10 pt
3	12 pt
4	14 pt
5	18 pt
6	24 pt
7	36 pt

Adding Superscript and Subscript

You can position selected characters using superscript (above the line) or subscript (below the line). To do so, select the characters and press Alt + Enter (or choose Font from the Format menu). In the Font dialog box, click Special Styles. In the Vertical Position area, select Superscript or Subscript, and specify the distance from the baseline in the By box. Click OK to confirm.

Adding Color to Your Text

You can add color to your text, type and select the text, then click the Color button on the Format toolbar. (This color is in addition to default colors for normal text and hyperlinks discussed earlier in this chapter.)

19

Choosing Fonts

FrontPage Express enables you to format your text using any of the fonts installed on your system. Simply select the text, and choose a font from the Change Font list box on the Format toolbar. (You can also choose Font from the Format menu to display the Font dialog box.) Be careful in choosing fonts. Keep in mind that when people access your page on the Web, the fonts won't appear unless the same fonts are installed on their systems, and there's a good chance they won't be. While there's usually little lost if the user doesn't have the same font—the user's browser simply displays your text using the browser's default font setting—you'd be wise to avoid relying too much on fonts for your page design.

Using TrueType Fonts

To help improve the font situation, Microsoft designed several exceptionally attractive TrueType fonts and made them available to the public for free. Available for Windows and Macintosh systems, these fonts include Trebuchet MS, Georgia, Verdana, Comic Sans MS, Arial Black, and Impact, as well as a font containing cool symbols called Webdings (Figure 19-5). These fonts are specifically designed to look good on the relatively low-resolution display technology that characterizes the Web. (But frankly, they're so nice that you can use them for almost any purpose.) To obtain these fonts, download them from www.microsoft.com/typography.

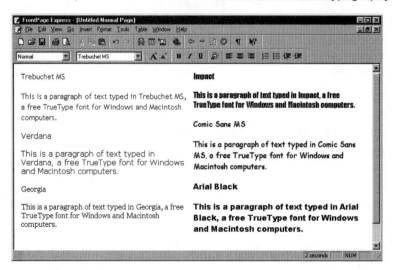

Figure 19-5

Microsoft makes several TrueType fonts available via its Web site.

PART

III

If you would like to use these TrueType fonts on your Web pages, include a link to
Microsoft's site so that users can download them, if they haven't already done so.

Aligning and Indenting Text

As the previous chapter explained, you build your document using the basic,
built-in styles, such as those for various lists and normal paragraphs. However, you can align and indent text in any style. (Almost all of the newer
browsers support these alignment and indentation options, although a few
older browsers might not.)

Use alignment and indentation options so that the page's white space
becomes part of the design. In Figure 19-6, you see how alignment and
indentations help to guide the eye through the document's message.

To align, select the text and click one of the alignment tools on the
Format toolbar. You can choose from flush left (smooth left margin and
ragged right), centered, and flush right (ragged left margin and smooth right).
Justification (smooth left and right margins) isn't supported yet by HTML.

To indent, select the text and click one of the indent tools (Decrease
Indent or Increase Indent) on the Format toolbar. Note that you can increase
the indent substantially by clicking the Increase Indent button more than once.

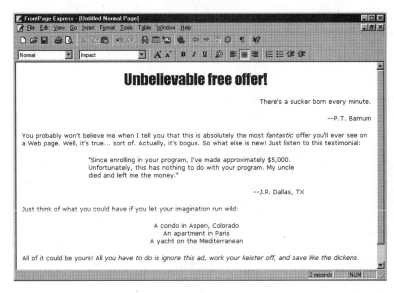

Figure 19-6

You can align and indent text that's entered in any style.

19

Publish

What's all that other stuff on the Special Styles page?

HTML contains a number of styles that aren't really supported by most browsers, including several character styles: Citation, Sample, Code, Variable, and Keyboard. Most browsers simply format these using the default monospace font—they're not differentiated in any visible way. FrontPage Express does make these visibly different, as you can see by selecting one of these options and looking at the Sample box. The problem is that there's no guarantee your text will look that way when displayed by another browser. If you want to display typewriter-like text, choose Courier New in the Font page of the Font dialog box, and click Typewriter, so that browsers that don't recognize fonts will display the text using the default monospace font. Also in the Special Styles page is the Blink option, which you should use sparingly—if at all. (It's annoying to readers.)

Adding a Marquee

Here's a quick way to add some visual spice to your page: add a marquee, or scrolling text. A *marquee* consists of a line of text that moves across your page. You can control the direction (left or right), speed of movement, behavior (scrolling, sliding, or bouncing back and forth), alignment with text (top, middle, or bottom), text size, repetition, and color. To insert a marquee, follow these steps:

1. Go to the Insert menu and choose Marquee. You'll see the Marquee Properties dialog box (Figure 19-7).

2. In the Text box, type the text you want to appear in the marquee.

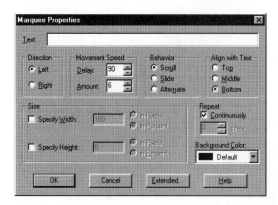

Figure 19-7
You can create scrolling text using this dialog box.

3. For the other settings, try using the defaults, for now. Later you can go back and change these until you get the effect you want.

4. Click OK. You'll see the marquee in your page, but FrontPage Express doesn't show how it scrolls. (To check the results, access your Web page through Internet Explorer.)

NOTE At this time, marquees aren't supported by browsers other than Microsoft Internet Explorer. If you add a marquee to your page and someone using another browser accesses it, the marquee text will appear, but it won't scroll.

Inserting Graphics

Enough about text! Let's add some visual appeal. You can add any JPEG or GIF graphic to your Web page, taking full advantage of the advanced features of these graphics formats that smooth the downloading process. You can also control the graphic's alignment, spacing, and size.

Inserting the Graphic

Start by adding a graphic to your page.

1. Position the cursor where you want the graphic to appear.

2. On the standard toolbar, click Insert Image, or choose Image from the Insert menu.

3. If necessary, click Other Location. You can specify your file's source by locating and naming a disk file, or you can type the URL of a graphic on the Web.

4. Specify your graphic file's location or choose a clip art image, and click OK.

You'll see the graphic in your document, positioned using the default layout and size options (Figure 19-8).

For the benefit of the many people who browse with images switched off, as well as people using text-only browsers, be sure to supply alternative text for each graphic you insert. This alternative text tells the user what the graphic would have shown. For those browsing with images switched off—a common method of speeding browser performance on slow modem connections—this option enables users to determine whether they'd like to use a special command that downloads this particular graphic.

19

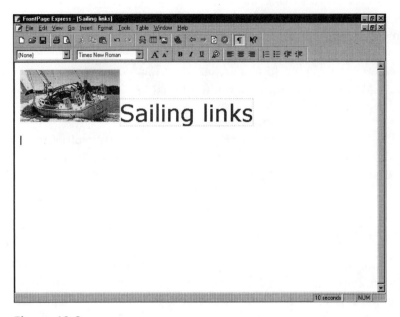

Figure 19-8

Adding graphics to your Web pages is easy.

To define alternative text, first select the graphic you've just inserted. Then press Alt + Enter, or choose Image Properties from the Edit menu, or click the right mouse button and choose Image Properties. In the Image Properties dialog box, click the General tab and type a brief description of your graphic in the Text box (Alternative Representations area).

Adjusting the Graphic Layout and Size

By default, FrontPage Express positions graphics flush left and aligns text to the right of the graphic; the text is aligned with the graphic's baseline. You can change these options, and you can specify the graphic's size.

To choose these options, first select the graphic. Then press Alt + Enter, or choose Image Properties from the Edit menu. (You can also point to the image, click the right mouse button, and choose Image Properties.) Click the Appearance tab to display the appearance options shown in Figure 19-9.

TIP

In case you haven't noticed by now, Alt + Enter is a cool keyboard command. If you select something and press these keys, you'll see the properties box for whatever you pointed to. If you point to a graphic, for example, you see the Image Properties dialog box.

Figure 19-9

You can control layout and size options for your graphic.

The following list explains the options you can choose:

🌐 **Alignment.** This option controls the position of the graphic in relation to surrounding text. You can align the text at the top, center, or bottom of the graphic, and you can also choose to position the graphic to the right or left of the text. You'll find some other options here, but they aren't supported by most browsers.

🌐 **Border spacing.** Here, you specify the width of the border surrounding the graphic. By default, this is zero (no border).

🌐 **Horizontal spacing.** This choice controls the amount of space between the graphic and surrounding text (to the left or right). By default, this is zero, but it's a good idea to change this to one or two so that there's a little blank space around the graphic.

🌐 **Vertical spacing.** With this option, you can add some space above and below the graphic. You may want to do this if the graphic looks crowded next to other graphics or text.

🌐 **Size.** If you would like to change the size of the graphic, click Specify Size and choose a width and height. (You can enter these in pixels or a percentage of screen width.) Note, though, that FrontPage Express doesn't automatically preserve the graphic's *aspect ratio* (the relation between the width and height), so making changes here might introduce unwanted distortions.

19

Understanding Graphics File Formats

You can include two types of graphics in your Web page.

JPEG is short for Joint Photographic Experts Group. This graphics format uses *lossy compression,* in which some of the original information is discarded in order to reduce the size of the file. This loss isn't apparent to the eye unless the compression ratio is pushed too far. JPEG graphics are used for complex visual images with many colors, such as photographs. Some JPEG graphics, called *progressive JPEG graphics,* are designed to download so that a quick, rough version of the image appears, then gradually takes on more definition. This feature enables viewers to get an idea of how the page will look without having to wait for the whole download.

GIF stands for Graphics Interchange Format (GIF), a graphic format originally developed by CompuServe. Although GIF graphics cannot store as many colors as JPEG graphics, they compress large single-color areas more efficiently. GIF graphics are a great choice if your graphic contains areas of solid color. There are two GIF standards, called GIF 87 and GIF 89a. The GIF 89a standard enables a single GIF file to contain more than one image, which makes it possible to create animations quickly and inexpensively. Another very cool feature of the GIF 89a format is transparency, the ability to define the background color so that it blends with the color of your Web page's background. To create GIF animations and transparent GIFs, you need a graphics editor such as Paint Shop Pro.

Making a Graphic into a Hyperlink

Any graphic can function as a hyperlink. To transform a graphic into a hyperlink, select the graphic and click Create Or Edit Hyperlink (on the standard toolbar). Specify the URL, and click OK.

Adding an Animated GIF

Want to add animations to your page? Would you believe it's as simple as adding a graphic, which you already know how to do? Animated GIFs are GIF files that contain more than one image, together with instructions on the display sequence and timing.

You can create your own animated GIFs using a commercial or shareware GIF animation program, but many Web sites offer free animated GIFs. These pages come and go. To see the current crop, try this AltaVista search: +"animated GIF" +free.

Please be careful. Just because you know how easy it is to add animated GIFs to your page, don't give into the temptation to overdo it. Pages that are full of little blinking, flapping, marching, and flying creatures can be very annoying.

Creating Tables

If you've ever created tables with a word processing program, you know how easy and useful they are. You define the number of rows and columns you want, and you get a matrix of *cells,* areas in which you can type text. Within each cell, you can type as much as you want, and the program automatically adjusts the table dimensions and boundaries. With FrontPage Express, it's just as easy to create and edit tables.

NOTE

Tables aren't just for entering tabular data. They're the key to effective Web page design. Short of using frames, which many users dislike, there's no other way to position text in two or more columns. You should learn how to create tables, even if you don't plan to publish tabular data. Using a simple, two-cell table, you can create a very cool Web page.

Inserting a Table

To add a table to your document, click the Insert Table button on the Format toolbar. When the pop-up window appears (Figure 19-10), drag across and down to create the number of rows and columns you want. (Figure 19-10 has two rows and two columns.) After you release the mouse button, you'll see table boundaries in your document. If the table boundaries don't appear, click Show/Hide Paragraph Marks.

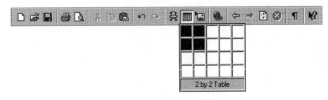

<u>Figure 19-10</u>
Click the Insert Table button and drag to create a table.

19

Typing Text in Table Cells

By default, FrontPage Express creates a table with invisible borders and dynamically sized cells. To create your table, simply start typing in one of the cells. FrontPage will expand the cell as needed to accommodate as much text as you type. If you run out of room, the program automatically starts a new line; you don't have to press Enter.

Within a table, the Tab key—useless elsewhere in an HTML document—finally takes on a meaningful function: You press it to move to the next cell. If you're at the end of the table, pressing Tab creates a new row.

Editing the Table Structure

When you created your table, you chose the number of rows and columns you wanted. But you're not stuck with this. You can add rows and columns, or you can delete them if you add too many. In addition, you can add cells anywhere you like, even if a given column has more or fewer cells than another. You can also split cells and merge cells. You'll quickly learn the steps you take to perform these table-editing tasks.

Adding rows, columns, or cells

To add a cell, position the cursor where you want the new cell to appear and choose Insert Cell from the Table menu.

If you want to add a new row at the end of your table, position the cursor in the last cell and press Tab. To insert a row or column within the table, position the cursor where you'd like the new one to appear, go to the Table menu, and select Insert Rows Or Columns. You'll see the Insert Rows Or Columns dialog box (Figure 19-11). Choose Columns or Rows, and do one of the following:

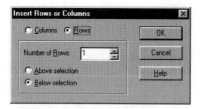

Figure 19-11

Use this dialog box to quickly insert rows or columns.

🌐 If you chose Columns, indicate the number of columns you want to add and choose where you'd like the new columns inserted (left or right of the selection). Click OK.

🌐 If you chose Rows, indicate the number of rows you want to add and choose where you'd like the new rows inserted (above or below the selection). Click OK.

Deleting rows, columns, or cells

To delete rows, columns, or cells, you must first select them. Use the selection commands on the Table menu—ordinary selection techniques won't work.

To select a cell, place the cursor in the cell and choose Select Cell from the Table menu. To delete the cell, press the Delete key.

To select a row or column, place the cursor anywhere in the row or column, go to the Table menu, and choose either Select Row or Select Column. Press Delete to remove the row or column.

You can also select rows and columns with the mouse, thanks to an invisible selection area positioned just outside the table area. To select a column, move the mouse to the white space just above the top of the column. When you see a down arrow, click the left mouse button. To select a row, move the mouse to the white space just to the left of the row until you see a right arrow. Then click the left mouse button.

Splitting a cell

You can split a cell into two or more rows or two or more columns. Place the cursor in the cell, go to the Table menu, and choose Split Cells. You'll see the Split Cells dialog box (Figure 19-12). Choose Split Into Columns or Split Into Rows, and specify the number. Click OK when you're done.

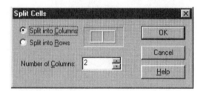

Figure 19-12

Use this dialog box to split an existing cell.

Merging cells

You can also merge two cells into one. Select the cells by dragging across them, and choose Merge Cells from the Table menu.

Choosing Table and Cell Properties

You can choose a variety of properties for the entire table or for individual cells. These properties include alignments, border size, extra space, absolute widths, and more. You can even add a background graphic or color to the whole table or to a particular cell.

19

Looking at common properties

You can choose many of the same properties for tables and individual cells. The following options are common to both:

🌐 **Horizontal alignment.** This option formats text as flush left, center, or flush right. The default setting leaves this up to the browser, which usually formats table text flush left.

🌐 **Custom background.** You can use a background graphic or choose a background color.

🌐 **Custom colors.** If your table has a border width greater than 1 pixel, you can create a three-dimensional border effect by specifying the color to use for the light border (the top and left borders for the table, bottom and right for cells) and the dark border (bottom and right for the table, top and left for cells). See Figure 19-13 for an example.

If you choose alignment, background, or color options for an individual cell, your choice overrides the current table properties. For example, suppose you've chosen a blue background for your whole table, but you select a red background for one of the cells within the table. Only that cell appears red. In Figure 19-13, you see a table with a white background, but with some cells in a different color.

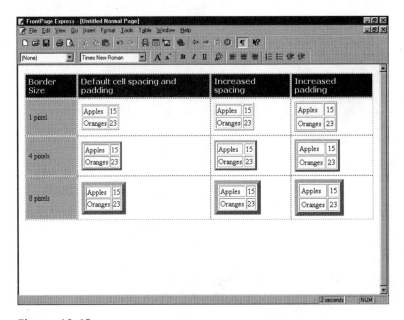

Figure 19-13

This table illustrates some of the table border, spacing, and padding options.

PART
III

362

Choosing table properties

To choose properties for your whole table, choose Table Properties from the Table menu or right-click the table and choose from the pop-up menu. You'll see the Table Properties dialog box (Figure 19-14). In addition to the properties shared with cells, tables use the following options:

🌐 **Border size.** By default, FrontPage Express omits the border. If you add a border, you can choose custom colors, including a light and dark border for three-dimensional effects.

🌐 **Cell padding.** The cell padding setting enables you to offset the text from the table border. By default, the program inserts 1 pixel of padding, which is enough to separate the text from the border. You can "open up" the table by increasing this measurement. (Don't make it smaller than 1.)

🌐 **Cell spacing.** The cell spacing setting enables you to add additional space between cells. If you add a border, this option splits the border, producing an effect in which each cell appears to be surrounded by a frame.

🌐 **Minimum width.** You can specify the minimum width of your table in pixels or as a percentage of the window width. To make sure your table always spans the browser's window, specify a width of 100 and click In Percent.

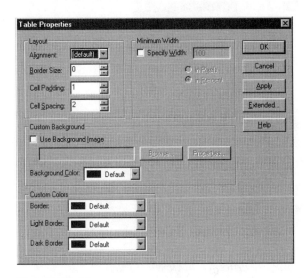

Figure 19-14

In this dialog box, you choose properties for the whole table.

19

To see how the borders, cell padding, and cell spacing work together, create a small table and try varying the options. Create the table, and then choose Table Properties from the Table menu. Select an option, and click Apply to see the results without leaving the Table Properties dialog box. (Move the dialog box to one side so you can see your table). Figure 19-14 shows some of the effects you can create with borders, spacing, and padding, as well as three-dimensional borders (light and dark colors).

Choosing cell properties

Once you've chosen properties for the whole table, you can choose properties for individual cells. To do so, place the cursor in a cell and choose Cell Properties from the Table menu. (You can also point to the cell, click the right mouse button, and choose Cell Properties from the pop-up menu.) You'll see the Cell Properties dialog box shown in Figure 19-15. A number of the same properties appear in the Table Properties dialog box, including horizontal alignment, minimum width, custom background, and custom colors. In addition, you'll find these properties:

- **Vertical alignment.** The default is Middle, but you can choose Top or Bottom.

- **Header cell.** Click this option to format this cell's text in bold.

- **No wrap.** Click this option to prevent text wrapping in this cell.

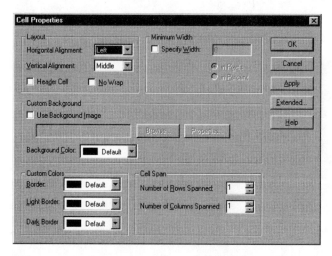

Figure 19-15
In this dialog box, you choose properties for individual cells.

🌐 **Cell span.** You can enlarge a cell so that it spans a specified number of rows or columns. To make a cell span rows, columns, or both, increase the settings in the cell span area. After you span rows or columns, you'll have some extra cells, since the program pushes them aside to make room for the cell that spans two or more rows or columns. Simply delete these extra cells.

Adding a Table Caption

To add a caption to your table, go to the Table menu and choose Insert Caption. FrontPage Express positions the cursor at the top of the table and enables you to type a centered caption. If you'd prefer to place the caption at the bottom of the table, go to the Table menu, choose Caption Properties, and select Bottom Of Table.

Using Table Layout Tricks

Tables aren't just for tabular data, as the previous section stressed. Professional Web designers use them to control document layout, and so can you. To see how Web authors use tables, find any nonframed page that appears to have a multiple-column layout, click Edit, and take a look at the page in FrontPage Express. Microsoft's own Start Page turns out to be a table made up of cells that span rows and columns as needed. Cool trick, isn't it?

Try this yourself. Create a simple 2-by-2 table—two rows, two columns, with no borders, spanning 100 percent of the screen. Delete one of the cells in the first row, and then define the remaining one so that it spans two columns. Color it black. In the second row, type the names of the pages in your site, pressing Shift + Enter after each one. Define each of these names as hyperlinks to pages with the same name. Color this cell silver, and set the minimum width to 135 pixels. What's left? One big cell. Format this cell so that its minimum size is 75 percent of the screen width (Figure 19-16).

The big cell will hold the page's content, but don't write the content yet. Add one or two inline graphics, and save this page to your hard disk so that you can use it as a template. To create each of the pages in the site, open the template and add content. Then save the page with its own, unique file name. In this way, each page of your site will have the same overall design, and people will compliment you on what a fantastic job you've done.

A two-column, one-row table at the beginning of your document gives you control over the placement of a graphic next to text. The page shown in Figure 19-17 uses this technique to allow for a multiple-line title next to the graphic—something you can't do with HTML's standard tools for aligning graphics and text.

19

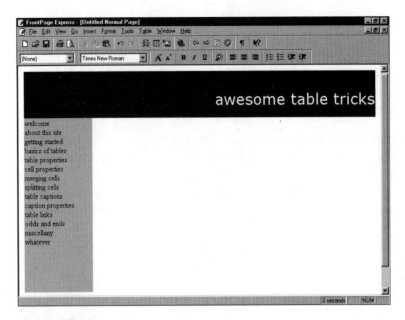

Figure 19-16

This simple site design template uses a table with three cells.

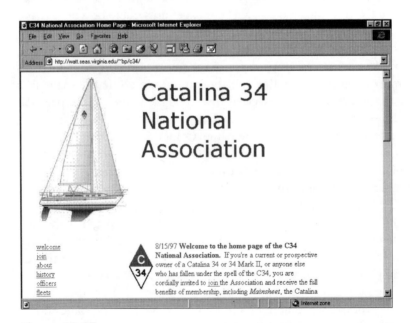

Figure 19-17

Tables enable you to place more than one line of text next to a graphic.

Inserting Active Content

If you're not a programmer, you won't be able to create your own JavaScripts or ActiveX controls. But you can still include active content on your pages, thanks to the easy-to-use tools of FrontPage Express.

As you'll see, FrontPage Express enables you to add active JavaScript content to your pages by dragging and dropping scripts and applets. However, as with the ability to drag and drop graphics, this capability doesn't give you unlimited license to appropriate other peoples' intellectual efforts without permission. Always ask permission before copying a JavaScript from the Web—unless the page you're dragging from specifically indicates that the script or applet is free for your use.

Including a JavaScript

JavaScript is a scripting language for the Web. Originally developed by Netscape Communications and recently standardized, JavaScript is loosely based on Java, but it's much easier to use. Unlike Java applets, which aren't readable on screen, JavaScripts are typed directly into a Web document. On the Web, you'll find hundreds of free JavaScripts, which you can add to your document using FrontPage Express's nifty drag-and-drop capabilities.

Look for JavaScripts that you can use on your page without modifying the underlying code. For example, there are a number of freebie JavaScripts that display the current date and time. These need no modification to be used on your page.

Adding the JavaScript with drag and drop

You can easily include a JavaScript in your Web page using these steps:

1. Using Internet Explorer, display the page that contains the JavaScript.

2. Click Edit. You'll see the page in FrontPage Express. The JavaScript appears as a small J in a box with a yellow background.

3. Drag the JavaScript to your page, and release the mouse button.

Viewing the script's properties

After you've added a JavaScript to your page, you'll want to view the script. Select the script's icon, and press Alt + Enter. You can also point to the script's icon and click the right mouse button, or choose WebBot Component

19

Properties from the Edit menu. You'll see the Script dialog box, with the JavaScript shown in plain text (Figure 19-18). If you know a little JavaScript language, you can modify the code.

Figure 19-18
You can view (and even modify) any JavaScript code.

Inserting a script by typing it

You may run across JavaScripts in books or magazines. If so, you can type them into the Script dialog box and add them to your pages. Just be sure to copy the script exactly. All the funny-looking symbols are important!

1. Choose Insert Script. You'll see a blank Script dialog box.

2. In the Language area, choose JavaScript.

3. In the Script area, type your script.

4. Proofread your typing carefully.

5. Click OK.

Adding a Microsoft Visual Basic script (VBScript) to your page is just as easy. You can add VBScripts using drag-and-drop techniques, just as you would a JavaScript. If there's a VBScript on your server that you'd like to use, add it by going to the Insert menu, selecting Script, and choosing VBScript. If the script is intended to run on the server rather than the client (check the script's documentation), click Run Script On Server.

Adding an ActiveX Control

FrontPage Express provides great tools for including ActiveX controls on your Web page. You can use ActiveX controls for a number of cool things, including three-dimensional buttons, animations, and pull-down menus. Bear in mind, though, that users won't be able to view the page unless they're using a browser capable of running ActiveX and a Windows computer.

In order to insert ActiveX controls on your page, you must first obtain and install the control. Be sure to read the control's documentation thoroughly. Once you've installed the control on your system, you can add it to your page by following these steps:

1. Place the cursor where you want the ActiveX control to appear.

2. Go to the Insert menu, choose Other Components, and then select ActiveX Control. You'll see the ActiveX Control Properties dialog box (Figure 19-19).

3. In the Pick A Control box, click the down arrow to see a list of the ActiveX controls installed on your system and choose the control you want to add.

4. Accept the default layout settings for now. (If you'd like to adjust the alignment and other position settings later, select the control and press Alt + Enter.)

5. Click OK to add the control to your page.

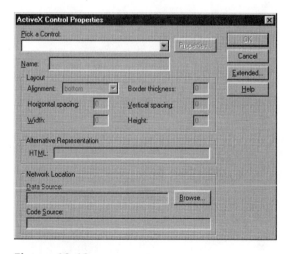

Figure 19-19

Adding an ActiveX control to your page is simple.

19

From Here

Use the skills you've learned about Web pages to customize your computer! You can treat every folder on your computer as if it were a Web page, replete with sounds, animations, color, rich text formatting, ActiveX controls—the works! Find out how easy it is to do this in the next chapter.

20

Bring
It Home

Many people believe that personal computing ought to be truly personal, and it ought to include more than choosing your favorite applications or Web sites. Since you spend so much time working with your computer, it should reflect your tastes, interests, and preferences. You spend a lot of time in your home, after all, and you don't use motel decor. Instead you can hang your favorite pictures, decorate with your best-loved colors, and play the music that you enjoy. Why should your computer be any less of an individual statement?

With Microsoft Internet Explorer 4, you can personalize your computer to a degree that's completely unprecedented. Of course, Microsoft Windows has always enabled you to choose a few sounds and colors, and you could choose wallpaper to decorate your computer's screen background. But Internet Explorer takes customizing much further. As you'll learn in this chapter, Internet Explorer does far more than extend the browsing metaphor to your files and folders. It also transforms every disk and folder on your computer into the equivalent of an HTML page. You can transform your computer into a multimedia experience—one that expresses your personal interests. Every folder on your system can have its own distinctive background graphic, background sound, and font.

TIP To make use of the techniques discussed in this chapter, you need to switch your desktop to the Web style, in which your computer looks and acts like the Web. To do so, open any Windows Explorer or My Computer window and choose Folder Options from the View menu. Click the General tab, choose Web Style, and click OK.

Adding Backgrounds to Folders

Get started the easy way by adding a background graphic to a frequently used folder. Avoid background graphics that have a full tonal range, going from stark white to solid black; you'll have a tough time reading your icon captions. Go for a graphic that's all or mostly all dark or light, and choose an icon caption color that will show up against this background.

To add a background to a folder, follow these steps:

1. In Windows Explorer, display the folder.

2. Go to the View menu, and choose Customize This Folder. You can also point to the folder background, click the right mouse button, and choose Customize This Folder from the pop-up menu. You'll see the first page of the Customize This Folder wizard (Figure 20-1).

3. Click Choose A Background Picture, and click Next. You'll see a list of background pictures. If you don't see a picture you'd like to use, click Browse to locate one. After you've selected the picture, you'll see a preview.

4. Consider whether your icon captions will show up. To make sure they do, choose an appropriate text color and, optionally, a text caption background color. When you're finished choosing background picture options, click Next.

5. Click Finish. You'll see your background graphic in the folder (Figure 20-2).

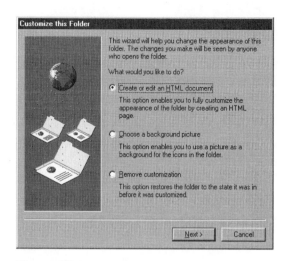

Figure 20-1

The Customize This Folder wizard lets you do folders your way.

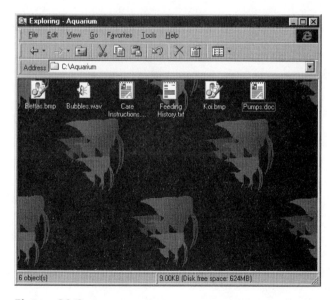

Figure 20-2

You can add a background graphic to each folder.

20

I can't read the icon captions!

It's tempting to choose a complex graphic for your folders, but it's really hard to read icon captions if the graphic has lots of detail or a wide tonal range. To change the graphic, repeat the steps you followed to add the background graphic; then choose a more even-toned, less complex graphic. Be sure to choose a text caption color that will show up against the background. To restore the folder to its appearance before you started customizing it, start the wizard and choose Remove Customization.

Using HTML to Customize Folders

By using the technique just introduced, you can easily add a background graphic—with no knowledge of HTML. But if you know how to write HTML, you can add a whole slew of interactive features to your folders. Jazz them up using a background color (instead of a background graphic), different fonts, background sounds, marquees, and much more. But I must warn you: You should venture into this territory only if you are quite comfortable with writing HTML.

Getting Started

To start personalizing your folder, start the Customize This Folder wizard. In Windows Explorer, go to the View menu and choose Customize This Folder; you can also right-click the folder background and then click Customize This Folder. You'll see the Customize This Folder dialog box (Figure 20-1). Choose Create Or Edit An HTML Document, and click Next until you see Windows Notepad.

You already have a bunch of HTML code, and you haven't typed a single tag! What you see is the code that produces the default Web view. Don't make any changes yet. Simply close Notepad. The Customize This Folder wizard notes that you've finished editing; click Finish to close the wizard.

Your Windows Explorer window now looks similar to Figure 20-3. (If you don't see the new version of your window, choose Refresh from the View menu or press F5.) The file you saw briefly in Notepad creates three "panes": one across the top that displays the icon and name of the folder, one down the left side that displays information about each icon you select, and one that displays the file icons themselves. Now that you've seen the default Web view, start the Customize This Folder wizard again, display the HTML code in Notepad, and try adding some features. Be careful! It's easy to break the JavaScripts if you insert text in the wrong locations.

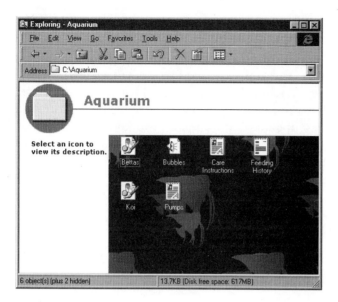

Figure 20-3

Your Windows Explorer window has been transformed into a Web document.

Reversing the Customization

If you're tired of your custom folder view—or if you've added some HTML code that causes Windows Explorer to complain—you can easily reverse the customization. Start the Customize This Folder wizard, and select Remove Customization. Click Next. The wizard warns you that all your customization is about to be removed. Click Next and then click Finish. Your window returns to its usual appearance.

Technical Stuff

So how does Windows Explorer remember how each folder should appear? It uses two files that normally stay hidden in your folder. To view these files, choose Folder Options from the View menu and then click the Advanced tab. Under Hidden Files, click Show All Files and then click OK. You'll see two files, Desktop and Folder. Desktop's full name is Desktop.ini; it contains the unique identifier of the folder and any special attributes, such as the background graphic you added earlier. The full name of the Folder is Folder.htt; it is an HTML template that contains the code you saw in Notepad.

NOTE Although the Customize This Folder wizard says that it will use your HTML editor, you won't be able to use FrontPage Express because some of the features used by Windows Explorer aren't supported by FrontPage Express.

20

From Here

You've done it! You've completed this edition of the Official Microsoft Internet Explorer 4 Book, and you've learned more than enough skills to qualify you as a capable Internet user. Now you can browse, communicate, and publish with the best. You're ready to take in information from around the world and or to send updates to old friends. You know how to speak your mind to large audiences, as well as how to keep private messages private. You can shop, search, create, and converse. With Internet Explorer 4, you're prepared for cyberspace.

See you on the 'Net!

Index

Bryan Pfaffenberger, Ph.D., is a bestselling author of dozens of books on computer and Internet subjects, including Microsoft Internet Explorer (all the way back to the pre-frame version 1.0). He is a recognized expert on Web searching, Web page design, and Internet security and privacy issues. Reviewers and readers alike praise his works for explaining complex technical subjects with clarity, accessibility, and wit. He is currently Associate Professor of Technology, Culture, and Communication at the University of Virginia, where he has taught technical writing and the history of technology since 1985. When not involved in such serious activities, Pfaffenberger enjoys sailing his Catalina sailboat, Juliana, on Virginia's beautiful Rappahannock River and Chesapeake Bay. He lives in the countryside of Albemarle County, Virginia, with his family and a very spoiled cat.

The manuscript for this book was prepared and submitted to Microsoft Press in electronic form. Text files were prepared using Microsoft Word 97 for Windows. Pages were composed using Adobe PageMaker 6.51 for Windows, with text in Garamond and display type in Frutiger. Composed pages were delivered to the printer as electronic prepress files.

Cover Graphic Designer
Greg Erickson

Interior Graphic Designer
Kim Eggleston

Compositors
Abby Hall, Elizabeth Hansford

Principal Proofreader
Teri Kieffer

Indexer
Lynn Armstrong

Discover
a new standard—
built on success!

U.S.A. **$29.99**
U.K. £27.99 [V.A.T. included]
Canada $39.99
ISBN 1-57231-746-9

The MICROSOFT® WINDOWS® 98 OFFICIAL PREVIEW KIT is an inside guide to how Windows 98 will look, work, and act. You'll see how the Active Desktop™ will connect your PC to the larger world of networks, intranets, and the Internet. You'll also discover exciting new ways to interact with your computer—ways that will dramatically improve your productivity. If you're interested in seeing the new face of personal computing and getting a sneak preview of Microsoft's future systems software strategy, you'll want this book.

Microsoft *Press*

IMPORTANT—READ CAREFULLY BEFORE OPENING SOFTWARE PACKET(S). By opening the sealed packet(s) containing the software, you indicate your acceptance of the following Microsoft License Agreement.

MICROSOFT LICENSE AGREEMENT

(Book Companion CD)

This is a legal agreement between you (either an individual or an entity) and Microsoft Corporation. By opening the sealed software packet(s) you are agreeing to be bound by the terms of this agreement. If you do not agree to the terms of this agreement, promptly return the unopened software packet(s) and any accompanying written materials to the place you obtained them for a full refund.

MICROSOFT SOFTWARE LICENSE

1. GRANT OF LICENSE. Microsoft grants to you the right to use one copy of the Microsoft software program included with this book (the "SOFTWARE") on a single terminal connected to a single computer. The SOFTWARE is in "use" on a computer when it is loaded into the temporary memory (i.e., RAM) or installed into the permanent memory (e.g., hard disk, CD-ROM, or other storage device) of that computer. You may not network the SOFTWARE or otherwise use it on more than one computer or computer terminal at the same time.

2. COPYRIGHT. The SOFTWARE is owned by Microsoft or its suppliers and is protected by United States copyright laws and international treaty provisions. Therefore, you must treat the SOFTWARE like any other copyrighted material (e.g., a book or musical recording) except that you may either (a) make one copy of the SOFTWARE solely for backup or archival purposes, or (b) transfer the SOFTWARE to a single hard disk provided you keep the original solely for backup or archival purposes. You may not copy the written materials accompanying the SOFTWARE.

3. OTHER RESTRICTIONS. You may not rent or lease the SOFTWARE, but you may transfer the SOFTWARE and accompanying written materials on a permanent basis provided you retain no copies and the recipient agrees to the terms of this Agreement. You may not reverse engineer, decompile, or disassemble the SOFTWARE. If the SOFTWARE is an update or has been updated, any transfer must include the most recent update and all prior versions.

4. DUAL MEDIA SOFTWARE. If the SOFTWARE package contains more than one kind of disk (3.5", 5.25", and CD-ROM), then you may use only the disks appropriate for your single-user computer. You may not use the other disks on another computer or loan, rent, lease, or transfer them to another user except as part of the permanent transfer (as provided above) of all SOFTWARE and written materials.

5. SAMPLE CODE. If the SOFTWARE includes Sample Code, then Microsoft grants you a royalty-free right to reproduce and distribute the sample code of the SOFTWARE provided that you: (a) distribute the sample code only in conjunction with and as a part of your software product; (b) do not use Microsoft's or its authors' names, logos, or trademarks to market your software product; (c) include the copyright notice that appears on the SOFTWARE on your product label and as a part of the sign-on message for your software product; and (d) agree to indemnify, hold harmless, and defend Microsoft and its authors from and against any claims or lawsuits, including attorneys' fees, that arise or result from the use or distribution of your software product.

DISCLAIMER OF WARRANTY

The SOFTWARE (including instructions for its use) is provided "AS IS" WITHOUT WARRANTY OF ANY KIND. MICROSOFT FURTHER DISCLAIMS ALL IMPLIED WARRANTIES INCLUDING WITHOUT LIMITATION ANY IMPLIED WARRANTIES OF MERCHANTABILITY OR OF FITNESS FOR A PARTICULAR PURPOSE. THE ENTIRE RISK ARISING OUT OF THE USE OR PERFORMANCE OF THE SOFTWARE AND DOCUMENTATION REMAINS WITH YOU.

IN NO EVENT SHALL MICROSOFT, ITS AUTHORS, OR ANYONE ELSE INVOLVED IN THE CREATION, PRODUCTION, OR DELIVERY OF THE SOFTWARE BE LIABLE FOR ANY DAMAGES WHATSOEVER (INCLUDING, WITHOUT LIMITATION, DAMAGES FOR LOSS OF BUSINESS PROFITS, BUSINESS INTERRUPTION, LOSS OF BUSINESS INFORMATION, OR OTHER PECUNIARY LOSS) ARISING OUT OF THE USE OF OR INABILITY TO USE THE SOFTWARE OR DOCUMENTATION, EVEN IF MICROSOFT HAS BEEN ADVISED OF THE POSSIBILITY OF SUCH DAMAGES. BECAUSE SOME STATES/COUNTRIES DO NOT ALLOW THE EXCLUSION OR LIMITATION OF LIABILITY FOR CONSEQUENTIAL OR INCIDENTAL DAMAGES, THE ABOVE LIMITATION MAY NOT APPLY TO YOU.

U.S. GOVERNMENT RESTRICTED RIGHTS

The SOFTWARE and documentation are provided with RESTRICTED RIGHTS. Use, duplication, or disclosure by the Government is subject to restrictions as set forth in subparagraph (c)(1)(ii) of The Rights in Technical Data and Computer Software clause at DFARS 252.227-7013 or subparagraphs (c)(1) and (2) of the Commercial Computer Software — Restricted Rights 48 CFR 52.227-19, as applicable. Manufacturer is Microsoft Corporation, One Microsoft Way, Redmond, WA 98052-6399.

If you acquired this product in the United States, this Agreement is governed by the laws of the State of Washington.

Should you have any questions concerning this Agreement, or if you desire to contact Microsoft Press for any reason, please write: Microsoft Press, One Microsoft Way, Redmond, WA 98052-6399.